Augsburg College
George Sverdrup Library
Minneapolis, Minnesota 55404

CHINA AT THE CONFERENCE
A REPORT

BY

WESTEL W. WILLOUGHBY

Professor of Political Science at the Johns Hopkins University;
Formerly Legal Adviser to the Chinese Republic;
Technical Expert to the Chinese Delegation to the Conference
on Limitation of Armament, at Washington, D. C.;
Author of "Foreign Rights and Interests in China"

BALTIMORE
THE JOHNS HOPKINS PRESS
1922

Copyright 1922 by
THE JOHNS HOPKINS PRESS

The Lord Baltimore Press
BALTIMORE, MD., U. S. A.

PREFACE

It is a remarkable fact that, with the exception of a part of one session which was devoted to the situation in Siberia, the entire work of the Conference at Washington, so far as it dealt with political questions in the Pacific and Far East, was concerned with the affairs of China.[1] An account, therefore, of China at the Conference will necessarily cover almost the entire proceedings of that body upon its purely political side as distinguished from its deliberations and discussions with reference to the reduction of existing, and the limitation of future, armaments.

The present work is in the nature of a report upon the work of the Chinese Delegation at Washington, but, not being official in character, there will be an opportunity for the author to speak, upon some points at least, rather more fully and frankly than it would be appropriate and expedient for the official representatives of the Chinese Government to do. It is, however, proper to say that the author served as Technical Expert to the Chinese Delegation throughout its work at Washington; that, in that capacity, he had access to all the records of the Conference so far as they related to China; that he was kept currently informed of the proceedings of the Conference and of its com-

---

[1] The discussion, or rather the statements made, in the conference relating to Siberia, are given in the Appendix.

mittees and subcommittees; and that the Chinese Delegates have made available to him their own confidential records, so that he feels justified in saying that, so far as a knowledge of the facts is concerned, he is in a position to give an adequate and accurate account of China's case at the Conference. Whatever opinions he may state as to the wisdom of the actions taken, whether upon the part of the Chinese Delegation or of the representatives of the other Powers, or whatever estimates he may express as to the general success or failure of the Conference in achieving the work for which it was convened, will necessarily be his own, and their value will be determined by the intelligence with which they have been formed.

Because it is hoped that this volume will serve as an authentic report of the work of the Conference, so far as China was concerned, the method will be followed of reproducing not only the texts of the final agreements reached, but also the carefully formulated statements which, from time to time, the Chinese Delegation made in order that it might not later be argued that, by silence, the representatives of China had given tacit acquiescence to the various treaty limitations upon, or violations of, the sovereignty, territorial integrity and administrative autonomy of China, the freedom or relief from which they were not able to obtain. And, in this connection, the author ventures to say that the reader of this volume will almost inevitably be impressed not only by the vigor with which the Chinese Delegates presented China's case to the Conference, but by the intelligent and scrupulous care which they took to avoid any admissions of principles, or unnecessary commitments upon the part of China which would unduly hinder her future freedom of action, or place obstacles in the way of her securing, at some later and more propitious time, action upon the part of the Powers which it was found impossible to obtain at Washington.

In result, it is hoped that this volume will be found to be a convenient supplement to the author's *Foreign Rights and Interests in China,* published in 1920, bringing to date, as it will, many of the statements of that work.

CONTENTS

Preface iii

CHAPTER I

The Convening of the Conference

	PAGE
Equality of the Powers..................................	1
Unanimity of Action Required...........................	2
Preliminary Correspondence	3
Japan's Hesitancy	5
The Formal Invitation to the Principal Allied and Associated Powers	7
The Invitation to China.................................	9
Belgium, Netherlands and Portugal Invited..............	11
The Delegates	11

CHAPTER II

The Need for the Discussion by the Conference of Pacific and Far Eastern Questions

China's Weakness and Japan's Ambitions.................	15
Interests of Western Powers............................	17

CHAPTER III

The Organization and Procedure of the Conference

Plenary Sessions	19
Committees of the Whole and Sub-Committees.............	19
Procedure	20
Agenda	25

CONTENTS

CHAPTER IV

China's Programme

	PAGE
China's Hopes	27
China's Fears	30
China's Ten Points	32

CHAPTER V

The Root Resolutions

General Discussion	37
China Defined	39
Root Resolutions	40

CHAPTER VI

China's Territorial and Administrative Integrity

Sovereignty	45
Territorial Integrity	48
Administrative Integrity	51
China's Rights as a Neutral	53

CHAPTER VII

Tariff Autonomy

Chinese Statement	55
Discussion	58
Sub-Committee Discussions	60
Japanese Statement	64
Discussion	65
Draft Agreement	67
Land Frontier Duties	69
Discussion in Committee of the Whole: Statement by Senator Underwood	72
Chinese Statement	75

CONTENTS

	PAGE
Drafting Committee: Report from	80
Discussion as to Russia	82
Grand Duchy of Luxemburg	83
Finland and Poland	83
Non-Treaty Powers	84
Draft of Treaty	86
Senator Underwood's View as to Power of China to Denounce Tariff Treaties	92
Maintenance of Existing Customs Administration	94
Banks for Deposit of Customs Receipts	95
Chinese Statements	103

CHAPTER VIII

RESOLUTION OF THE POWERS OTHER THAN CHINA REGARDING ARMED FORCES IN CHINA

Proposed Resolution	108
Chinese Statement	109
Statement by Sir Robert Borden	110
Resolution Adopted	112

CHAPTER IX

EXTRATERRITORIALITY

Chinese Statement	114
Resolutions Adopted	118

CHAPTER X

FOREIGN POST OFFICES IN CHINA

Chinese Statement	121
Discussion	129
Resolutions	131
Japanese Statement	132
Chinese Statement	133

CHAPTER XI

FOREIGN TROOPS AND POLICE IN CHINA

	PAGE
Chinese Statement	136
Japanese Statement	139
Chinese Rejoinder	143
Japanese Reply	150
Commission of Inquiry Proposed	151
Chinese Objection	152
Resolution Adopted	153
Chinese Statement	154

CHAPTER XII

WIRELESS AND OTHER ELECTRICAL COMMUNICATIONS INSTALLATIONS IN CHINA

Chinese Statement	157
Draft Resolution by Mr. Root	159
Discussion	160
In the Drafting Committee	161
Resolution of December 7	162
Viviani Resolution	164
Chinese Statement	166
Revised Root Resolution	168
Discussion	169
Resolution of December 7 Finally Approved	172

CHAPTER XIII

SPHERES OF INTEREST

Chinese Statement	174
Status of Question	175
Statements in the Conference	177
Resolution Adopted	179

CONTENTS

CHAPTER XIV

LEASED AREAS

	PAGE
Kwangchow-wan	183
Kiaochow and Kwantung District	185
Kowloon	186
Weihaiwei	188
Chinese Statement	190
Weihaiwei	191
Kwangchow-wan	192

CHAPTER XV

JAPAN'S CLAIM TO "SPECIAL INTERESTS" IN CHINA

Lansing-Ishii Agreement	193
Consortium	194
Manchuria	197
Mining Code	202

CHAPTER XVI

THE OPEN DOOR

Open Door Defined	206
Board of Reference	215
Chinese Statement	218

CHAPTER XVII

CHINESE RAILWAYS AND THE OPEN DOOR

Unification of Railways	222
The Open Door and the Chinese Railways	223

CONTENTS

CHAPTER XVIII

THE CHINESE EASTERN RAILWAY

	PAGE
Report of Technical Committee	227
Resolution Adopted	230

CHAPTER XIX

INTER-POWER AGREEMENTS RELATING TO CHINA

Chinese Statement	235
Discussion	238
Resolution Adopted	240

CHAPTER XX

ARMS EMBARGO

Draft Resolution	244
Discussion	244
Amended Resolution	246
Resolution Withdrawn	247

CHAPTER XXI

THE TWENTY-ONE DEMANDS: TREATIES AND AGREEMENTS OF MAY 25, 1915

Japanese Statement	250
Chinese Reply	253
Statement of the United States	256

CHAPTER XXII

CHINA'S COMMITMENTS

Chinese Proposals	261
Discussion	263

	PAGE
Draft Resolution	264
Discussion	265
Resolutions Adopted	271
Commitments without Time Limits	273
Construction of Commitments	274
China's Ninth and Tenth Points	274

CHAPTER XXIII

Shantung

Reasons for Resorting to the Conversations	280
Scope of the Conversations	284
The Status of the Shantung Question	285
Correspondence Between China and Japan	291
Japanese Note of September 7, 1921	293
China's Answer	294
Reasons why the Other Powers were Unwilling to have the Shantung Question brought before the Conference	297
Conversations Agreed Upon	299
Persons Participating in the Conversations	300
Restoration of Kiaochow	301
Customs	302
Public Properties	303
Vested Rights	306
Salt	306
Mines	307
Withdrawal of Japanese Troops	308
Wireless Stations	308
Submarine Cables	308
Renunciation by Japan of Preferential Rights in Shantung	309
The Shantung Railway	309
The Valuation of the Railway and Appurtenant Properties	310
Improvements and Additions	311
Joint Railway Commission	313
Mode of Payment and Conditions to be Attached Thereto	314

CONTENTS

	PAGE
Japanese Propose Loan by Japanese Capitalists and Employment of Japanese as Chief Engineer, Chief Accountant, and Traffic Manager	315
The Issue Drawn	321
Informal Conversations and Interviews	322
Agreement Reached	323
Understandings Recorded in the Minutes	323
Joint Commission	326
Results of the Conversations Communicated to Secretary Hughes and Mr. Balfour	326
An Estimate of the Merits of the Shantung Agreement	327

CHAPTER XXIV

RESULTS

No New Bonds upon China	336
Specific Results gained by China	339
Principles and Policies Relating to China	342
Anglo-Japanese Alliance	344
Siberia	349
Has a Fundamental Change of Policy on the Part of the Powers been Effected?	355
The Future	357

APPENDICES

APPENDIX I: TREATIES

A Treaty between the United States of America, The British Empire, France, and Japan, Signed December 13, 1921, Relating to their Insular Possessions and Insular Dominions in the Pacific Ocean	363
Declaration Accompanying the Above Four-Power Treaty	366
A Treaty between the Same Four Powers, Supplementary to the Above, Signed February 6, 1922	367

CONTENTS xv

PAGE

A Treaty between all Nine Powers relating to Principles and Policies to be followed in matters concerning China.... 368
A Treaty between the Nine Powers relating to Chinese Customs Tariff 374

APPENDIX II: RESOLUTIONS

Resolution Regarding a Board of Reference for Far Eastern Question 381
Resolution Regarding Extra-territoriality in China........ 381
Resolution Regarding Foreign Postal Agencies in China..... 383
Resolution Regarding Armed Forces in China............. 384
Resolution Regarding Radio Stations in China and Accompanying Declarations 385
Resolution Regarding Unification of Railways in China and Accompanying Declaration by China................. 387
Resolution Regarding the Reduction of Chinese Military Forces 388
Resolution Regarding Existing Commitments of China or with Respect to China................................. 389
Resolution Regarding the Chinese Eastern Railway, Approved by All the Powers Including China................... 390
Resolution Regarding the Chinese Eastern Railway, Approved by All the Powers other than China................... 391

APPENDIX III: TREATY FOR THE SETTLEMENT OF OUTSTANDING QUESTIONS RELATIVE TO SHANTUNG

Section	I.	Restoration of the Former German Leased Territory of Kiaochow...............	392
Section	II.	Transfer of Public Properties.............	393
Section	III.	Withdrawal of Japanese Troops...........	394
Section	IV.	Maritime Customs at Tsingtao............	394
Section	V.	Tsingtao-Tsinanfu Railway	395
Section	VI.	Extensions of the Tsingtao-Tsinanfu Railway	396
Section	VII.	Mines	397
Section	VIII.	Opening of the Former German Leased Territory of Kiaochow...................	397

CONTENTS

	PAGE
Section IX. Salt Industry	398
Section X. Submarine Cables	398
Section XI. Wireless Stations	398
Renunciation of Preferential Rights	399
Transfer of Public Properties	399
Maritime Customs at Tsingtao	400
Tsingtao-Tsinanfu Railway	400
Chefoo-Weihsien Railway	401
Opening of the Former German Leased Territory of Kiaochow	401

APPENDIX IV: STATEMENTS IN THE CONFERENCE REGARDING SIBERIA

Japanese Statement	401
Statement of the United States	406
French Statement	411

APPENDIX V: CHINA'S DELEGATION

Delegates	412
Superior Advisers	412
Secretary General	412
Assistant Secretary General	412
Advisers	412
Counselors	412
Technical Delegates	413
Directors of Departments	413
Assistant Director of Departments	413
Secretaries	413
Attachés	413
Translators	414
Clerks	414
INDEX	415

CHAPTER I

The Convening of the Conference

Equality of the Powers. As is well known the Washington Conference was called in order that two distinct, but related, purposes might be achieved. The first was that the five Powers, the United States of America, the British Empire, France, Italy and Japan—known during the World War as the Principal Allied and Associated Powers—might take common action with regard to a reduction of existing and a limitation upon future armaments. The second purpose was that existing political conditions in the Pacific and Far East might be so modified that, so far as possible, possibilities or probabilities of international controversies or even of war would be removed. In order that this second end might be obtained, the Governments of Belgium, China, the Netherlands and Portugal were invited to send representatives to the Conference who were to participate in its discussions and determinations insofar as they might relate to Pacific and Far Eastern political questions. Thus, while not invited to participate in the work of the Conference so far as matters of armament might be dealt with, the representatives of these four last named Powers took their seats in the Conference upon a basis of full equality with the representatives of the five

Principal Allied and Associated Powers so far as Pacific and Far Eastern questions were concerned.[1]

Unanimity of Action Required. With regard generally to the work of the Conference it is to be remembered that it was a meeting of sovereign Powers, each of which, by attending it, conceded no legal or even moral right upon the part of the other Powers to control its actions or politics by the determinations which they might arrive at. Therefore it was that no definite or treaty results could be expected from the Conference save such as might command the unanimous consent of the Powers concerned. In other words, as soon as the fact developed during the discussions in the Conference or outside of it in the informal conversations or communications between the several delegations, that unshakable objection to a proposition by even a single Power would be made, that proposition was almost always dropped, for its formal presentation to the Conference by the Powers especially interested could serve no other purpose than to place those Powers clearly upon record as to their views in the premises, and to obtain for them such support in the public opinion of the world as they might merit. These facts are to be constantly borne in mind in passing judgment either upon the work of the Conference as a whole or upon the wisdom of the actions of particular Delegations. No argument is needed to show that, as a general proposition, a Delegation would suffer a disadvantage by bringing forward a

---

[1] There is reason for saying that China would not have been willing to attend the Conference except upon this basis of equality, and that she received assurance that she would enjoy this status.

proposal which it was known in advance would not be favorably acted upon by the Conference, for, by failure to obtain action, the existing *status quo* would be rendered all the more fixed. Such being the case, a Delegation concerned would be justified in asking of the Conference action which it knew would be refused only if it were convinced that the disadvantage resulting from such refusal would be more than compensated for by the moral advantage of publicly asserting upon its part a policy that it deemed just and by thus, as it were, bringing before the bar of the conscience of the world those nations that would oppose it, or whose past actions had not been consistent with it. In two conspicuous instances the Powers concerned deemed it thus desirable to bring before the Conference matters upon which it was practically known that no favorable action could be obtained. The United States Delegation presented a severe indictment of Japan's policies in Eastern Siberia, and the Chinese Delegation brought forward the question of the fundamental validity of the Sino-Japanese Treaties and Agreements of May 25, 1915—those resulting from Japan's "Twenty-One Demands" upon China.

Preliminary Correspondence. For the purposes of this volume it is not necessary to speculate as to the more obscure causes which led to the convening of the Conference at Washington, nor to consider the diplomatic correspondence which preceded the issuance by the American President of the formal invitation to the Powers to participate in its deliberations and decisions. It is sufficient to say that, as was but proper, the American Government did not send its final and formal invitation until it had obtained assurance from the Powers to be addressed that they would give to it a favorable reply. All of the Powers addressed, with the exception of Japan, as will presently appear, gave full and prompt approval to the American proposal.

In an official statement given out July 10, 1921, by the American Department of State, it was said:

The President, in view of the far-reaching importance of the question of limitation of armament, has approached with informal but definite inquiries the group of Powers heretofore known as the Principal Allied and Associated Powers, that is, Great Britain, France, Italy and Japan, to ascertain whether it would be agreeable to them to take part in a Conference on this subject, to be held in Washington at a time to be mutually agreed upon. If the proposal is found to be acceptable, formal invitations for such a Conference will be issued.

It is manifest that the question of limitation of armament has a close relation to Pacific and Far Eastern problems, and the President has suggested that the Powers especially interested in these problems should undertake in connection with this Conference the consideration of all matters bearing upon their solution with a view to reaching a common understanding with respect to principles and policies in the Far East. This has been communicated to the Powers concerned and China has also been invited to take part in the discussion relating to Far Eastern problems.[2]

[2] In connection with this statement it is of interest to note the following statements made in the British House of Commons by the Prime Minister, Mr. Lloyd George:

On July 7 he was asked: "Whether at any time the suggestion of a Pan-Asiatic Conference has been brought to his notice; and whether if this is not the case he will consider the desirability of issuing the necessary invitations to the United States, Japan, and China with the object of terminating the controversies which threaten the peace of the Far East

Japan's Hesitancy. That the Japanese Government was not willing to give immediate and unreserved approval to the American project appeared when a memorandum was made public on July 23, which the American Chargé d'Affaires at Tokyo had handed to the Japanese Government. In this memorandum the

and the trade of this country." Questions were also asked as to the status of the Anglo-Japanese Alliance.

To these queries the Prime Minister replied that he hoped to be able to make a statement on the following Monday, July 11. "It depends," he said, "upon whether replies are received from the United States, Japan, and China."

On July 11 the Prime Minister said (in part):

"I am very glad to be able to inform the House today that the views of the government of the United States reached me last night, and are extremely satisfactory. The Chinese Government is also favorable. We have not yet had a formal reply from the government of Japan, but we have good reason to hope that it will be in the same sense. Now that these views have been received, I am glad to be at liberty to inform the House of Commons fully regarding the course which our discussions in the Imperial Cabinet took. I do this with particular satisfaction, because it will show how very valuable a step forward we have been able to take by common consent in the sphere of foreign affairs."

After discussing at some length the broad lines of policy in the Pacific and Far East as considered in the meetings of the Imperial Cabinet, and especially with reference to the Anglo-Japanese Alliance, the Prime Minister concluded:

"The views of the President of the United States were made public by the American Government this morning. As is known to the House, Mr. Harding has taken the momentous step of inviting the Powers to a Conference on the limitation of armaments, to be held in Washington in the near future, and he also suggests a preliminary meeting on Pacific and Far Eastern questions between the Powers most directly interested in the peace and welfare of that great region, which is assuming the first importance in international affairs. I need not say that we welcome with the utmost pleasure President Harding's wise and courteous initiative. In saying this I know that I speak for the Empire as a whole. The world has been looking to the United States for such a lead. I am confident that the House will esteem it as an act of farseeing statesmanship and will whole-heartedly wish it success. I need hardly say that no effort will be lacking to make it so on the part of the British Empire, which shares to the full the liberal and progressive spirit inspiring it."

American Government expressed the hope that the Japanese Government would not press its inquiry as to a fuller statement of the nature and scope of the Pacific and Far Eastern questions which were to be discussed. The precise agenda of the Conference, the American Government declared, could be later arrived at.

To this communication Japan replied on July 27, accepting the invitation, with, however, the understanding that the United States, prior to the meeting of the Conference, would proceed with exchanges of opinion regarding the nature and scope of the Pacific and Far Eastern questions to be discussed. The Japanese reply continued:

> The Japanese Government have been made aware through the communications and the published statement of the American Government and the conversations between the Secretary of State and Baron Shidehara that the proposition of the American Government to discuss the Pacific and Far Eastern problems is based on the close bearing they have on the question of the limitation of armament which is the original and principal aim of the Conference, and that therefore the main object of discussing these problems is to reach a common understanding in regard to general principles and policies in the Pacific and the Far East. Desiring, as they do, to contribute to the establishment of an enduring peace and to the advancement of human welfare, the Japanese Government earnestly hope that the proposed Conference may attain the expected results and their ideals may thereby be brought nearer to realization.
>
> In order to ensure the success of the Conference, the Japanese Government deem it advisable that the agenda thereof should be arranged in accordance with the main object of the discussions as above defined, and that introduction therein of problems such as are of sole concern to certain particular Powers or such matters that may be regarded accomplished facts should be scrupulously avoided.

Finally, on August 24, the Japanese Government expressed itself as in full accord with the purposes of the Conference, but nevertheless, in its communication of that date to the American Government, repeated its understanding that the scope of the Pacific and Far Eastern questions to be discussed was to be fixed by an exchange of opinions prior to the assembling of the Conference, and, furthermore, expressed the hope that the agenda of the Conference would in this way be arranged in harmony with the suggestions made in its prior memorandum.

The foregoing correspondence gives ample evidence to the fact that the government of Japan did not look to the Conference without misgivings. It was clearly evident that it felt that, so far as the discussion of Pacific and Far Eastern questions was concerned, it might be called upon to give justifications of certain of its acts which it would be difficult to give and that from the Conference might result policies or determinations which would not be agreeable to itself.

The Formal Invitation to the Principal Allied and Associated Powers. All of the Powers addressed having thus given their approval to the proposition that a Conference should be convened at Washington which should consider not only questions of Armament but Pacific and Far Eastern political questions as well, the President of the United States, on August 11, 1921, sent the following formal invitation to Great Britain, France, Italy, and Japan:

The President is deeply gratified at the cordial response to his suggestion that there should be a conference on the subject of limitation of armament, in connection with which Pacific and Far Eastern questions should also be discussed.

Productive labor is staggering under an economic burden too heavy to be borne unless the present vast public expenditures are greatly reduced. It is idle to look for stability, or the assurance of social justice, or the security of peace, while wasteful and unproductive outlays deprive effort of its just reward and defeat the reasonable expectation of progress. The enormous disbursements in the rivalries of armaments manifestly constitute the greater part of the encumbrance upon enterprise and national prosperity; and avoidable or extravagant expense of this nature is not only without economic justification, but is a constant menace to the peace of the world rather than an assurance of its preservation. Yet there would seem to be no ground to expect the halting of these increasing outlays unless the powers most largely concerned find a satisfactory basis for an agreement to effect their limitation. The time is believed to be opportune for these powers to approach this subject directly and in conference; and while, in the discussion of armament, the question of naval armament may naturally have first place, it has been thought best not to exclude questions pertaining to other armament to the end that all practicable measures of relief may have appropriate consideration. It may also be found advisable to formulate proposals by which in the interest of humanity the use of new agencies of warfare may be suitably controlled.

It is, however, quite clear that there can be no final assurance of the peace of the world in the absence of the desire for peace, and the prospect of reduced armaments is not a hopeful one unless this desire finds expression in a practical effort to remove cause of misunderstanding and to seek ground for agreement as to the principles and their application. It is the earnest wish of this Government that through an interchange of views with the facilities afforded by a conference, it may be possible to find a solution of Pacific and Far Eastern problems of unquestioned importance at this time, that is, such common understandings with respect to matters which have been and are of international concern as may serve to promote enduring friendship among our peoples.

It is not the purpose of this Government to attempt to define the scope of the discussion in relation to the Pacific and Far East, but rather to leave this to be the subject of suggestions to be exchanged before the meeting of the Conference in the expectation that the spirit of friendship and a cordial appreciation of the importance of the elimination of sources of controversy will govern the final decision.

Accordingly, in pursuance of the proposal which has been made, and in the light of the gracious indication of its acceptance, the President invites the Government of Great Britain to participate in a conference on the subject of Limitation of Armament, in connection with which Pacific and Far Eastern questions will also be discussed, to be held in Washington on the 11th day of November, 1921.

The Invitation to China. Upon the same date—August 11—an invitation was sent to the Chinese Government, which, it will appear, was worded similarly to that sent to the other Powers except that the paragraph referring specifically to the limitation of armaments was omitted, and China was invited to participate only in the discussion of Pacific and Far Eastern questions. The invitation ran:

Accordingly, in pursuance of the proposal which has been made, and in the light of the gracious indication of its acceptance, the President invites the Government of the Republic of China to participate in the discussion of Pacific and Far Eastern questions, in connection with the Conference on the subject of Limitation of Armament, to be held in Washington, on the 11th day of November, 1921.

The reply of the Chinese Minister at Washington addressed to the American Secretary of State was prompt, and was as follows:

August 17, 1921.

Sir.—I have the honor to acknowledge the receipt of your Department's memorandum of the 11th instant, which gives the text of the invitation of the President of the United States transmitted to the Government of the Republic of China on that date through the American Legation at Peking.

I am instructed by my Government, in a cablegram dated August 16, 1921, to communicate to you the following reply:

"On the 13th instant a note was received from the American Chargé d'Affaires at Peking transmitting the invitation of the President of the United States to the Government of the Republic of China to participate in a conference to be held in Washington on the 11th day of November, 1921.

"A conference for the purpose stated meets with the hearty concurrence of the Government of the Republic of China. Since the conclusion of the war in Europe the fear is general that there may again be a recurrence of the horrors of war. Furthermore, the center of gravity in matters international has recently shifted to the Pacific and the Far East. China occupies an important place not only on account of the extent of its territory and the density of its population, but also on account of its geographical position. The Pacific and Far Eastern questions as viewed by the Chinese people are questions affecting the peace of the world of the present day.

"This Conference at Washington, called by the President of the United States for the promotion of peace, cannot but contribute in a large measure to the accomplishment of results that will enable the people of the world to enjoy prosperity and happiness and obtain permanent release from the calamities of war. It is with special satisfaction that the Government of the Republic of China makes known its desire to co-operate on a footing of equality with other governments in this beneficent movement.

"The American Government by declaring that it is not its purpose to attempt to define the scope of the discussion in relation to the Pacific and Far East gives evidence of its readiness to be fair to all without any preconceived bias. The Government of the Republic of China desires to take the same position, and will participate in the Conference in the spirit of friendship and with a cordial appreciation of the importance of the elimination of the sources of controversy as stated in the American Chargé's note and observe perfect frankness and cordiality in the exchange of views and in arriving at decisions to the end that the purpose of the President of the United States to promote universal peace may be fulfilled."

Accept, Sir, the renewed assurance of my highest consideration.

SAO-KE ALFRED SZE.

CONVENING OF CONFERENCE 11

Belgium, Netherlands and Portugal Invited. In view of their several interests in the Far East invitations were later extended to and accepted by Belgium, the Netherlands and Portugal to participate in the work of the Conference so far as it might relate to Pacific and Far Eastern questions. Thus, in result, the Conference became one of five Powers so far as the limitation of armaments was concerned; and one of nine Powers, so far as Pacific and Far Eastern questions were concerned.

The Delegates. The following are the names of the Delegates sent by the participating Governments to the Conference:[3]

FOR THE UNITED STATES OF AMERICA:
Charles Evans Hughes.
Henry Cabot Lodge.
Oscar W. Underwood.
Elihu Root.
   Citizens of the United States.
FOR BELGIUM:
Baron de Cartier, Belgian Ambassador to the United States.
FOR THE BRITISH EMPIRE:
The Right Honorable A. J. Balfour, O. M., M. P., Lord President of the Council.
The Right Honorable Lord Lee of Fareham, G. B. E., K. C. B., First Lord of the Admiralty.
The Right Honorable Sir Auckland Geddes, K. C. B., British Ambassador.
   Canada—
      The Right Honorable Sir Robert Borden, G. C. M. G., K. C.

[3] The complete list of the Chinese Delegation, including Advisers, Secretaries, Counselors, etc., will be found in the Appendix.

12 CHINA AT THE CONFERENCE

Australia—
: Senator the Right Honorable G. F. Pearce, Australian Minister for Defense.

New Zealand—
: The Honorable Sir John Salmond, Judge of the Supreme Court of New Zealand.

India—
: The Right Honorable Srinivasa Sastri, member of the Indian Council of State.

FOR CHINA:
Mr. Sao-Ke Alfred Sze, Envoy Extraordinary and Minister Plenipotentiary to United States of America.
Mr. V. K. Wellington Koo, Envoy Extraordinary and Minister Plenipotentiary to the Court of St. James.
Mr. Chung-Hui Wang, Chief Justice of the Supreme Court of the Republic of China.

FOR FRANCE:
M. Aristide Briand, President of the Council, Minister for Foreign Affairs.
M. René Viviani, Deputy, Former President of the Council.
M. Albert Sarraut, Senator, Minister of Colonies.
M. Jules Jusserand, Ambassador of France to the United States.

FOR ITALY:
Signor Carlo Schanzer, Senator.
Signor Vittorio Rolandi-Ricci, Senator, Italian Ambassador to the United States.
Signor Luigi Albertini, Senator.

FOR JAPAN:
Baron Tomasaburo Kato, Minister of Navy.
Baron Kijuro Shidehara, Ambassador at Washington.
Prince Iyesato Tokugawa, President of House of Peers.
Mr. Masanao Hanihara, Vice Minister for Foreign Affairs.

FOR THE NETHERLANDS:
Jonkheer H. A. van Karnebeek, Minister for Foreign Affairs.
Jonkheer F. Beelaerts van Blokland, Envoy Extraordinary and Minister Plenipotentiary, Chief of the Political Division of the Ministry for Foreign Affairs.

Dr. E. Moresco, Vice President of the Council of the Netherlands East Indies.
Dr. J. C. A. Everwijn, Netherlands Minister to the United States.
Jonkheer W. H. de Beaufort, Minister Plenipotentiary.

FOR PORTUGAL:
Viscount d'Alte, Portuguese Minister to the United States.
Captain E. de Vasconcellos.

CHAPTER II

THE NEED FOR THE DISCUSSION BY THE CONFERENCE OF PACIFIC AND FAR EASTERN QUESTIONS

As is well known the Conference in its primary conception was to be one for arriving at a programme whereby the five Powers—America, Great Britain, France, Italy and Japan—might obtain relief from the heavy economic burdens imposed upon them by their competitive struggle to create and maintain vast military and naval establishments. That, as auxiliary to this, it was necessary to remove, as far as might be done, possible causes of war was, however, early seen, and, furthermore, it was appreciated that, possibly nowhere more than in the Far East, were there conditions existing and policies in operation which, if uncorrected or unchanged, would be provocative of international controversies and possibly of war. The President of the United States in his letter of invitation to the Powers to participate in the Conference referred in careful language to this fact but did not attempt to specify the conditions that needed to be corrected or the policies that needed to be changed. We may quote again his words upon this point:

> It is the earnest wish of this Government, that through an interchange of views with the facilities afforded by a conference, it may be possible to find a solution of Pacific and Far Eastern problems of unquestioned importance at this time, that is, such common

understandings with respect to matters which have been and are of international concern as may serve to promote enduring friendship among our peoples.

The specific matters regarding which common understandings among the Powers concerned needed to be arrived at can best be considered *seriatim* in the account which will be given of the work of the Conference. It will, however, be appropriate and advisable to give here a general characterization of the situation in the Far East in order to show, in broad outlines, the reasons why it was felt necessary that there should be a joint discussion of it by the nine Powers concerned.

China's Weakness and Japan's Ambitions. Two elements united to raise a serious international situation in the Far East. Upon the one hand was China with its vast territory, its millions of population, its considerable natural resources, its potential market for the manufactured goods of the world and for the investment of foreign capital; its special civilization, but, withal, its lack of an effective administrative system and its great military weakness. Upon the other hand there was Japan, with a strong, centralized, bureaucratic, monarchical government, largely under the control of militarists, with undisguised imperialistic policies eager to widen Japanese political and economic influence and control if not Japanese sovereignty, and exhibiting little regard for the legal or ethical rights of other peoples whose interests might stand in the way of the realization of its own ambitions. Thus, by a series of actions dating from the Sino-Japanese War of 1895, but especially from the Russo-Japanese War of 1905, Japan had shown to the world her desire and intention, if not checked, to dominate Eastern Asia and possibly the entire Far East. In 1895 she annexed Pescadores group of islands and the great island of Formosa lying off the southern coast of China and, before that time, belonging to China, and would have annexed the southern portion of the province of Fengtien and appurtenant islands,[1] had not France, Germany and Russia intervened.[2] In 1905 Japan expelled Russia from South Manchuria and installed herself in Russia's place, and from that time forward showed herself determined to exercise political as well as railway and other forms of economic control in that vast and rich area of China. At this time also she again obtained possession, by way of lease, of the southern portion of the Province of Fengtien —known as the Liaotung Peninsular or Kwantung District. In that same year Japan also brought Korea under her effective administrative control, and, in 1910, despite repeated assurances that the sovereignty and independence of that country would be respected, formally annexed it and made it an integral part of the Japanese Empire. In 1915 came the Twenty-One Demands by Japan upon China, by the presentation of which Japan made it no longer possible for her to deny, without insulting the intelligence of those to whom the denial might be addressed, that it was her desire to dominate China politically

[1] See Treaty of Peace of April 17, 1895. MacMurray's *Treaties with and Concerning China*, p. 18.
[2] See MacMurray, pp. 50-53.

as well as economically. Finally, by her conduct in Eastern Siberia since the Allied intervention in that country, Japan has given clear evidence of her desire to obtain a paramount economic and political position in that portion of Eastern Asia.

The significance of these series of acts by Japan was such that even he who ran could read, and it is therefore but fair to say that the Far Eastern Problem has been due to two factors, the one passive and the other active. The political and military weakness of China, and, after the Russian Revolution of 1917, of Eastern Siberia as well, has furnished the opportunity; the natural resources and agricultural products of China and Russia have furnished the temptation; and her own increasing population and lack of mineral resources have furnished Japan with the incentive for her aggressive imperialistic policies.

Interests of Western Powers. It may, however, be asked: What have been, or are, the direct interests of the Western Powers which have caused them to view with concern these developments in the Far East, and which have been deemed sufficient to make it desirable that the general situation should be discussed in a Conference in which they should all participate? The answer to this question is as follows:

In the first place, the Western Powers participating in the Conference, with the exception of Italy and Belgium have important territorial possessions in the Pacific and Far East which need to be protected, and Belgium has in China extensive financial investments. All of the Powers have in China commercial interests already considerable in amount but potentially still greater if reference be had to the future. Added to these interests, material in character, are two other factors psychological or ethical in character. So far as China is concerned, the Western Powers have undoubtedly been influenced, though not controlled, by an unwillingness to see that country unjustly and oppressively treated. So far as Japan is concerned, the Western Powers, especially since 1914, have viewed with disfavor the paramount influence exerted by the Japanese militarists, the continued maintenance of monarchical bureaucratic government, and the adoption by the Japanese Government of policies which, in political and ethical character, it has been difficult to distinguish from those of monarchical Prussia. It is not surprising that the Japanese people should have objected to being termed the Prussians of the East, but that they have been so viewed, and that by the actions of their Government justification has been given for this characterization, there can be little doubt.

Reduced then, to its simplest and baldest terms, the chief political problem which the Conference was called to solve was to find means of placing a restraint upon the imperialistic ambitions of Japan. In addition it was hoped that policies could be framed and declarations made that would be acceptable to all the Powers having treaty relations with China whereby harmonious and mutually beneficial political and economic relations with China could be established and maintained.

CHAPTER III

The Organization and Procedure of the Conference

Plenary Sessions. For final authoritative action, the Conference met in what were termed Plenary Sessions of which seven in all were held. The limitations of space of the room in which the sessions were held made it necessary that only persons obtaining tickets of admission could be permitted to attend. The sessions were, however, public in the fullest sense of the word. That is, newspaper reporters were present and no restrictions were placed upon what they might publish regarding the proceedings. In fact, however, the work of these sessions, aside from a number of formal addresses, as, for example, by the President of the United States, by Secretary of State Hughes, by Mr. Arthur Balfour, by M. Briand and others, and formal announcements, was almost wholly limited to the approval, without debate, and only occasionally with comments and explanatory statements, of the decisions which had been previously arrived at in Committees of the Whole.

Committees of the Whole and Sub-Committees. These Committees of the Whole were two in number, the one devoted to the consideration of matters of armament, and the other to Pacific and Far Eastern Questions. The Delegates of Powers, including China, which had not been invited to participate in the discussion of armaments of course did not attend the meetings of the Committee of the Whole which dealt with that subject.

These Committees of the Whole, it may be further observed, found it expedient, in a number of cases, to create sub-committees or drafting committees for the preliminary and detailed discussion of special topics. Thus it happened that some of the resolutions or agreements finally adopted by the Conference in Plenary Session had been first discussed in sub-committees of the Committee of the Whole, referred to drafting committees, perhaps again referred to a sub-committee then reported to and adopted by the Committee of the Whole, and, by that Committee, reported to the Conference in Plenary Session.[1]

Procedure. The meetings of the Committees of the Whole were not open to the public, nor were verbatim reports of all their proceedings published. However, in accordance with the general policy adopted by the Conference of giving as much publicity to its work as was possible, press " *Communiques* " were issued after each session of the

[1] Among such sub-committees were the following: On Post Offices, on Chinese Revenues (Tariff), on Extraterritoriality, and the Drafting Committee, which, in addition to its drafting functions, considered the matters of foreign troops and wireless installations in China. At the first plenary session there were also appointed two committees on Programme and Procedure to report respectively upon the programme and procedure to be followed by the two Committees of the Whole.

Committees which, in some cases, were practically verbatim statements of what was said, and, in all cases, were detailed in character. Sometimes press communiques were issued of the proceedings of even the sub-committees. It does not need to be said, however, that an important part of the work of the Delegates to the Conference took the form of highly confidential interviews between themselves and the representatives or spokesmen of the other Powers whereby preliminary understandings were arrived at before final action was taken either in the sub-committees or Committees of the Whole.

In connection and close association with the Conference, a number of highly important treaty agreements were arrived at and reported to the Conference. These treaties, the two most important of which were the so-called " Four Power Pact " and the Sino-Japanese Shantung Treaty, were reported to the Conference and noted upon its official records, and thus obtained, morally and politically, if not juristically, a more solemn recognition than if they had been negotiated and signed by the Powers concerned under ordinary circumstances. But they did not result from approving votes in and by the Conference itself. The relation to the Conference of the Shantung Treaty and of the Conversations leading to its drafting and signing, will be more particularly discussed in the chapter devoted to the Shantung Question.

The Conference, following the precedent of all other similar gatherings, created for itself a General-Secretariat, headed by a Secretary-General, whose function it was to keep the official records of the Conference, and who, it is announced, will prepare and distribute to the participating Governments an official report of the proceedings and determinations of the Conference. The Honorable John W. Garrett was elected Secretary-General. The American Secretary of State, Honorable Charles Evans Hughes, was unanimously elected Chairman of the Conference, and of such committees as he might be a member. It was agreed that, at the Committees' meetings, each Delegation should be accompanied by one secretary and one technical adviser. It was understood that each Delegation, through its own secretary, should keep minutes of the proceedings: also that the Secretary-General should keep a fairly full record, and should, in consultation with the secretaries of the several Delegations, draw up a résumé thereof which should be subject to the approval of each Delegation. It was further agreed that, at any time, a Delegate might call upon a stenographer to take down verbatim any statement which he might wish to make and have it thus recorded in the minutes. In actual practice statements or declarations by the Delegations were frequently mimeographed and distributed to the other Delegations, sometimes in advance of their presentation.

It should also be said that not infrequently, in exercise of the right of each Delegation to revise the reports made by the Secretary-General of what was said by them, considerable elisions were made. As it was not known to the other Delegations that these elisions would be made, the result is that, in the Secretary-General's minutes there occasionally appear gaps or instances of what seem to be irrelevancy.

It was decided that Technical Experts might be called upon to supply information asked of them by sub-committees but that they were not to decide questions of policy.

Regarding press Communiques, it was agreed that each Delegation could make public its own statement. Not infrequently, however, there was an agreement by all the Delegations that certain portions of the discussions in committee should not be thus made public.

With regard to the relationship between the adjustment of the Pacific and Far Eastern questions and the limitation of armaments, Secretary of State Hughes, in his opening address at the first Plenary Session of the Conference, said:

The inclusion of the proposal for the discussion of Pacific and Far Eastern questions was not for the purpose of embarrassing or delaying an agreement for limitation of armament, but rather to support that undertaking by availing ourselves of this meeting to endeavor to reach a common understanding as to the principles and policies to be followed in the Far East and thus greatly to diminish, and if possible wholly to remove, discernible sources of controversy. It is believed that by interchanges of views at this opportune time the Governments represented here may find a basis of accord and thus give expression to their desire to assure enduring friendship.

In the public discussions which have preceded the Conference, there have been apparently two competing views; one, that the consideration of armament should await the result of the discussion of Far Eastern questions, and another, that the latter discussion should be postponed until an agreement for limitation of armament has been reached. I am unable to find sufficient reason for adopting either of these extreme views. I think that it would be most unfortunate if we should disappoint the hopes which have attached to this meeting by a postponement of the consideration of the first subject. The world looks to this Conference to relieve humanity of the crushing burden created by competition in armament, and it is the view of the American Government that we should meet that expectation without any unnecessary delay. It is, therefore, proposed that the Conference should proceed at once to consider the question of the limitation of armament.

This, however, does not mean that we must postpone the examination of Far Eastern questions. These questions of vast importance press for solution. It is hoped that immediate provision may be made to deal with them adequately, and it is suggested that it may be found to be entirely practicable through the distribution of the work among designated committees to make progress to the ends sought to be achieved without either subject being treated as a hindrance to the proper consideration and disposition of the other.

The heads of the several Delegations made appropriate replies to Secretary Hughes' address, Mr. Sze, in behalf of the Chinese Delegation, saying:

Mr. Chairman and Gentlemen: The Chinese Government desires to record its gratification that this meeting of the nations has been called. It is convinced that the present is an auspicious time for bringing into accord the political and economic interests of the Powers in the Pacific. That the invitation to participate in this gathering should have come from the great American nation, and that the sessions are to be held in its capital city, is a source of additional gratification to the Chinese people. They and their Government will cordially co-operate in bringing to successful conclusion the work of the Conference.

We are all anxious that results beneficial to the world shall crown the work of this Conference. Mr. Chairman, with you guiding the meetings of the Conference, we feel confident that this end will be reached.

The proposition of Secretary Hughes that the two subjects of Armaments and Pacific and Far Eastern Questions should be synchronously considered being accepted, Committees on Programme and Procedure with respect to these two matters were appointed, each of which reported a recommendation, which was accepted by the Conference, that, before final action by the Conference, these matters should be discussed in Committees of the Whole. The result was that thenceforth armaments and Pacific and Far Eastern Questions were discussed separately, each in its own Committee of the Whole, the results of these committee discussions being reported from time to time to the Conference in Plenary Session, which sessions were convened only when resolutions had been adopted which were ready for final and authoritative action upon the part of the Conference.

Agenda. Prior to the convening of the Conference, the American Government drew up an Agenda which, though put forward as tentative in character, was, in fact, accepted unchanged by the Powers. Upon receiving this Agenda, the Chinese Government at Peking recommended to its Minister at Washington that certain changes and additions to it might be suggested to the American Government. Having received, however, verbal assurances as to the liberal spirit in which the heads of the proposed Agenda would be interpreted, and being therefore assured that China would have full opportunity to bring before the Conference the matters which she would wish to have discussed, these recommendations upon the part of the Peking Government were not pressed.

The Agenda followed by the Conference for the discussion of Pacific and Far Eastern Questions was, therefore, as follows:

1. Questions relating to China.
    First—Principles to be applied.
    Second—Application.
        Subjects—
            (a) Territorial integrity.
            (b) Administrative integrity.
            (c) Open door—equality of commercial, industrial opportunity.
            (d) Concessions, monopolies or preferential economic privileges.
            (e) Development of railways, including plans relating to Chinese Eastern Railway.
            (f) Preferential railroad rates.
            (g) Status of existing commitments.
2. Siberia (similar headings).
3. Mandated islands (unless questions earlier settled).
    Electrical communications in the Pacific.

Under the heading of "Status of Existing Commitments" it is expected that opportunity will be afforded to consider and to reach an understanding with respect to unsettled questions involving the nature and scope of commitments under which claims of rights may hereafter be asserted.

CHAPTER IV

China's Programme

China's Hopes. It has been pointed out in the first paragraph of this volume that the Conference, so far as the discussion of Pacific and Far Eastern Questions was concerned, devoted itself almost exclusively to a consideration of Chinese affairs. It is, however, important to remember that the primary purpose of the Conference was not to furnish relief to China. Its primary purpose was so to alter conditions in the Pacific and Far East generally as to make less likely international controversies in the future, and thus to reduce, as far as possible, the likelihood of war. If, from the action to be taken by the Conference, China was expected to receive especial benefit this would be because, fortunately for her, the existing situation could be bettered only by freeing her from certain of the treaty bonds which limited the autonomous use of her sovereign powers, and by obtaining a cessation of acts which had been in violation of her territorial sovereignty and administrative integrity. It was, indeed hoped, and, to some extent, this hope was realized, that the Powers participating in the Washington Conference would, in their actions, exhibit less national selfishness, and a higher regard for principles of pure justice than had previously found play in their international policies. It was, however, too much to expect that nationalistic interests would not be predominantly potent in the Conference. It was, therefore, not to be expected that China would obtain from the Conference all that she might desire to obtain, or all that, upon a basis of abstract justice, she ought to obtain. It was to be hoped, however, that she would obtain substantial relief from existing violations of her sovereign rights as well as a removal or loosening of some of the bonds which, by treaties, had restrained her freedom of political and administrative action.

For many years China had been unfortunately circumstanced as regards her relations to the other Powers. Very early she developed a civilization which, in many respects, has compelled the admiration of the world, and along with this civilization a form of government and methods of administration which, as their long persistence showed, were well suited to the simple economic life which her people led. When, however, she was brought into close contact with the Western World, and was forced, whether she wished it or not, to conform to their standards of international intercourse, to receive within her borders their merchants and missionaries, and to adopt many of the features of their intense commercial and industrial life—when this had come about, it soon transpired that China had not a governmental organization that would enable her to defend herself against attacks upon her sovereignty and territorial integrity. Because of her very size, as well as because of her lack of a strong executive authority in her central government, China found herself compelled to surrender the suzerainty or sovereignty which she had previously exercised over certain areas lying outside of her eighteen Provinces, and also to consent to the exercise within her borders of various forms of jurisdiction which have lessened the efficiency of her government over her own people and derogated from her dignity as a great State.

This had been her misfortune, but it was her good fortune that when, in the Conference at Washington, there was to be a general consideration by all the Powers concerned of their future policies in the Far East, China was able to come to the council table with no acts of aggression of her own toward other friendly Powers which needed to be explained or defended, and that she was able to appear as a petitioner for the recognition of and adherence to principles which were not only just in themselves but which in their application would be of benefit to all and promotive of international peace and good will.

In other words, China, at the Conference, did not have to ask that she be given any territory the legal title of which was not already conceded to be hers. She needed to ask for no rights other than those universally conceded to attach to sovereign States. She needed to ask only that certain wrongs done to her in the past should be corrected, and that she be made more fully the mistress in her own household. And even these claims she could put forward, not in absolute terms, but as warranted by the progress which she could demonstrate she had made in bringing her institutions and administrative methods into consonance with the standards of right and efficiency which the Western Nations exact of themselves. Thus supported, China believed that she would be able to show that what she sought would be beneficial to the Western Powers as well as to herself.

China's Fears. One very serious disadvantage China rested under at the Conference—one which was ever present in the minds of other Delegations and which undoubtedly operated powerfully to prevent China from securing much of the relief which she failed to obtain. This disadvantage was due to the fact of the disturbed political conditions in China itself, and the slight degree of effective control over the country which the central government at Peking was able to exert. It was not simply that there was an organization in the south, with its headquarters at Canton, which claimed to be the " constitutional " government of China and which denied legal legitimacy to the Peking Government, but that, throughout the Provinces, there were bodies of troops, aggregating, according to some estimates, more than a million men, many of whom were not under sufficient discipline, and all of whom were commanded by Tuchuns who paid only the slightest attention to the orders or wishes of the civil authorities, who fought against one another, and, not infrequently, committed acts of violence against persons and property within the regions in which they were stationed. Because of its weakness, the Peking Government for several years had not been able to obtain from the Provinces their normal contributions to the Central Treasury with the result that, deprived of an adequate revenue,

China had been obliged to rely upon loans for its current administrative expenses. Furthermore, the Peking Government, because of a lack of confidence by the Chinese people themselves in its efficiency and stability, had not been able, except in small measure, to obtain these loans from Chinese financial interests, but had been compelled to obtain them from abroad, and under very disadvantageous conditions. Finally, to make matters still worse, just before the convening of the Conference, the Peking Government had been compelled to make default upon certain of its foreign loans.

It is not surprising, therefore, that China came to the Conference with mixed feelings of hope and fear. It hoped for relief from past and existing wrongs by foreign Powers against herself. It feared lest these Powers would take advantage of her undeniable domestic disorder and administrative weakness to take concerted action to impose new restraints upon the autonomous exercise of her administrative powers which would amount to a political receivership, and which, though declared to be temporary in character, might easily prove permanent and thus mark the beginning of the end of China's status as a sovereign and independent nation. Upon this point it will be found that China won a complete victory, for not only were no new limitations imposed upon her by the Powers, but joint declarations by all the other Powers at the Conference were obtained to the effect that they would not take advantage of the existing conditions in China to obtain for themselves special rights, and that China was to have the fullest and most unembarrassed opportunity to develop and maintain for herself an effective and stable government.

China's Ten Points. The Chinese Delegates early considered among themselves whether it would be the best policy first to bring before the Conference specific proposals for action upon the part of the Powers, and then to endeavor to have adopted certain general principles and policies which it was hoped the Powers might formally adopt for the guidance and control of their future actions in the Far East and especially with reference to China; or whether it would be wiser first to seek the adoption by the Powers of these general principles, and then to bring forward the specific applications which China would desire. It was decided that this latter procedure would be likely to lead to the best result, and, therefore, at the opening of the first meeting of the Committee of the Whole on Pacific and Far Eastern Questions, on November 16, the Chinese Delegation presented what have since been known as China's Ten Points.

This maneuver upon the part of the Chinese Delegation was undoubtedly a wise one, since the result was that, from that time forward, the work of the Committee assumed almost exclusively the character of an examination of the Pacific and Far Eastern situation from the point of view of China. That is, China appeared as the proponent of the matters which were discussed. At the same time this meant that upon the Chinese Delegation was thrown by far the greatest burden of work which any of the Delegations at the Conference had to bear. Fortunately

CHINA'S PROGRAMME 33

it was in a position to assume this burden, and carry it with satisfaction to the Conference throughout the twelve weeks it was in session in Washington.

The Ten Points of China, together with the introductory statement of His Excellency Mr. Sze, Doyen of the Chinese Delegation, were as follows:

In view of the fact that China must necessarily play an important part in the deliberations of the Conference with reference to the political situation in the Far East, the Chinese delegation have thought it proper that they should take the first opportunity to state certain general principles which, in their opinion, should guide the Conference in the determinations which it is to make. Certain of the specific applications of the principles which it is expected that the Conference will make it is our intention later to bring forward, but at the present time it is deemed sufficient simply to propose the principles which I shall presently read.

In formulating these principles the purpose has been kept steadily in view of obtaining rules in accordance with which existing and possible future political and economic problems in the Far East and the Pacific may be most justly settled and with due regard to the rights and legitimate interests of all the powers concerned. Thus it has been sought to harmonize the particular interests of China with the general interests of all the world.

China is anxious to play her part not only in maintaining peace, but in promoting the material advancement and the cultural development of all the nations. She wishes to make her vast natural resources available to all peoples who need them, and in return to receive the benefits of free and equal intercourse with them. In order that she may do this, it is necessary that she should have every possible opportunity to develop her political institutions in accordance with the genius and needs of her own people. China is now contending with certain difficult problems which necessarily arise when any country makes a radical change in her form of government.

These problems she will be able to solve if given the opportunity to do so. This means not only that she should be freed from the danger or threat of foreign aggression, but that, so far as circumstances will possibly permit, she be relieved from limitations which now deprive her of autonomous administrative action and prevent her from securing adequate public revenues.

In conformity with the agenda of the Conference, the Chinese Government proposes for the consideration of and adoption by the Conference the following general principles to be applied in the determination of the questions relating to China:

1. (a) The Powers engage to respect and observe the territorial integrity and political and administrative independence of the Chinese Republic.

(b) China upon her part is prepared to give an undertaking not to alienate or lease any portion of her territory or littoral to any Power.

2. China, being in full accord with the principle of the so-called open door or equal opportunity for the commerce and industry of all nations having treaty relations with China, is prepared to accept and apply it in all parts of the Chinese Republic without exception.

3. With a view to strengthening mutual confidence and maintaining peace in the Pacific and the Far East, the Powers agree not to conclude between themselves any treaty or agreement directly affecting China or the general peace in these regions without previously notifying China and giving to her an opportunity to participate.

4. All special rights, privileges, immunities or commitments, whatever their character or contractual basis, claimed by any of the Powers in or relating to China are to be declared, and all such or future claims not so made known are to be deemed null and void. The rights, privileges, immunities and commitments, not known or to be declared are to be examined with a view to determining their scope and validity and, if valid, to harmonizing them with one another and with the principles declared by this Conference.

5. Immediately or as soon as circumstances will permit, existing limitations upon China's political jurisdictional and administrative freedom of action are to be removed.

6. Reasonable, definite terms of duration are to be attached to China's present commitment which are without time limits.

7. In the interpretation of instruments granting special rights or privileges, the well-established principle of construction that such grants shall be strictly construed in favor of the grantors, is to be observed.

8. China's rights as a neutral are to be fully respected in future wars to which she is not a party.

9. Provision is to be made for the peaceful settlement of international disputes in the Pacific and the Far East.

10. Provision is to be made for conferences to be held from time to time for the discussion of international questions relative to the Pacific and the Far East, as a basis for the determination of common policies of the Signatory Powers in relation thereto.

By the Sub-Committee on Programme and Procedure, composed of the heads of the nine Delegations, it was decided that, in the Committee of the Whole, there should first be a general discussion of the questions relating to China and then an examination of the various particular topics in the order listed in the Agenda which had been suggested by the American Government, together with a consideration of the Chinese proposals in so far as they might relate to, or come within the scope of, the heads of that Agenda. It was, however, agreed, when this programme was reported to the Committee of the Whole, that the fact that certain of China's ten points might not seem to be within the scope of these agenda heads, would not prevent their consideration at appropriate times. In accordance with this arrangement it was agreed, at the fourth meeting of the Committee on Pacific and Far Eastern Questions that No. 1 (a) of the Chinese proposals had been embodied in the Resolutions already adopted; that No. 1 (b) was a statement of China's policy and did not need discussion by the Conference;[1] that 3, 5, and 8 of the

[1] The approval by the other Delegations of China's proposals was, however, given in a formal vote which was taken.

Chinese proposals related to the territorial and administrative integrity of China; that numbers 2, 6 and 7 related to the headings Open Door and Concessions on the Agenda; and that number 4 related to sub-head G of the Agenda (Status of Existing Commitments), and that, therefore, these proposals would be considered in connection with these agenda topics as they were reached.

CHAPTER V

THE ROOT RESOLUTIONS

General Discussion. At the second meeting of the Committee of the Whole on Pacific and Far Eastern Questions, held November 19, Baron Kato, speaking in behalf of the Japanese Delegation, declared that the existing difficulties in China seemed to lie no less in her domestic situation than in her external relations. " We are anxious," he said, " to see peace and unity re-established at the earliest possible moment, but we want to avoid all action that may be construed as an intervention in the internal affairs of China. All that this Conference can achieve is, it seems to us, to adjust China's foreign relations, leaving her domestic situation to be worked out by the Chinese themselves." " We are solicitous," he added, " of making whatever contributions we are capable of towards China's realization of her just and legitimate aspirations. We are entirely uninfluenced by any policy of territorial aggrandizement in any part of China. We adhere without condition or reservation to the principle of the open door and equal opportunity in China. We look to China in particular for the supply of raw materials essential to our industrial life and for food stuffs as well. In the purchase of such materials from China, as in our trade relations with that country, we do not claim any special rights or privileges, and we welcome fair and honest competition with all nations."

The spokesmen for the other Delegations responded with equal sympathy and general approval to the propositions which the Chinese Delegation had advanced.

Baron de Cartier, speaking for Belgium, said his country unreservedly favored the policy of the open door, and that its Government would "take part willingly in all the measures that this Conference may adopt to insure that territorial integrity of China and to furnish her with the means to overcome her present difficulties."

Mr. Balfour, for the British Empire, said that "he had nothing to add to the frequent declarations of his Government with regard to its support of the open door in China, the integrity of China, and the desirability of leaving China to work out its own salvation and to maintain control over its own affairs and of substituting, when circumstances warranted, the normal processes of law for extraterritoriality."

Senator Schanzer stated that Italy would "give its support to the solutions that shall appear to be best suited to assure the free development of China and to guarantee an equality in footing of the different nations in their efforts to promote the progress of China and of commerce with that country."

M. Briand said that France was "disposed to consider in the most favorable light the Chinese claims in their entirety," but that in order to reach a practical result it would be necessary to make a thorough examination of each claim.

THE ROOT RESOLUTIONS

Jonkheer van Karnebeek declared that the Netherlands would consider the principles which China had laid down and the problems themselves "from the standpoint of the world's general welfare and to examine them in a spirit of sympathy and friendship towards China."

Viscount d'Alte, in behalf of Portugal, said that his Delegation was in full agreement with the views that the other Delegations had given expression to.

Mr. Root, of the American Delegation, then called attention to the fact that, from the expression of views which had been given, it appeared that there was a substantial agreement upon certain fundamental principles and that he therefore suggested that these be formulated in Resolutions to be adopted by the Conference. With reference to these Resolutions he thought that existing facts should be recognized and that the agreements should be framed as expressions of a common purpose, as evidencing no intention to interfere with valid treaties and agreements which, after examination, might be found to create existing rights, but leaving the possessors of these rights with full powers to make changes in them for the benefit of China.

China Defined. The question "What is China?" having been incidentally raised, Dr. Koo, of the Chinese Delegation, said that the territories of the Chinese Republic were defined in its Constitution and that these were to be considered as an entity to which the principle of territorial integrity should be applied. As regarded administrative integrity, he pointed out that there was some difference in the existing status of administration in the different parts of China; that, generally speaking, the administration of China proper, composed of the twenty-two Provinces, formed one unit, and that of the other parts of the Republic constituted other units; but that this was an internal arrangement within the Republic, and, so far as the outside world was concerned, the principle of administrative integrity should be confirmed for the Chinese Republic as one unit; and that, in the framing of the proposed Resolutions, these observations should be taken into consideration.

Root Resolutions. At the third meeting of the Committee,[1] held November 21, Mr. Root presented the following four Resolutions which he had drafted:

It is the firm intention of the Powers attending this Conference:

(1) To respect the sovereignty, the independence, and the territorial and administrative integrity of China.

(2) To provide the fullest and most unembarrassed opportunity to China to develop and maintain for herself an effective and stable government, overcoming the difficulties incident to the change from the old and long-continued imperial form of government.

(3) To safeguard for the world, so far as it is within our power, the principle of equal opportunity for the commerce and industry of all nations throughout the territory of China.

(4) To refrain from taking advantage of the present conditions in order to seek special rights or privileges which would abridge the rights of the subjects or citizens of friendly states and from countenancing action inimical to the security of such states.

---

[1] Hereafter the Committee of the Whole on Pacific and Far Eastern Questions will usually be referred to as "the Committee of the Whole," or simply as "the Committee."

Upon inquiry upon the part of Mr. Sze of the Chinese Delegation, Mr. Root declared that the word "respect" as used in the first resolution, was intended as a stronger word than "observe."[2]

Upon inquiry from Baron Kato, of the Japanese Delegation, Mr. Root said that the words "administrative integrity" "did not affect any privileges accorded by valid or effective grants; that, on the contrary, respect for the administrative integrity of a country required respect for the things that are done in the exercise of its full sovereignty by an independent State." To this, Mr. Balfour, of the British Delegation, added the statement that this in no way barred the Committee in future discussions from either leaving things as they were or modifying them. The Chairman, Mr. Hughes, also declared that "it was not contemplated to preclude discussion of any question relating to China; that China was a sovereign and independent State, and had her administrative autonomy except as limited by restrictions which might have been placed upon it through valid engagements; that it might be possible for the Committee to remove or modify some of these restrictions, but that those would be particular questions."

Regarding the second Resolution it was agreed that the words "overcoming the difficulties incident to the change from the old and long-continued imperial form of government," added nothing to the substance of the Resolution, and they were therefore deleted.

[2] The Chinese Delegation in the first of its Ten Points had used the phrase "respect and observe."

Regarding the third Resolution, it was declared by Mr. Root that the words " so far as it is within our power " were used in order to make it certain that no nation was attempting to do anything outside its competency. Upon the suggestion of Mr. Balfour, it was then agreed that the wording should be so changed as to make the Resolution read that the Powers would " use their influence for the purpose of effectually establishing and maintaining the principle of equal opportunity," etc.

As to the fourth Resolution, Mr. Root pointed out that the phrase " abridge the rights " did not refer exclusively to a particular vested right of an individual because the nations had treaties with China which authorized them or their citizens to acquire further rights;—" that it was broader and went beyond that particular case having to deal with cases where there were rights guaranteed by China and protected by these treaties; that any attempt to obtain rights for one Power that would detract from rights already vested in the nationals of another Power, by some valid engagement with the government of China, would constitute an abridgement." In other words that, in the future, no nation might attempt to do, what Japan in 1915 by her Twenty-One Demands had done,—to obtain rights that would be in derogation of the existing rights of the other Treaty Powers.

As finally adopted by the Committee and later approved by the Conference at its fourth plenary session, held December 10, 1921, and embodied in a draft treaty to which all the nine Powers gave their

THE ROOT RESOLUTIONS

assent at the sixth plenary session on February 4, the Root Resolutions ran as follows:

It is the firm intention of the Powers attending this Conference hereinafter mentioned, to wit, the United States of America, Belgium, the British Empire, France, Italy, Japan, the Netherlands and Portugal:

1. To respect the sovereignty, the independence and the territorial and administrative integrity of China.
2. To provide the fullest and most unembarrassed opportunity to China to develop and maintain for herself an effective and stable government.
3. To use their influence for the purpose of effectually establishing and maintaining the principle of equal opportunity for the commerce and industry of all nations throughout the territory of China.
4. To refrain from taking advantage of the present conditions in China, in order to seek special rights or privileges which would abridge the rights of the subjects or citizens of friendly States and from countenancing action inimical to the security of such States.

With regard to the fourth of these Resolutions the observation may be made that it was distinguishable from the other three Resolutions in that it was not based, as were they, upon statements previously made in the Committee by the several Delegations, and that thus, in fact, Mr. Root had received no specific instruction from the Committee to frame and introduce it. The Resolution therefore represented a proposition to which the Powers were asked to commit themselves which was initiated by the American Delegation upon its own responsibility. For this action China owes a debt of gratitude to the American Government, for its adoption at the very outset of the Conference meant a decisive victory of China, tending as it did, to allay its fears that the Powers at the Conference might propose forms of concerted action that would mean further encroachments upon China's administrative autonomy.

The Ten Points of China and the Root Resolutions had fallen under the heading of the Agenda " Questions Relating to China: Principles to be Applied." The Points having been presented and the Root Resolutions adopted, the Committee was prepared to discuss the second of the Agenda heads—" Applications." For purposes of convenience it was decided that the two sub-heads of this chief head " Territorial Integrity " and " Administrative Integrity " might be considered together and the Chinese Delegation was asked to bring forward the specific matters coming under these titles which it wished to have discussed.

CHAPTER VI

CHINA'S TERRITORIAL AND ADMINISTRATIVE INTEGRITY

Before proceeding to an examination of the matters presented by the Chinese Delegation under these two heads of the Agenda, it will be advisable to consider for a moment the significance of these terms and their relation to the more comprehensive term "Sovereignty."

Sovereignty. This term is employed in both Constitutional (or national) and International Jurisprudence. In International Law the concept indicated by the word is practically synonymous with independence; that is, a State which is recognized by other States as Independent and as a member of the "Family of Nations," is conceded to have the right, free from foreign interference, to exercise the rights which, as a sovereign State in a constitutional sense, it is conceded by constitutional law to have over its own territory and the persons living or sojourning within its territorial limits. To fix the meaning of the term Sovereignty it is therefore necessary to first determine its constitutional implications.

Under all systems of modern public law a State, viewed as a sovereign political entity, is regarded as the possessor of a legally supreme will which is, therefore, the source of all the legal rights, public and private, which exist within its territory, and which can be claimed by those over whom its jurisdiction extends. This absolute principle, has, perhaps, never been better stated than by the great American jurist and judge, Chief Justice Marshall. In the case of *The Exchange,* decided in 1812 by the United States Supreme Court, Marshall said:

The jurisdiction of the nation within its own country is necessarily exclusive and absolute. It is susceptible of no limitation not imposed by itself. Any restriction upon it, deriving validity from an external source, would imply a diminution of its sovereignty to the extent of the restriction, and an investment of that sovereignty to the same extent in that Power which would impose such restriction. All exceptions, therefore, to the full and complete power of a nation within its own territory, must be traced up to the consent of the nation itself. They can flow from no other source.

Thus, as Marshall goes on in this case to show, even the privileges of extraterritoriality which, in all the States of the civilized world, are enjoyed by diplomatic officials, and which are strenuously insisted upon by their home governments, are declared to owe their existence to the implied consent of the States within which such international rights, or other privileges, are claimed.

International Law, as has been said, recognizes this principle of constitutional law and therefore lays down the rule that, except where permission has been explicitly or by necessary implication granted by a nation, other nations will respect its exclusive jurisdiction over its own territory, reserving only the right upon their part to intervene, in extreme cases, when the State in question has made a clearly unjust and offensive use of its legal powers.

The generality of the foregoing principle of International Law leads to another fundamental doctrine of international jurisprudence, namely, the legal equality of all members of the Family of Nations. Thus Oppenheim, the eminent English authority, says:

In entering into the Family of Nations a State comes as an equal to equals; it demands that certain consideration be paid to its dignity, the retention of its independence, its territory and its personal supremacy. Recognition of a State as a member of the Family of Nations contains recognition of such State's equality, dignity, independence, and territorial and personal supremacy. The States are International Powers because they recognize these qualities in one another and recognize their responsibility for violations of these qualities.[1]

Because of its very sovereignty and independence every State has the right, acting in conformity with the provisions of its own constitutional law, to enter into agreements with other States providing that it will permit those other States, under specified conditions or limitations, to exercise within its own territory, certain political powers. These agreements, owing their existence and continuance to the will of the agreeing State, are not in derogation of that State's sovereignty and independence. There are, therefore, no *a priori* limits to the extent to which a State may thus go in permitting other States to exercise jurisdiction, through their own officials, within its own area. Thus a given State may not only agree that it will itself exercise certain of the powers only in a specified way, but may consent that

[1] International Law, 2d ed., p. 113.

certain of its own public revenues shall be supervised or administered by officials of other States, or that their citizens, being within its borders, shall be legally amenable only to the orders of tribunals maintained by these other States, which tribunals may, according to the understanding entered into, apply in such cases the local law or that of their own countries.

It does not need to be said that only imperative necessity disposes a State to grant to other States the right to exercise jurisdictional powers within its own territory, and that that State is justified in seeking at the first opportunity to obtain from other States a release from the concessions which it has made. It would seem, also, but an act of international amity and good will that those States should yield to this legitimate desire as soon as, in their judgment, objective circumstances reasonably justify their doing so. In other words, their own selfish interests or desire for authority does not justify them in retaining these jurisdictional powers in another State which is their technical equal as a member of the Family of Nations, when the conditions which originally led to their concession no longer exist.

Territorial Integrity. To the term " Territorial Integrity " two meanings may properly be given.

(1) In the first place it means that, without its consent, no portion of the territory belonging or subject to the jurisdiction of a sovereign and internationally independent State, may justly be taken from it by other States. This consent may be voluntarily given by the State, as, for example, when it cedes by

way of sale or exchange, or for any other reason deemed good and sufficient, a portion of its soil to another State, or recognizes the political independence of any of its colonies or dependencies or of its own local subdivisions; or the consent may be wrung from it at the conclusion of an unsuccessful war.

(2) In the second place "Territorial Integrity" has reference to the fact of the exclusiveness of political jurisdiction which a State has over its own territory. As thus used, the "Territorial Integrity" of a State is violated whenever, without its consent, any foreign Power exercises jurisdiction within its borders, or when, what amounts to the same thing, it gives official support to the refusal of its nationals to obey the laws of the local sovereign.

Thus, in this sense of the term, in the case of China, her "Territorial Integrity" is violated by the maintenance, without her consent, of foreign troops upon her soil; by the establishment and operation within her borders of foreign post-offices; by the erection and operation of wireless stations; by the refusal of a foreign Government to permit postal parcels entering China to be examined by the Chinese customs officials; or, by the practice of certain Legations at Peking in granting asylum to fugitives from Chinese justice.

Due respect to China's territorial integrity is not paid by other nations which seek to exercise a political influence or to claim without treaty right preferential or monopolistic economic interests within specified geographical areas of her territory, for such a claim necessarily impairs the supreme and exclusive authority of China within such areas, or limits her freedom to develop them economically and industrially according to her own judgment in specified cases as they arise. Thus the claims of various of the Treaty Powers to " Spheres of Interest " and " Special Interests " in China are, and have been recognized to be, in derogation of China's Territorial Integrity. That this is so has been repeatedly declared by Great Britain and the United States in their communications with regard to the Open Door, and especially with reference to the efforts made by Japan to have Manchuria and Eastern Inner Mongolia excepted from the operations of the new Consortium.

The Territorial Integrity of a State is limited, even if not violated, when it is compelled to lease portions of its area to other Powers, or to grant to them any other form of extraterritorial jurisdiction. Thus, in the case of China, the existence of the leased areas of Weihaiwei, Liaotung Peninsula, Kowloon, and Kwangchouwan; the municipal " Settlements " at Shanghai and the " Concessions " at other of her cities; and the extraterritorial rights enjoyed by foreigners throughout her limits, are all limitations upon her Territorial Integrity.[2]

---

[2] In his note of July 3, 1900, to the Powers, Secretary Hay referred to the policy of the United States as one to preserve Chinese territorial and administrative "Entity." It would not appear, however, that it was intended that the word should have any other effect than would have followed from the use of the term "integrity." It is probable that Secretary Hay used the word entity because of some special feeling held by him that, under the given circumstances, it was, as a matter of verbal nicety, the appropriate term to use. As to this see the article by J. B. Moore, "Hay's Work in Diplomacy," in the American *Review of Reviews*, August, 1905.

Administrative Integrity. The terms " administration " and " administrative " have, in political science, two distinct meanings. In the one, which is restrictive, they relate to the operations of the executive branch of a government; in the other, they refer generally to all the operations of a government, that is, to the actual conduct of the affairs of all of its departments—legislative, judicial, and executive.

It is quite clear that, as used in the Agenda for the Washington Conference, the term Administrative Integrity had reference to all the operations of the Chinese Government. This had been the meaning many times attached to it by the Powers in their communications with each other with reference to China and, therefore, it was understood that this was the idea of the American Government when it employed the term in its Agenda for the Conference.

This being established, it is clear that any restraint placed upon the Government of China in the exercise of its sovereign powers would be treated as *pro tanto* an impairment of its Administrative Integrity. The restraints based upon treaty or other agreements which China had made, were to be regarded as *limitations;* those having no contractual basis, as *violations* of this Integrity.

With reference to its executive operations or administrative powers within the narrower sense of the word, China's Administrative Integrity is impaired when one of its services, as, for example, its maritime customs or its salt tax, is under foreign control or supervision. With regard to its legislative functions, China's Administrative Integrity is impaired when she is not permitted to determine her policies, fiscal or of other character, according to her own judgment as to what her interests require. Thus, in so far as China is not permitted to fix the rates of her maritime customs, or to vary these rates according to the commodities to which they apply, her Administrative Integrity upon its legislative side, is seriously limited. So, also, the existence of foreign "Settlements" and "Concessions" in various of her Treaty Ports, operate as a limitation upon her local administrative powers. Furthermore, the whole system of extraterritorial jurisdiction is in derogation of her exclusive right as the local sovereign to administer justice.

It is thus seen that the concepts of Territorial Integrity and Administrative Integrity are so closely related that, in very many cases, a violation or limitation of the one is almost necessarily a violation or limitation of the other. It was therefore almost unavoidable that, in the proceedings of the Conference, the two subjects of Territorial Integrity and Administrative Integrity should be treated as a single indivisible topic.

The matters which the Chinese Delegation brought forward under these two heads were the following: Tariff Autonomy, Extraterritoriality,[2] Leased Areas, Spheres of Interest, Foreign Troops, Police Boxes, Postal Services, Electrical Communications upon her soil, and the Agreements and Notes of May 25, 1915.

[1] Under this title was of course included municipal concessions and settlements which would be expected automatically to disappear with the abrogation of extraterritorial rights in China.

In order that the consideration of these subjects might be expedited, the Conference or Committee did not attempt fully to dispose of one of these topics before another was taken up. That is, several were under consideration at the same time, but in different sub-committees which reported from time to time to the Committee of the Whole. The discussions that were had and the actions taken can, however, be most clearly presented if we take up these subjects one after another, and show as to each of them what was done regarding them.

China's Rights as a Neutral. The eighth of the Points presented by the Chinese Delegation to the Committee on November 16 read:

> China's rights as a neutral are to be fully respected in future wars to which she is not a party.

At the thirteenth meeting of the Committee of the Whole, Dr. Wang, stated that this proposition was an obvious one and clearly embraced within the first of the four Root Resolutions that had already been adopted. However, in view of the fact that, in the past, China's rights as a neutral had been greviously disregarded,—conspicuously in the Russo-Japanese War, the land operations of which were carried on wholly upon Chinese soil and in the recent war when Japan had landed her troops at a point one hundred and fifty miles from their military objective—the leased area of Kiaochow,—he felt that it was appropriate that the Powers should pledge themselves to this proposition.

Secretary Hughes, Mr. Balfour, and M. Viviani said that their governments fully concurred in the Chinese declaration of principle. Mr. Hanihara, speaking for Japan, said that he associated himself with these views, but added: "No country now desires to assail the neutrality of another country, but when a country is not in a position to fulfill its obligations as a neutral, then the other Powers must defend themselves." The point of this remark, in view of the circumstances under which, in 1915, Japan had violated China's rights as a neutral, is somewhat obscure.

Without further discussion, China's proposition was unanimously adopted, but, as finally adopted by the Conference at its fourth plenary session, held December 10, and as embodied as Article VI in the Nine Power Treaty Relating to Principles and Policies to be Followed in Matters Concerning China, the resolution was made to read:

The Contracting Powers, other than China, agree fully to respect China's rights as a neutral in time of war to which China is not a party; and China declares that when she is a neutral she will observe the obligations of neutrality.

CHAPTER VII
Tariff Autonomy

Chinese Statement. The matter of obtaining for China a fuller control of her own maritime Customs as regards the rates to be charged and their apportionment among different classes of articles was first raised at the fourth meeting of the Committee, but China's proposals with regard to this subject were not formally presented to the Committee until its fifth meeting on November 23, when Dr. Koo made in substance the following statement:[1]

Prior to the year 1842, China had enjoyed the full right of fixing her customs duties. But in that year and in the subsequent years, she had made treaties with Great Britain, France and the United States, in which for the first time a limitation was imposed on this full right. The rule of 5 per cent ad valorem was thereby established, and later a schedule was fixed upon the basis of the current prices then prevailing. In the years preceding 1858, prices began to drop, and the 5 per cent customs duty collected appeared consequently to be in excess of the 5 per cent prescribed. A revision was therefore asked for by the Treaty Powers and was effected in 1858. From that time until 1902, however, as prices mounted and the Chinese Government had been receiving less than the 5 per cent rate, no request was made on the part of the Treaty Powers for a revision. If the Chinese Government did not at that time press for a revision, it was only because the needs of the Government were

[1] See "Conference on the Limitation of Armament" published by the American Government as Senate Document No. 126, 67th Congress, 2d session, pp. 469-473.

then comparatively few and the revenues collected, small as they were, were not inadequate to meet the requirements.

It was only in 1902, as a result of the Boxer uprising, that another revision was made with a view to raising sufficient revenue to meet the newly imposed obligations arising out of the protocol of 1901. In that tariff, however, the rates were calculated on the basis of the average prices of 1897-1899, the then prevailing prices not being taken into account. But the revenue collected according to this increased tariff was hardly sufficient to meet the obligations of the indemnity. In 1912, another attempt was made to revise the tariff in order to bring it more in accord with actual prices. It proved to be a failure, as the unanimous consent of some 16 or 17 Powers was not obtained. It was only after six years of protracted negotiation that another revision was effected in 1918. The purpose of this revision was to increase the rate to an effective 5 per cent, but the resulting tariff, which was now in force, yielded only $3\frac{1}{2}$ per cent in comparison with the prices of commodities actually prevailing.

Dr. Koo asked on behalf of the Chinese delegation for the recovery by China of the right to tariff autonomy. He said that in the first place the existing régime in China constituted an infringement of the Chinese sovereign right to fix the tariff rate at her own discretion—a right enjoyed by the States throughout the world.

Again, it deprived China of her power to make reciprocity arrangements with the Powers and ran counter to the principle of equality and mutuality. While foreign goods imported into China had to pay only 5 per cent of import tax, goods of Chinese origin imported to foreign countries had to pay customs duties of maximum rate. For instance, Chinese tea imported to the United Kingdom had to pay 1 shilling per pound, which meant 25 per cent, as the price there was about 4 shillings per pound; Chinese tobacco on importation into Japan had to pay 350 per cent; raw silk into Japan, 30 per cent; and manufactured silk into the United States, 35 to 60 per cent. Such a régime constituted a serious impediment to the Chinese export trade and to China's economic development.

Moreover, a uniform rate for all kinds of commodities without latitude to differentiate rates between luxuries and necessaries had

TARIFF AUTONOMY

obvious disadvantages. For example, it was evident that machinery and similar merchandise so much needed by China ought to pay a low rate, while on the other hand luxuries, such as cigars and cigarettes, should be more heavily taxed, as much for mitigating or preventing the injurious effects on the morals and social habits of the people from the use of these luxuries as for raising more revenue. The Chinese tariff was therefore not a scientific one, as it failed to take into consideration the economic and social as well as the fiscal needs of the Chinese people.

Continuing, Dr. Koo said that the present tariff caused a serious loss of revenue to the Chinese exchequer. Customs duties formed one of the most important sources of revenue of a country. Great Britain, for example, received 12 per cent out of her total revenue; France, 15 per cent; United States, 35 per cent. (In giving these figures, he said he would be glad to hear his colleagues correct him, if they were not accurate to date.) The Chinese customs revenue, on the other hand, played, for nearly 100 years, a comparatively insignificant part in the national revenue. Besides, a large part of China's customs revenue was pledged to meet various foreign loans secured thereon, and this fact again reduced the amount available for the needs of the Government.

Furthermore, under the existing customs régime it was exceedingly difficult to revise the tariff, even for the modest purpose of raising it to an effective 5 per cent. The revision of 1902 was the first revision in 44 years, and the resulting tariff yielded only $2\frac{1}{2}$ per cent in comparison with the market value of the imports, *i. e.*, $2\frac{1}{2}$ per cent less than what could have been collected if the tariff schedule had been revised to date. The revision of 1918, as was pointed out, was effected only after six years of negotiation, and being based on the average prices of 1912-1916, the new tariff of 1918 was yielding only $3\frac{1}{2}$ per cent. But even an effective 5 per cent import tariff, which would probably produce an additional revenue of nearly 15,000,000 taels, might, however, still prove inadequate to meet the manifold needs of the Chinese Government, such as those for education, road building, sanitation, and public welfare.

In view of the foregoing reasons, Dr. Koo asked the Powers to agree to the restoration to China of her tariff autonomy. In making this request, the Chinese Government entertained no desire to interfere with the present administration of the maritime customs, which was generally considered to be efficient and satisfactory, nor to interfere with the devotion of the funds of the maritime customs to the liquidation of foreign loans secured thereon. What he had uppermost in mind in asking for the recognition of China's tariff autonomy was the right to fix and differentiate the tariff rates. As the establishment of such a new régime would require time, it should come into force only after a period to be agreed upon. Before that period, a maximum rate should be agreed to, and within that maximum rate China should enjoy full freedom of differentiating rates, for example between luxuries and necessaries. But negotiation for the purpose of fixing a maximum rate might take months, and as the present Chinese financial condition needed some immediate relief, it was proposed that on and from January 1, 1922, the Chinese import tariff should be raised to $12\frac{1}{2}$ per cent, a rate mentioned in the Chinese treaties with Great Britain, the United States, and Japan.

Discussion. Mr. Root stated that the treaty of 1903 between the United States and China contained a provision concerning the abolition of likin and proceeded to read Article IV of the treaty as follows:

The Chinese Government, recognizing that the existing system of levying dues on goods in transit, and especially the system of taxation known as likin, impedes the free circulation of commodities to the general injury of trade, hereby undertakes to abandon the levy of likin and all other transit dues throughout the Empire and to abolish the offices, stations, and barriers maintained for their collection and not to establish other offices for levying dues on goods in transit. It is clearly understood that after the offices, stations, and barriers for taxing goods in transit have been abolished no attempt shall be made to re-establish them in any form or under any pretext whatsoever.

Continuing, Mr. Root stated that the treaties of 1902 and 1903 between China and Great Britain and

TARIFF AUTONOMY

Japan, respectively, contained provisions of similar effect, and that the increase in customs duties to $12\frac{1}{2}$ per cent, as proposed in those treaties, was clearly intended as a consideration for the abolition of likin, and inquired of Mr. Koo what proposal, if any, he was ready to make with regard to "likin."

Mr. Koo answering said that likin was a handicap to the internal, as well as the external trade of China, and that the substantial classes in China favored its abolition. He added that the Government would be prepared to abolish likin if tariff autonomy were granted, and if it were possible to agree on an increase in customs duties, which would compensate for its abolition. He considered the original proposition of an increase to $12\frac{1}{2}$ per cent as hardly sufficient today, in view of the great increase in public expenses.

Senator Underwood called attention to the fact that stable conditions in China would be for the benefit of all those nations who did business with China and that such conditions were desirable. Pointing out that it was recognized as axiomatic that no government can function effectively without revenue, he said that the committee, in working to secure ample revenue for China, was laying the cornerstone for stabilization in that country. He remarked that he did not consider the transportation tax as a tax on imports and added that the United States had had a similar tax. Continuing, Senator Underwood pointed out the necessity of refraining, as far as possible, from disturbing existing trade conditions: readjustment and revision should be made with a view to avoiding any disturbance of established channels of trade. It seemed advisable, in view of the efficiency of the present system of administration, that it should not be disturbed. In his opinion no arbitrary rates, such as 12½ per cent, should be decided upon, but rather such changes should be made as to assure a revenue sufficient to keep China out of debt. It was important that every cent collected should go to meet the expenses of government. He added that Mr. Koo's suggestion that China should have the right to charge more duty on luxuries than on necessities was a reasonable one, but argued that a simple and not a complicated tariff was desired. Finally, the needs of the Government should be clearly known and the customs levies changed to meet them.

Sub-Committee Discussions. The matter of Tariff Autonomy for China having thus been presented and discussed in general terms by the Committee, it was decided that, for its further and detailed consideration, a sub-committee[2] should be appointed.

Six meetings of this sub-committee were held.

At the first meeting, held November 29, Dr. Koo presented the following specific proposals on behalf of China:

1. The present import duty of 5 per cent shall be forthwith increased to 12½ per cent.

2. China agrees to abolish likin on January 1, 1924, and the Powers agree to put in force on the same day the levy of certain

[2] Upon this sub-committee the following were appointed by the Chairman of the Committee: Senator Underwood (Chairman) for the United States; Baron de Cartier, with M. Cattier as alternate, for Belgium; Sir Robert Borden, with Sir John Jordan as alternate, for the British Empire; Dr. Koo, for China; M. Serraut, for France; Senator Albertini, with Signor Fileti as alternate, for Italy; M. Hanihara, for Japan; Jonkheer Beelaerts van Blokland, for the Netherlands; Captain Vasconcellos, for Portugal.

surtaxes on import and export duties provided for in the Treaty of 1902 with Great Britain and in that of 1903 with the United States and that of 1903 with Japan; and the Powers further agree to the levy of an additional surtax to be put in force on the same day for articles of luxury over and above the import tariff rate of $12\frac{1}{2}$ effective. In all other respects, the undertakings of China and the Powers herein stipulated are to be carried out in accordance with the terms of the Treaties above mentioned.

3. Within five years from the date of agreement, a new customs régime shall be negotiated and concluded by treaty on the basis of a maximum rate of 25 per cent *ad valorem* for any article imported into China, within which rate China is to be free to regulate and arrange the import tariff schedule. This new régime is to be in force until the end of the period referred to in paragraph 5 below.

4. The reductions now applicable to the customs duty collected on goods imported into and exported from China by land shall be abolished.

5. The treaty provisions between China and the Powers by which the levy of customs duties, transit dues and other imposts is regulated shall be abrogated at the end of 10 years from date of agreement.

6. China voluntarily declares that she is not contemplating to effect any fundamental changes in the present system of customs administration, or to disturb the devotion of the customs revenue to the services of the foreign loans secured thereon.

In support of the propositions which he had presented, Dr. Koo called attention to the fact that the significance to China of a competency upon her part to control her import customs rates was peculiarly great since Chinese industries were as yet largely undeveloped, that Chinese communities were still largely agricultural in character, and that, therefore, China, for a considerable time, could not depend to any considerable extent upon sources of revenue other than maritime customs. Also, he pointed out that the facts should not be overlooked that already a large portion of her present receipts from impost duties was pledged for the payment of the interest upon foreign loans and that the Chinese Government had imperative need for increasing her present revenues in order to meet the legitimately increased expenses for education, public health, and provision for additional public utilities.

The discussion of specific forms of relief to be granted to China with regard to her tariff almost immediately revealed certain of the peculiar conditions of fact which were to render impossible the obtaining by China, in the immediate future, of her desire with respect to a considerable increase in her customs rates. The matter of this increase was indissolubly bound up with the abolition by China of Likin charges upon imported and exported commodities, and doubt was expressed whether, so long as present political conditions should persist in China, the Chinese Government at Peking would be able to take effective action throughout the Provinces with regard to this matter. Doubt was also felt by some of the representatives of the other Powers whether, aside from this, it would be advantageous to China to give to her an increased revenue which might find its way into the hands of the various military commanders, or Tuchuns, in China and thus tend to strengthen these leaders who, as yet, had not been brought into due subordination to the civil authorities. Thus, even those Delegations which were desirous of enabling China to increase her customs revenues, were inclined to impose the condition that China should give the undertaking that the increased revenue to be derived by her should be devoted to certain specific purposes. There is reason for believing that the American Government was not disposed to require such an undertaking, but that Japan was insistent that, out of this increase, provision should be made for the payment of outstanding debts to foreign financial interests which had already matured, and that Great Britain desired that this increase should be devoted to specific productive enterprises. There was also some discussion in the sub-committee as to whether the increased customs revenues which China might receive might be divided into allotments,—certain percentages to be devoted to debt payments, education and productive enterprises, and the remainder to be available for the current administrative expenses of the Chinese Government. This plan, however, came to nought when it was finally decided that China was not to be given the immediate treaty right to levy more than an effective five per cent upon imports.

It should further be said that, even when it was proposed that the immediate increase of import duties should be limited to $7\frac{1}{2}$ per cent, the Japanese Delegation protested that this would have such serious effects upon Japanese industries that it could not give its assent. The matter was referred to the Japanese Government at Tokyo and this position of its Delegation affirmed.

From the very beginning it appeared certain that, the domestic conditions of China being what they were, no promise would be given by the Powers of a definite date at which China was to obtain complete tariff autonomy.

At the second meeting of the sub-committee, held November 30, Sir Robert Borden, in behalf of the British Delegation, definitely proposed that the present tariff of China should be immediately increased so as to make it an effective five per cent, and that, after a general revision of the valuations of imports into China had been obtained, the rate should be raised to $7\frac{1}{2}$ per cent.

Japanese Statement. Mr. Odagiri, in behalf of the Japanese Delegation, submitted the following statement:

Taking into consideration the views and suggestions made by our colleagues at yesterday's meeting, as well as of the commercial relations between Japan and China, the Japanese sub-committee states its views regarding the increase of tariff as follows:

As the Japanese trade with China covers more than 30 per cent of China's foreign trade and represents the same percentage of Japan's oversea trade, the country which would suffer most by the revised tariff would be Japan.

Japan supplies those articles which are mostly sold to the lower class of people in China to satisfy their daily need. Those goods imported from Japan represent the production of a large number of comparatively small Japanese manufacturers.

Therefore, this sudden and big increase of tariff would mean on the one hand forcing high prices, to the purchasers in China—the majority of the common people—causing a higher cost of living, and, on the other hand, would mean a serious effect upon the industry of Japan. In consequence it is very important that the tariff revision should follow a gradual process, allowing enough time to enable the people of the countries concerned to adjust their economic life accordingly.

In the foregoing circumstances the Japanese sub-committee declares, much to its regret, that in its opinion the abrupt increase of tariff to an effective $7\frac{1}{2}$ rate—more than doubling duties of the present 3½ per cent tariff—is impossible to put into practice, and as to a 12½ per cent tariff, it is absolutely impractical.

The revision which the Japanese sub-committee believes proper is an increase of the present tariff to an effective 5 per cent in accordance with the agreement between the Chinese Government and the diplomatic bodies in Peking.

But in order to avoid the delay of 6 months to one year required for the establishment of the aforesaid conversion, the Japanese sub-committee would propose the alternative measure which will avoid unnecessary delay and will result in greater advantage to the Chinese Government.

As an alternative measure, it is proposed to levy a surtax, of say 30 per cent, upon export, import and coastwise trade, which should bring in to the Chinese Government an additional revenue of approximately silver $20,000,000.

The fruit of raising the tariff to an effective 5 per cent, on imports would be an increase of revenue of about silver $16,000,000.

This suggested surtax is not an entirely new idea, for this year all the Powers agreed to the imposition of a surtax of 10 per cent, levied on all customs dues for one year, as a measure of temporary famine relief, and it was estimated by the customs authorities that this surtax would produce about taels 5,000,000.

Of course, the Japanese sub-committee would not mean absolutely and permanently to refuse its assent to the proposal to increase the tariff. On the contrary it would say that Japan is ready to assist the Chinese in revising the tariff as is shown in the supplementary Treaty of Commerce and Navigation which was concluded during the year 1903.

There is no objection whatever on the part of Japan to the suggestion to appoint an international committee to proceed to China and study the condition of tariff, the likin, and related matters, in order to solve this difficult question and present to the respective Governments any workable scheme for increasing the tariff.

Discussion. Dr. Koo, replying to Sir Robert Borden and M. Odagiri, pointed out that an increase of the Chinese tariff rates to 7½ per cent would be but a slight one, and that, assuming that Japan's share of China's foreign trade was 30 per cent, such an increase would mean scarcely more than six million dollars gold to be spread annually throughout all parts of the Japanese Empire, and should, therefore, not be a cause of anxiety to Japanese traders and manufacturers.

Dr. Koo also presented statistical tables showing: (1) The Actual Percentages of Import Duties Collected in Comparison with the Value of Imports; and (2) The Average Percentage which the Import Duties Collected by Certain Countries Bear to the Value of Their Imports; and (3) The Average Percentage which the Import Duties Collected by Japan Bear to the Value of her Imports. These tables showed, as Dr. Koo pointed out, that, because of a discrepancy between the actual valuations and those used for the purpose of assessing tariff duties, there had been an annual net loss of revenue to China approximating 27,000,000 Chinese dollars, and that this fact should be taken into consideration in determining the relief which China in the future should obtain.

After some discussion Dr. Koo, on behalf of the Chinese Delegation, expressed his willingness to accept Sir Robert Borden's proposals with an amendment to the effect that, pending the revision of the import tariff to $7\frac{1}{2}$ per cent effective, a surtax should be immediately applied which would yield a revenue equivalent to $7\frac{1}{2}$ per cent effective. Dr. Koo also accepted Sir Robert's corollary proposition that a higher rate, say a maximum of $12\frac{1}{2}$ per cent, might be levied on articles that might be fairly denominated luxuries.

Further discussion showed some objection upon the part of the French Delegation to the higher charge upon luxuries since, M. Sarraut said, it would be difficult to draw a line of demarkation between necessities and luxuries; also objection upon the part of Sir Robert Borden to the proposition of levying forthwith a surtax until there had been a revaluation of commodities and an effective $7\frac{1}{2}$ per cent rate established. But all the Delegations, Japan alone excepted, gave their approval to the proposition that China should be given the right to levy $7\frac{1}{2}$ per cent tariff duties. The Japanese Delegation said that, before giving her approval to this, they would have to communicate with their Government at Tokyo.

Draft Agreement. At the third meeting of the sub-committee, held December 27, Sir Robert Borden submitted a draft of agreement upon the Chinese tariff which he hoped would bring together the conflicting viewpoints and especially those of the Chinese and Japanese Delegations. It is not necessary to quote this tentative draft, which was discussed at the fourth meeting of the sub-committee, it being sufficient to give the text of the report prepared by Senator Underwood based upon that draft and the discussion that was had upon it. This report, submitted at the fifth meeting of the sub-committee, held January 3, 1922, was as follows:

The Powers attending this Conference agree:

I. That immediate steps be taken through a Special Conference representing China and the Powers which accept this agreement to prepare the way for the speedy abolition of likin and the fulfillment of the other conditions laid down in Article VIII of the Anglo-Chinese Commercial Treaty of September 5, 1902, and the corresponding Articles of the United States and Japanese Treaties, with a view to the levying of the surtaxes as provided in those Articles.

II. That the present tariff on importation shall be forthwith revised and raised to a basis of 5 per cent effective.

That this revision shall be carried forthwith by a Revision Committee at Shanghai on the general lines of the last revision. The revision shall proceed as rapidly as possible with a view to its completion within four months from the conclusion of the present Conference, and the revised tariff shall become effective two months after publication without awaiting ratification.

III. That the interim provisions to be applied until the Articles referred to in paragraph I come into operation be considered by the aforesaid Special Conference which shall authorize the levying of a surtax on dutiable imports as from such date, for such purposes, and subject to such conditions as they may determine. The surtax shall be at a uniform rate of $2\frac{1}{2}$ per cent *ad valorem* except in the case of certain articles of luxury which in the opinion of the Conference can bear a greater increase without unduly impeding trade, and upon which the total surtax shall not exceed 5 per cent.

IV. (1) That there shall be a further revision of the tariff to take effect at the expiration of four years following the completion of the immediate revision herein authorized, in order to ensure that the rates shall correspond to the *ad valorem* rates fixed.

(2) That following this revision there shall be periodical revisions of the tariff every seven years for the same purpose.

(3) That in order to prevent delay such periodical revisions shall be effected in accordance with rules to be settled by the Special Conference provided in paragraph I.

V. That in all matters relating to customs duties there shall be effective equality of treatment and of opportunity for all nations parties to this Agreement.

VI. That reductions now applicable to the customs duties collected on goods imported into and exported from China by land shall be abolished.

TARIFF AUTONOMY

VII. That the charge for transit passes shall be at the rate of 2½ per cent *ad valorem* except when the arrangements contemplated in paragraph I are in force.

VIII. That the Treaty Powers not here represented shall be invited to accept the present Agreement.

IX. That this Agreement shall over-ride all provisions of Treaties between China and the Powers which accept it which are inconsistent with its terms.

The Delegate for China submitted the following communication which it was unanimously agreed should form a part of the foregoing Agreement as an Appendix thereto:

The Chinese Delegation has the honor to inform the Committee on the Far Eastern Questions of the Conference on the Limitation of Armament that the Chinese Government have no intention to effect any change which may disturb the present administration of the Chinese Maritime Customs.

Land Frontier Duties. Discussion of these proposals revealed the fact that the French Delegation was unwilling to accept Section VI which provided for the abolition of the reductions provided for by existing treaties on goods imported by land into China, and that the American Delegation was equally insistent upon the retention of this provision in order that the principle of equality of treatment might have full application to all of China's imports.[3]

---

[3] In explanation with regard to China's land frontier tariff duties, the following statement, taken, in the main, from Willoughby's *Foreign Rights and Interests in China,* pp. 152, is given:

Special Arrangement Regarding Trade between Korea and Manchuria. Japan has with China a special arrangement whereby she secures a reduction in customs dues on goods imported into Manchuria from or through Korea (Chosen) and exported from Manchuria to or through Chosen, by rail via Antung. On dutiable goods leaving Manchuria by rail for places beyond that point, only a two-thirds customs rate is charged. The

The French Delegate took strongly the view that the special terms which China had given to imports from Indo-China were correlative to the considerable special personal, civil and commercial privileges which France had given to Chinese nationals residing in Tongking—some 400,000 in number.

"Transit" charges on these goods are one-half of the customs charges, that is, one-half of the two-thirds normal rate. Goods from Manchuria for local consumption in Hsin Wiju or which within two years are carried by rail beyond that point pay the full rate but obtain a rebate of one-third.

Russian Frontier Trade. By certain regulations attached to the St. Petersburg Treaty of 1881 between China and Russia it was provided that no duties should be levied on the frontier of the two countries within a limit of one hundred li (33 miles). This zone was abolished in 1912 to take effect on January 1, 1913. By regulations agreed upon by the two countries, under date of July 8, 1907, it was provided that China was to establish customs stations on the frontier, but was to collect no duties upon goods shipped by rail to stations within this former zone. Also that certain areas were to be fixed within which goods shipped by rail should be required to pay but two-thirds of the regular Chinese import duty. Thus at Harbin the two-thirds duty area was to extend to all points within a radius of ten li from the station. At other designated stations the radius was to be five li. For all its smaller stations on the Eastern Railway the radius was to be three li. Goods shipped out of these areas were to pay the full duty. It was further provided that while this was a special arrangement between China and Russia, not only Russia but all foreign merchandise shipped to China over the Chinese Eastern Railway should enjoy the same treatment.

Russia on her part agreed to a reduction of one-third on goods imported across her frontier from China.

According to Article 10 of the Regulations for trade between China and Russia by Railway promulgated September 8, 1896, goods carried by rail were to pay one-third less than the regular customs dues. A little later (July 8, 1907, and May 30, 1908) it was agreed that in determining the duties to be paid at the ports of Manchuli and Suifenho there should be the same reduction.

Frontier Trade with Indo-China. By Article III of the amended Trade Regulations for trade between China and France of 1887 it was provided that with a view to developing as rapidly as possible the commerce between China and Tonkin the rights of exportation and importation stipulated in Articles VI and VII of the treaty of April 23, 1886, should be provisionally modified so that all foreign goods entering the Chinese provinces of

TARIFF AUTONOMY

The British Delegation indicated that, while India was prepared to accept the principle that the rates of customs duties levied on all land frontier should be the same as the maritime customs, it was expected

Yunnan, Kwangtung and Kwangsi (the Kwang Provinces) across the frontier should pay three-tenths less duties than the regular tariff, and that the goods from China across the frontier should pay four-tenths less than the regular rate. It has since been further agreed that the rates fixed by the Revised Tariff of 1903 should not be followed, but those of 1858. This agreement is still in force.

In 1895 by a treaty signed at Peking on June 20 between France and China it was provided that "Chinese goods in transit from one or the other of the four towns open to commerce on the frontier, Lungchou, Mengtse, Ssumao and Hokou, in passing through Annam, will pay on leaving, duties reduced by four-tenths"; and also that "Chinese goods exported from the four above-named locations and transported to Chinese maritime or river ports, open to commerce, shall pay on passing the frontier export duty reduced by four-tenths. A special certificate will be delivered setting forth the payment of this duty, and destined to accompany the goods. When they shall arrive at one of the maritime or river ports open to commerce, they shall pay the half re-importation duty in conformity with the general rule for all goods of like nature in the maritime or river ports open to commerce."

Chinese goods transported from Chinese martime or river ports open to commerce, by way of Annam, towards the four above-named localities, shall pay on crossing (the frontier) full duty. A special certificate will be delivered, setting forth the payment of this duty, and destined to accompany the goods. When they shall arrive at one of the frontier customs stations they shall pay on entry half re-importation duty based on the reduction by four-tenths.

By Article VIII of the Anglo-Chinese Convention of March 1, 1894 (MacMurray, p. 1), it was provided that Chinese products and manufactures, with the exception of salt, should enter Burmah by land free of duty; that British and Burmese produce, with the exception of rice, should be exported to China by land free of duty, and that the import duty on salt and the export duty on rice should not be higher than the duties on import or export by sea. By Article IX of the same Convention it was provided that the duty on goods imported by land by certain specified routes from Burmah to China should be less by three-tenths than the duties specified in the general tariff of China's Maritime Customs; and that the duty on goods exported from China by those routes should be less by four-tenths than those specified in the general maritime customs.

that, if this was done, arrangements would be made to restore to India the right to impose import duties on Chinese goods entering Burmah, and export duties on Burmese products and British manufactures exported by land to China.

In order to meet these views of France and Great Britain, the following provision, drafted by Sir Robert Borden to replace Article VI of the draft of agreement previously reported by Senator Underwood, was proposed at the sixth meeting of the sub-committee, held January 4, 1922:

> That the principle of uniformity in the rates of customs duties levied on all the frontiers, land and maritime, of China be recognized, and that it be referred to the Special Conference mentioned in paragraph I [of the Draft Heads of Agreement of December 28], to make arrangements to give practical effect to this principle, with power to authorize any adjustments which may appear equitable in cases in which the customs privilege to be abolished was granted in return for some local economic favor. In the meantime, any increase in the rates of customs duties or surtax imposed in pursuance of the present agreement shall be levied at a uniform rate *ad valorem* on all frontiers, land and maritime.

Discussion in Committee of the Whole: Statement by Senator Underwood. This proposal received the unanimous approval of all the members of the sub-committee, which thereupon terminated its work upon the Chinese tariff, and submitted its conclusions to the Committee of the Whole.

Thereupon, at the seventeenth meeting of the Committee on Pacific and Far Eastern Questions, held January 5, the consideration of the conclusions of the sub-committee which have been above given was

TARIFF AUTONOMY

taken up. In submitting them to the Committee, Senator Underwood said, in part:[4]

The importance of this Agreement in reference to trade conditions in China, which to a large extent were controlled by the duties levied at the customs house, went, Senator Underwood thought, much further than the mere question of the money involved. As he had stated some time ago, he thought one of the principal causes of irritation and difference between the nations of the world arose from their trade conditions, and when one nation felt that it was not standing on an equality with another nation it was likely to bring about conditions of unrest and might lead in the end to war; and the great purpose of this convention was to eliminate the causes of war. Therefore Senator Underwood thought that the members of the committee could congratulate themselves at this time that they had reached, in the report that he would present, an understanding to wipe out the discriminations on the border of China in reference to customs duties and that would make all the countries of the world feel that they would hereafter have an open door that meant equal opportunity of trade.

The agreement in its present form, Senator Underwood said, contained provisions relating to two distinct phases of tariff readjustment, namely, those which might become immediately applicable without taking treaty form requiring ratification and those which must be embraced in a treaty and which would require ratification. The first of these related to the immediate revision of the present tariff to a basis of 5 per cent effective and the second related to subjects to be dealt with in a special conference which would be charged with taking measures looking to the speedy abolition of likin and the application of surtaxes, together with the realization of the principle of uniformity in the rates of customs duties on all frontiers whether land or maritime.

The stages, therefore, of applying the terms of the agreement were as follows:

1. A committee of revision would meet forthwith at Shanghai to revise the present tariff to a basis of 5 per cent effective. This

[4] What follows is quoted or paraphrased from the report given in U. S. Senate Document No. 126, 67th Congress, 2d session, pp. 589 ff.

revision would become effective two months after publication without awaiting ratification. It would provide an additional revenue amounting to about $17,000,000 silver.

2. Immediate steps would be taken for a special conference representing China and the Powers charged with the duty of preparing the way for the speedy abolition of the likin and the bringing into effect of the surtaxes provided for in the treaties between China and Great Britain of 1902 and China and the United States and Japan of 1903. The Special Conference would likewise put into effect a surtax of 2½ per cent *ad valorem,* which would secure additional revenue amounting to approximately $27,000,000 silver, and a special surtax on luxuries, not exceeding 5 per cent *ad valorem,* which would provide a still further revenue amounting to $2,167,000 silver. The additional revenue from customs duties provided in the present agreement would fall into four categories, as follows:

1. Increase to 5 per cent effective, $17,000,000 silver.
2. Surtax of 2½ per cent, $27,000,000 silver.
3. Surtax not exceeding 5 per cent on luxuries, $2,167,000 silver.
4. Total additional revenue, $46,167,000 silver.

With the completion of the work of the Special Conference carrying into effect the abolition of likin and the application of the surtaxes provided in the treaties with Great Britain, Japan, and the United States, the additional revenue provided should amount to $156,000,000 silver. The present tariff produced revenue at the rate of $64,000,000 silver for 1920. If to this were added the additional revenue provided for in the agreement, the total yield from customs duties would amount to $110,167,000 silver. Aside from these measures, there were important provisions in the agreement relating to future revisions of the tariff with a view to maintaining it on a correct basis of valuation so that it might produce revenue at the effective rates to which China was entitled. Following the immediate revision there would be a second revision in four years and subsequent revisions every seven years.

Heretofore there had been some difficulty encountered in securing revisions regularly. The special conference was charged with the duty of providing means whereby future delays in revision might be avoided. Carrying into effect the general agreement already adopted by this Conference, there was a provision in the present agreement for effective equality of treatment and of opportunity. This provision carried with it an important recognition of the principle of uniformity in the rates of customs duties levied on all frontiers, which meant the abolition of discriminatory practices in relation to goods imported by land.

Senator Underwood said he felt that for the first time measures had been taken which effectually removed the highly unjust and controversial preferences with which the foreign trade of China had heretofore been encumbered. Those nations which had enjoyed the advantages of preferential treatment across their land frontiers had acted with commendable foresight and altruism in surrendering those minor advantages in trade to the broader principles of equality of treatment and the general betterment of the conditions of friendly trade competition. This appeared to him to represent a signal achievement, not only in the interest of China and of each of the Treaty Powers, but also in the interest of trade in general and of peace itself.

Chinese Statement. Dr. Koo, responding to the remarks and report of Senator Underwood, took the opportunity of making the following formal statement, in behalf of the Chinese Government, regarding the re-establishment of China's tariff autonomy—a matter to which, he said, the Chinese people attached great importance:

On November 23 last, I had the honor, in behalf of the Chinese Delegation, to lay the tariff question of China before the committee. Three propositions were submitted. The principal one of them was for the restoration to China of her tariff autonomy: the other two being intended merely as provisional measures to prepare the ground for the early consummation of the main object. At the same time I stated that it was not the intention of the Chinese Government to effect any change that might disturb the present administration of the Chinese maritime customs, though this statement obviously could not be reasonably construed to preclude China's legitimate aspirations gradually to make this important branch of the Chinese Government more national in character.

I explained the reasons why China was desirous of recovering her freedom of action in respect to the matter of levying customs duties. The committee, after some discussion, referred the whole question to a sub-committee, of which Senator Underwood has been the distinguished chairman. The results of the discussions in the sub-committee are embodied in an agreement which has just been laid before you. It is a valuable agreement, embodying, as it does, a number of important points connected with the effective application of the present régime of treaty tariff. But it will be noted that the question of the restoration of tariff autonomy to China is not included, it being the opinion of some members of the sub-committee that it would not be practicable to fix at present a definite period within which the existing treaty provisions on tariff were to be brought to an end, and that the question should be decided in the light of conditions that might arise in the future.

The Chinese Delegation, however, cannot but wish, that a different view had prevailed. Tariff autonomy is a sovereign right enjoyed by all independent states. Its free exercise is essential to the well-being of the state. The existing treaty provisions, by which the levy of customs duties, transit dues, and other imports is regulated, constitute not only a restriction on China's freedom of action, but an infringement on her sovereignty. Restoration to her of tariff autonomy would only be recognition of a right which is hers and which she relinquished against her will.

The maintenance of the present tariff régime means, moreover, a continued loss of revenue to the Chinese Government. The customs import duty under this régime is limited to the very low rate of 5 per cent *ad valorem* for all classes of dutiable goods, compared with the average rate of 15 per cent to 60 per cent levied by other countries. In fact, because the duties are levied on the basis of a previously fixed schedule, the actual collections amount to only $3\frac{1}{2}$ per cent effective. The customs revenue, therefore, constitutes only about $7\frac{1}{2}$ per cent of China's total revenue, while the average for the principal countries in the west ranges from 12 per cent to 15 per cent at present, and still higher before the war. When the proposed surtax of 2½ per cent for ordinary articles and of 5 per cent on certain luxuries eventually goes into effect, more revenue will be produced, but even then it will hardly be commensurate with the rapidly growing needs of the Chinese Government. Much of the elasticity of the fiscal systems of other States depends upon their freedom to regulate their customs duties. To provide the fullest and most unembarrassed opportunity to China to develop and maintain for herself an effective and stable government, it is necessary to restore tariff autonomy to her at an early date.

The necessity to levy a uniform low duty has encouraged a disproportionate increase in the import of luxuries such as wine and tobacco; and apart from the loss of revenue consequent upon giving these things the same rate as is levied on the necessaries of life, the effect on the social and moral habits of the Chinese people has been altogether deleterious. A beginning has been made in the agreement before the committee in authorizing a levy of an additional surtax of 2½ per cent on certain articles of luxury, but it is apparent that a greater increase is needed if a restraining influence is to be exercised in the use of these articles of luxury.

Nor is it to be overlooked that the present treaty tariff régime is an impediment to China's economic development. Under this régime China enjoys no reciprocity from any of the Powers with which she stands in treaty relations. Though every Treaty Power enjoys the advantage of having its wares imported into China at the exceptionally low rate of 5 per cent *ad valorem,* the Chinese produce and merchandise, on entering into any of these countries, is subjected to the maximum rates leviable, which are in some cases 60 or 70 times the rate which she herself levies on foreign imports. The necessity of levying uniform duties on all articles imported into China, on the other hand, makes these duties on such articles as machinery and raw materials for Chinese industries a handicap to China's industrial development. At present there are more than 1000 Chinese factories employing foreign machinery and methods and engaged in over 30 different kinds of important industries. To enable them to live and develop and thereby contribute to the growth of China's foreign trade in which all nations are deeply interested, some latitude is necessary in the regulation of the customs duties.

Besides, regulation of China's tariff by treaty must inevitably, in the nature of things, work unjustly and to her great detriment. Thus, whenever China makes a proposal, be it for revision of the tariff to bring it more into harmony with the prevailing prices or for an increase of the customs duty to meet her increased needs, the unanimous consent of more than a dozen Treaty Powers is necessary. As each country naturally desires to protect and promote its own commercial interests in China, and as the industries of these Treaty Powers vary in character and export different kinds of merchandise, they all seek to avoid the burden of the new revision or increased rate falling upon the industries of their own countries. With this end in view, different conditions are not infrequently attached by different Powers to their consent to revise the customs tariff or increase the rate.

Thus, though this matter of custom tariff is intimately connected with the well-being of the Chinese State, the interests of the Treaty Powers appear to be placed at times before the legitimate interests of China. Under such circumstances the difficulty of effecting any adjustment or arrangement favorable to China can easily be conceived, and it has at times been well nigh insurmountable. On one occasion or another there is always some Power who considers its own interest in the matter of Chinese customs tariff more important than the supreme interests of China. The experience of the Chinese Delegation in the sub-committee on tariff, much as it has accomplished, has not altogether removed the ground for this opinion. But as unanimity is required, the dissent of one Power is sufficient to defeat and upset a general arrangement agreed to by all the others, while by virtue of the most favored nation clause, a concession or privilege granted by China to one nation for a specific consideration is at once claimed by all without regard to the *quid pro quo.*

In view of the inherent difficulty and injustice of the present régime, and of the wholesome and desirable effect which restoration of tariff autonomy is sure to have upon the trade and economic development of China, as well as upon the evolution of her fiscal system, the Chinese Delegation feel in duty bound to declare that though this committee does not see its way to consider China's claim for the restoration of her tariff autonomy, it is not their desire, in assenting to the agreement now before you, to relinquish their claim; on the contrary, it is their intention to bring the question up again for consideration on all appropriate occasions in the future.

Senator Underwood, with reference to what Dr. Koo had said, declared that he did not desire to discuss the pending resolution further than he had already done, but he wished to make one statement before the committee adjourned that morning. He had listened with much interest to the statement read by Mr. Koo in reference to the desire of China for tariff autonomy, which was a very natural and proper desire. Any great government naturally wished the time might come when she might control her own finances, notwithstanding that she yielded the control herself. So far as he was concerned, he gladly welcomed an opportunity, when it could be done, of restoring to China her entire fiscal autonomy; but he thought it was fair to the sub-committee and to the members of this committee to say this—and it was in line with the resolution pending—that he was sure this sub-committee and the committee to which he was now addressing himself would gladly do very much more for China along all lines if conditions in China were such that the outside Powers felt they could do so with justice to China herself. He did not think there was any doubt in the minds of the men on the sub-committee as to the question that if China at present had the unlimited control of levying taxes at the customs house, in view of the unsettled conditions now existing in China, it would probably work, in the end, to China's detriment and to the injury of the world; and he thought that had more to do with the sub-committee's not making a full and direct response to Mr. Koo's request than anything else. He was sure there was no desire on the part of the other powers to be selfish, or not to recognize the full sovereignty of China, and he only rose to say this, that if he was a judge of the situation, a judge of the temper of conditions in the balance of the world, he felt sure that when China herself established a parliamentary government of all the Provinces of China and dispensed with the military control that now existed in many of the Provinces of China, so that the outside Powers might feel that they were dealing with a government that had entire and absolute and free control of the situation, China could expect to realize the great ideals of sovereignty that she asked for at this table.

Senator Underwood, in behalf of the sub-committee, then recommended that, as the agreements which had been reported related to two different matters, namely, (1) the immediate revision of the present tariff in accordance with existing treaties, and (2) other matters involving the modification of existing treaties, they should be referred to the Drafting Committee with a view to putting the agreement into final form and separating the principles which could go into immediate force from those which would require treaty ratification by the Powers.

Drafting Committee: Report from. This suggestion was adopted and the resolutions referred to the Drafting Committee, which reported them back to the eighteenth session of the Committee of the Whole, held January 16, 1922.

Mr. Root, who made the report in behalf of the Drafting Committee, said that the sub-committee on Chinese Revenue had suggested that those of its recommendations which were declaratory in nature should be separated from those which modified existing treaties and would therefore need to be put into treaty form. As to the first, the Drafting Committee reported as follows:

Agreement on the Revision of the Chinese Tariff.

With a view to providing additional revenue to meet the needs of the Chinese Government, the Powers represented at this Conference, namely, the United States of America, Belgium, the British Empire, China, France, Italy, Japan, the Netherlands, and Portugal, agree:

That the customs schedule of duties on imports into China adopted by the tariff revision commission at Shanghai on December 19, 1918, shall forthwith be revised so that the rates of duty shall be equivalent to 5 per cent effective as provided for in the several commercial treaties to which China is a party.

A revision commission shall meet at Shanghai, at the earliest practicable date, to effect this revision forthwith and on the general lines of the last revision.

This commission shall be composed of representatives of the Powers above named and of representatives of any additional Powers who have treaties with China providing for a tariff on imports and exports not to exceed 5 per cent *ad valorem* and who desire to participate therein.

The revision shall proceed as rapidly as possible with a view to its completion within four months from the date of the adoption of this resolution by the Conference on the Limitation of Armament and Pacific and Far Eastern Questions.

The revised tariff shall become effective as soon as possible, but not earlier than two months after its publication by the revision commission.

7

The Government of the United States, as convener of the present Conference, is requested forthwith to communicate the terms of this resolution to the Governments of Powers not represented at this Conference, but who participated in the revision of 1918, aforesaid.

Discussion as to Russia. Mr. Root said [5] that, since the above agreement had been authorized by the subcommittee on drafting, the suggestion had been made that the terms of the clause which provided that the revision commission should be composed of representatives of the Powers present, and of representatives of any additional powers who had treaties with China providing for a tariff on imports and exports not to exceed 5 per cent, would include Russia, but that it would be impossible to send notice to Russia or to collaborate with Russia in such a commission because Russia had no government which had been recognized by any of the Powers here present. In conversation upon this subject with several members of the subcommittee on drafting the suggestion had been made that an amendment should be added to the resolution inserting after the words " additional powers " the words " having governments at present recognized by the Powers represented at this conference "; and, if that met the views of the members of this committee, it would hardly be worth while to call the sub-committee on drafting together again, as all its members were present. Mr. Root therefore suggested that the committee amend the report by the inclusion of these words.

[5] The report of the discussion that follows is that given in Senate Document No. 126.

Grand Duchy of Luxemburg. Baron de Cartier said he wished to raise the question of the position in which the Grand Duchy of Luxemburg would be placed by the resolution just read by Mr. Root. On September 2, 1861, a treaty of commerce and navigation was concluded between China and the King of Prussia, the latter acting in his own name as well as in the name of other members of the Zollverein, among which was the Grand Duchy of Luxemburg. When war had been declared between China and Germany, the Netherlands minister in Peking, Jonkheer Beelaerts van Blokland, in charge of the interests of the Grand Duchy in Peking, made representations to the Chinese Government, in order to protect Luxemburg interests, as the Grand Duchy did not go to war with China. It was Baron de Cartier's impression that the Grand Duchy was embraced in the "additional governments" mentioned in the resolution, but this should be made clear.

The chairman, Secretary Hughes, said that, subject to any observation to the contrary which might be made, he supposed that the Grand Duchy would be embraced within this clause and would be adequately represented. If there was no objection, the committee would so assume.

Finland and Poland. Sir Robert Borden inquired whether the drafting committee had considered the effect of the wording of paragraph 4 on States which were formerly part of the Russian Empire, but which were not independent Powers whose governments had been recognized. He presumed that it was intended that these Powers should have the right to be represented on the revision commission and at the special conference, if they so desired.

Mr. Balfour remarked that Finland and Poland had both been recognized.

Non-Treaty Powers. Senator Underwood said that he was not sure that his viewpoint was the correct one, but, as he understood the situation, China was sovereign as to her right to levy taxes except in so far as she had given away that right by treaty. Now it was proposed to change the treaty right by which the power of the Republic of China was at present limited and to offer an increase in taxation at the customs house. No country that had not treaty relations with China and obligations from China growing out of those treaties had any right to make any complaint whatever as to what China did in reference to taxes at the customs house. Her only binding obligation was in respect to the Governments with whom she had signed treaties. As to the other Governments, who would not be represented, they could not complain as a matter of right, because they had no established right in regard to China (any more than in regard to the United States or Japan) to control the customs taxation of China.

On the other hand, they could not complain of any undue advantage being taken of them, because these two papers, this resolution and the treaty that was to follow, prescribed everything to their advantage in providing that the " open door " into China should in the future mean equal opportunity to all, whether treaty powers or non-treaty powers, whether they sat at the table to reform this tariff or not. Every one of them would go into China under the same conditions and, therefore, he could not see that any power that was not represented at the table could have any right to complain, especially as to this resolution, since in it the treaty powers were only complying with their contract with China heretofore made.

The chairman said that he supposed this clause of the resolution defined those who were to be represented in the proposed commission. They were the Governments who were at present recognized by the powers represented at this conference and who had treaties with China providing for a tariff.

Mr. Koo said he wished to add a few words in regard to the actual situation in China with reference to non-treaty powers. According to the paragraph under discussion, for a country to have a representative on the commission mentioned therein it was necessary for several conditions to be present at the same time. One of these conditions was that the power in question should have a treaty with China in regard to import customs duties. Other powers (*i. e.*, those not having such treaties) were necessarily precluded. As a matter of fact, the Chinese Government had already promulgated and put in force some time before a special tariff for non-treaty powers. If a lower rate than the 5 per cent authorized by the existing treaties had been granted to one of these non-treaty Powers, such a reduction would probably have to be made applicable to all under the most-favored-nation clause. But the present rate of import duties on the goods of the non-treaty powers was higher than 5 per cent. In that respect the principle of the " open door," under the present Chinese law, could not be invoked to include non-treaty powers.

Sir Robert Borden reverted to the point which he had already raised. He said that if the Government of Russia were recognized Russia would obviously be entitled under Paragraph IV of the resolution to be invited to send representatives to the proposed conference. But the present Russian Government was not recognized. On the other hand two States whose territories were formerly part of the Russian Empire —namely, Finland and Poland—were recognized, and the question the committee had to decide was whether the convening power would be bound to ask these two States to send representatives to the conference. The question might be taken into consideration afterwards, but in his opinion it would be necessary at some stage to determine whether or not Poland and Finland had succeeded to Russia's rights in respect of treaties which the former Russian Empire had concluded with China.

The delegations being polled, each voted affirmatively, and the chairman announced that the resolution had been unanimously adopted.

Draft of Treaty. With regard to matters that would require a treaty or convention between the Powers, Mr. Root, on behalf of the Drafting Committee, then submitted the following resolutions regarding revision of Chinese customs duties:

With a view to increasing the revenues of the Chinese Government, the United States of America, Belgium, the British Empire, China, France, Italy, Japan, the Netherlands, and Portugal agree:

I. That immediate steps be taken through a special conference, to be composed of representatives of the contracting Powers and other Powers which adhere to this convention, to prepare the way for the speedy abolition of likin and for the fulfillment of the other conditions laid down in Article VIII of the Treaty of September 5, 1902, between Great Britain and China, in Articles IV and V of the Treaty of October 8, 1903, between the United States and China, and in Article I of the Supplementary Treaty of October 8, 1903, between Japan and China, with a view of levying the surtaxes provided in those articles.

The special conference shall meet in China within three months after the date of the ratification of this convention on a day and at a place to be designated by the Chinese Government.

II. The special conference shall consider the interim provisions to be applied prior to the abolition of likin and the fulfillment of the other conditions laid down in the articles of the treaties above mentioned; and it shall authorize the levying of a surtax on dutiable imports as from such date for such purposes and subject to such conditions as it may determine.

The surtax shall be at a uniform rate of $2\frac{1}{2}$ per cent ad valorem, except in the case of certain articles of luxury, which, in the opinion of the special conference, can bear a greater increase without unduly impeding trade, and upon which the total surtax shall not exceed 5 per cent.

III. That following the immediate revision of the customs schedule of duties on imports into China as provided for in a resolution adopted by the representatives of all powers signatory to this convention at a plenary session of the Conference on the Limitation of Armament held in the City of Washington on the — day of January, 1922, there shall be a further revision to take effect at the expiration of four years following the completion of the aforesaid revision in order to insure that the customs duties shall correspond to the ad valorem rates fixed by the special conference herein provided for.

That following this revision there shall be periodical revisions of the customs schedule of duties on imports into China every seven years for the same purpose in lieu of the decennial revision authorized by existing treaties with China.

That in order to prevent delay such periodical revisions shall be effected in accordance with rules to be settled by the special conference mentioned in Article I herein.

IV. That in all matters relating to customs duties there shall be effective equality of treatment and of opportunity for all Powers parties to this convention.

V. That the principle of uniformity in the rate of customs duties levied at all the land and maritime frontiers of China is hereby recognized; that the special conference above provided for shall make arrangements to give practical effect to this principle; and it is authorized to make equitable adjustments in those cases in which the customs privilege to be abolished was granted in return for some local economic advantage.

In the meantime, any increase in the rates of customs duties resulting from tariff revision or any surtax hereafter imposed, in pursuance of the present convention, shall be levied at a uniform rate ad valorem at all land and maritime frontiers of China.

VI. That the charge for transit passes shall be at the rate of $2\frac{1}{2}$ per cent ad valorem, until the arrangements contemplated in Article I herein come into force.

VII. That the powers not signatory to this convention, but whose present treaties with China provide for a tariff on imports and exports not to exceed 5 per cent ad valorem, shall be invited to adhere to the present convention, and upon such adherence by all of them this convention shall override all provisions of treaties between China and the respective contracting powers which are inconsistent with its terms.

That the United States Government, as convener of the present conference, undertake to make the necessary communications for this purpose and to inform the Governments of the contracting powers of the replies received.

VIII. Ratification clause of usual form.

Mr. Root said that, in accordance with the resolution already adopted, there should be inserted some words in Article VII, so that it would read:

That the powers not signatory to this convention having Governments at present recognized by the powers represented at this conference, but whose present treaties with China provide for a tariff on imports and exports not to exceed 5 per cent ad valorem, shall be invited to adhere to the present convention, and upon such adherence by all of them this convention shall override all provisions of treaties between China and the respective contracting powers which are inconsistent with its terms.

Mr. Root said, with reference to the first paragraph of Article III, that the sense of the paragraph was that, following the immediate revision of the schedules or duties which the commission would raise under the resolution that had been adopted, there should be a further revision to take effect at the expiration of four years following the completion of the aforesaid revision in order to insure that the customs duties should correspond to the ad valorem rates fixed by the special conference as in the treaty. It was not to make the customs duties correspond to the ad valorem rates in force, but to the ad valorem rates fixed by the special conference, and to make the customs duties correspond to the new ad valorem rates, if there should be any, not the ad valorem rates already in force.

Mr. Sarraut said that he would ask to be enlightened with respect to Article I, especially with respect to the phrase " and other powers which adhere to this convention to prepare the way for the speedy abolition of likin and for the fulfillment of the other conditions laid down in Article VIII of the treaty of September 5, 1902, between Great Britain and China, in Articles IV and V of the treaty of October 8, 1903, between the United States and China, and in Article I of the supplementary treaty of October 8, 1903, between Japan and China, with a view to levying the surtaxes provided in those articles."

Mr. Sarraut said he believed that there had been certain changes from the first text prepared by Mr. Kammerer in which special reference had been made to " Articles IV and VIII of the treaties between the United States and China and to Article I of the supplementary treaty of October 8 between Japan and China." These references had not been made in the original text. Referring to the text of these treaties, Mr. Sarraut said he would like to ask the following questions: Was it the intention of the articles as drafted to oblige all nations to bind themselves by the terms of the most-favored-nation clause or was this done by error? If an automatic application of the most-favored-nation clause was intended, he must make a reservation, as his own Government might not agree. He believed that it would be better to omit the clauses referring to the most-favored-nation clause or to say that it was not desired to apply them automatically.

Mr. Root said the treaties referred to in Article I were the same treaties which were referred to in the original report of the committee on Chinese revenue. The only difference was that this draft specified the particular articles of those treaties which were supposed to be relevant to the subject matter of this instrument. It was rather to limit than to enlarge the reference in the original report, and the conditions which were referred to in Article I were the conditions upon which the powers entering into these treaties with China undertook to consent to the increase of duties; *i. e.,* they agreed to consent to an increase of duties on condition that China did thus and so. No conditions were imposed upon any other power, so that no obligation whatsoever could be found in this article upon any of the powers other than China in respect of the most-favored-nation clauses. That was his understanding of it.

Mr. Sarraut said that he took note of Mr. Root's statements, and would refer to them, if necessary. He felt he must point out, however, that if the text of the resolutions alone was considered it did not directly appear that the most-favored-nation clause did not automatically apply. In view of Mr. Root's explanation, however, he would not insist further upon the matter.

Sir Auckland Geddes said he assumed that it was quite clear—this was the way in which he read this paragraph—that, so far as the treaties in question bound countries other than China at the present time, they would bind only those countries afterwards, and that the provisions, for instance, of the Chinese-American treaty would not be extended to Chinese-British? Mr. Root said he had no doubt of that.

A vote being taken, the draft agreements and resolutions were then unanimously approved by the Committee of the Whole. However, before being reported to the Conference in plenary session, these agreements were further discussed and amended in the last session of the Committee when they were brought before it in what was then expected to be their final form.

Mr. Balfour at that time raised the point that, as then drafted, the reform of the Chinese tariff which all the Delegations desired would not come into effect until every Power that had a treaty with China providing for an export and import tariff of not greater than five per cent had given its adherence to the agreements then before the Committee. He suggested, therefore, that there should be inserted in the draft the words " the provisions of the present treaty shall override all stipulations of treaties between China and the respective Powers which are inconsistent therewith, other than stipulations according most-favored-nation treatment." The effect of this provision would of course be that so long as any Power, not party to the proposed treaty, should refuse adherence to it, and therefore, under its treaties with China, be entitled to claim of China that imports from itself to China or exports from China to itself should not bear a tariff higher than five per cent, the other Powers, signatory to the treaty would themselves be entitled to make the same claim upon China.

Senator Underwood's View as to Power of China to Denounce Tariff Treaties. This proposal gave to Senator Underwood an opportunity, in supporting Mr. Balfour's amendment, to make an argument with regard to China's obligations under her tariff treaties that is of sufficient interest to deserve quotation. As reported in the Minutes of the Committee, Senator Underwood said:

He might be wrong in this matter, but he believed this treaty was not on the same basis as many other treaties involving great national rights. This was a trade agreement, a trade contract, which China had made with the other nations of the world, and he thought China had a right to denounce these treaties when she thought proper. He thought this was clearly her right, because no question of national right was involved; it was merely a question of trade agreements, and agreements of that kind had been made in the past to extend over a period of time, or an indefinite period of time, and when conditions changed so that they worked a great disadvantage to one or others of the contracting parties it had been recognized in the past that such trade conventions might be eliminated.

This might not meet with the approval of all, and he did not say it for that purpose; he was only stating his own viewpoint. China must have this money if she was going to function as a government. She had asked the powers at this table to grant her the right to raise these taxes. The nine powers had agreed with China on a plan which increased taxes. It seemed to him that if one nation in the world stood out alone against the sentiment and the consensus of opinion of the nationals sitting at the table and tried to prevent China from getting this additional money—this revenue which was necessary for her national life—the Chinese Government would be entirely justified in denouncing that treaty or that agreement.

He said this because this question might arise; one of the contracting parties might say that China must stand for the future on her 5 per cent tariff, which would endanger the life of the Chinese Government.

His opinion was that no one power in the world had the right, as against the sentiments expressed by the nine powers at the table and against the desires of China, to take such a position, and he believed that in the high courts of national morality such a position could well be maintained. If it were not, all the work of the committee was futile; if it were not, it meant that, simply because a nation 60 years before, when she did not feel that she needed more than 5 per cent revenue, had had her customs houses enter into an agreement, that nation must be bound for the years, for the decades and the centuries to come, unable to maintain her governmental life.

He did not feel, however, that the matter was so serious, since under this agreement the opportunity would be given (for example) to Spain and to Sweden to become parties to it, and he thought they would accept; but if they did not become parties to it or stood as dogs in the manger preventing China from having the opportunity of life to which she was entitled, then he thought the way to carry out this agreement would be to denounce it.

But the nations represented on the committee were entitled to protect their rights to equal terms, and if China did not denounce her treaties and allowed imports from Spain and Sweden to enter China under a 5 per cent duty—if these countries did not give their adherence—then China must recognize her duty to the nations represented at the table and let them continue their imports into China under the 5 per cent duty.[6]

As a result of this discussion, the following Article, numbered IX was inserted in the draft treaty.

The provisions of the present treaty shall override all stipulations of treaties between China and the respective Contracting Powers which are inconsistent therewith, other than stipulations according most favored nation treatment.

Maintenance of Existing Customs Administration. At this session there was also a discussion of the declaration upon the part of the Chinese Delegation that China had no intention to effect any change which might disturb the present administration of the Chinese Maritime Customs. The question was whether this declaration should be signed by the Chinese representatives and be made an annex to the treaty.

Dr. Koo pointed out that the declaration was a voluntary one on the part of the Chinese Govern-

[6] Senator Underwood repeated these views in the United States Senate when the treaty was before that body for approval.

ment; that there was no international treaty or convention in which it had been stipulated; that it occurred only in two loan contracts to which the Chinese Government was a party; and that, therefore, there was no reason why China should now be called upon to put the declaration into treaty form, that is, have it included in the body of or as an annex to a treaty which the Powers at the Conference, including China, were to sign. This view was strongly supported by Senator Underwood. He even intimated that if the declaration were made a part of the treaty, he might find it difficult to defend the treaty before the American people since there were many good people in the United States who were strongly opposed to having China coerced into an obligation that was not entirely satisfactory to her, especially as to a matter relating to the administration of her local affairs.

It was then agreed that the declaration should simply be placed upon the records of the Conference at the plenary session.

Banks for Deposit of Customs Receipts. In connection with the question of China's customs tariff there was brought up by Mr. Underwood, at the twenty-ninth meeting of the Committee of the Whole, the matter of the deposit in the banks of China of the moneys collected.

It had been originally provided that certain portions of the Chinese customs receipts should be set apart for meeting the interest and amortization charges on the bonds issued in payment of the Boxer

Indemnities. These had been deposited entirely, or almost entirely, in the Hongkong and Shanghai Bank and the Russo-Asiatic Bank. This, of course, had been of great advantage to those institutions, as compared with the other banks in China which had received no such deposits. In this connection he he would read the following statement which had been submitted to the sub-committee by Mr. Odagiri in behalf of the Japanese Government:

> Japan not only has no objection to, but welcomes, the proposal that the existing customs system of China should not be disturbed. In the meantime she must express the hope, in view of the important position which her Chinese trade occupies in the entire foreign trade of China and Japan's resulting large contribution to the Chinese customs revenues, that a fair and suitable adjustment may be effected with the above fact in view in regard to the future operations of the customs system; that is to say, concerning such matters as the custodian banks and the proportion of foreign nationals to be employed in the customs staff. We desire to make it clear, however, that this is not proposed as a condition of our acceptance of this agreement, but only as a frank expression of our desire. It is hoped that such special conference as is mentioned above in its deliberations upon the conditions involving questions such as custody and supervision of tariff revenue should take into consideration the above expressed desire of Japan.

The delegates of France, Italy, Belgium, and Holland had associated themselves in this matter with the Japanese delegation.

Senator Underwood said that the deposit of the revenues that had already been allocated to the Chinese debts could not be changed since that was a part of the contract, but that the surplus revenues were free to be deposited in such banks as might be determined upon. Providing for the additional surtax of 2½ per cent the Special Conference which was to be convened at Shanghai would have the right, with, of course, the consent of China, to a reallocation of these funds in the various solvent banks in China. The Conference at Washington, he thought, was not in a position to settle the matter.

Dr. Koo upon this point spoke as follows:

Prior to the revolution of 1911 the customs revenue that was collected in the ports was all deposited in the so-called Chinese Customs Bank, under the supervision of Chinese authorities, and the customs administration itself did not have the handling of the money. They issued receipts and clearance only on the production by the merchant of the receipts issued by the Customs Bank certifying that the customs duties had been paid. As the time arrived, from month to month, for the payment and discharge of obligations incurred for the Boxer indemnity and also for the foreign debts, the money was paid over. That arrangement proved very satisfactory, and there was the testimony of the inspector general of the customs on record that that arrangement would work very satisfactorily, and that there never was a single instance in which there was any difficulty in meeting the foreign obligations promptly and on the day they were due.

In the course of the revolution of 1911 various disturbances broke out in various part of China, and lest there might be delays or interference with the discharging of the foreign obligations, it was proposed that the customs revenues should be deposited temporarily in certain foreign banks to which Senator Underwood made reference a little while ago. While that arrangement was intended to be merely provisional, however, the practice of depositing customs revenues in those designated foreign banks continued. It had this effect on the commercial and financial situation in the various cities of importance, that, prior to the revolution, when money was deposited in the Chinese Customs Bank, of course it flowed into the various channels of the market to meet commercial and industrial needs in each community, and in that way the money market was always more or less easy and there were very few occasions when crises of a financial character arose. Since the new arrangement was introduced, however, of course all the customs revenue went into the foreign banks, and the money was now no longer quickly accessible to Chinese customers for legitimate purposes of commerce and trade as it had been heretofore with the result that from time to time constant anxiety prevailed in the Chinese commerce and trading communities because money was scarce and tight. Therefore, the Chinese bankers had made the suggestion more than once, and had drawn the attention of the Chinese Government to the fact, that some steps should be taken to modify the present provisional arrangement. He, therefore, wished not only to associate himself with Senator Underwood in his suggestion but to add that when the time came for considering the question on the reallocation, if in the opinion of the representatives at that time conditions were not yet such as to permit a complete reversion to the former practice, at least a part of the deposits should be allocated to those Chinese banks which were generally recognized as being sound and solvent.

The various resolutions relating to China's customs revenues were reported to the Conference at the sixth plenary session, held February 4, 1922. Senator Underwood, who made the report, introduced it with the following explanatory statements which are worthy of reproduction as an admirable historical summary of the facts leading to the situation which the proposed treaty was intended to improve if not wholly to correct.

It may seem an anomaly to the people of the world who have not studied this question that this Conference, after declaring that it recognizes the sovereignty and territorial integrity of China, should engage with China in a compact about a domestic matter which is a part of her sovereignty. To announce the treaty without an explanation may lead to misunderstanding, and therefore I ask the patience of the Conference for a few minutes that I may put in the record a statement of the historic facts leading up to present conditions, which make it necessary that this Conference should enter into this agreement.

The conclusions which have been reached with respect to the Chinese maritime customs tariff are two in number, the first being in the form of an agreement for an immediate revision of existing schedules, so as to bring the rate of duty up to a basis of 5 per cent effective. The second is in the form of a treaty, and provides for a special conference which shall be empowered to levy surtaxes and to make other arrangements for increasing the customs schedules above the rate of 5 per cent effective.

In order to understand the nature and the reasons for these agreements, it is well to bear in mind the historical background of the present treaty adjustment, which places such a large control of the Chinese customs in the hands of foreign powers.

The origin of the Chinese customs tariff dates back to the fourteenth century, but the administrative system was of such a nature that constant friction arose with foreign merchants engaged in trade with that country, and culminated in an acute controversy relating to the smuggling of opium, sometimes known as the Opium War of 1839-1842.

This controversy ended in 1842 with the Treaty of Nanking, between China and Great Britain. The Treaty of Nanking marked the beginning of Chinese relations on a recognized legal basis with the countries of the Western World, and is likewise the beginning of the history of China's present tariff system.

By the Treaty of Nanking it was agreed that five ports should be opened for foreign trade, and that a fair and regular tariff of export and import customs and other dues should be published.

In a subsequent treaty of October 8, 1843, a tariff schedule was adopted for both imports and exports, based on the general rate of 5 per cent ad valorem.

In 1844 the first treaty between China and the United States was concluded. In this treaty the tariff upon which China had agreed with Great Britain was made an integral part of its provisions, and most-favored-nation treatment was secured for the United States in the following terms:

"Citizens of the United States resorting to China shall in no case be subject to other or higher duties than are or shall be required of the people of any other nation whatever, and if additional advantages or privileges of whatever description be conceded hereafter by China to any other nation, the United States and the citizens thereof shall be entitled thereupon to a complete, equal, and impartial participation in the same."

In the same year a similar treaty between China and France was concluded, and in 1847 a like treaty was entered into with Sweden and Norway.

After an interval of a little over a decade, friction again developed and a war ensued.

In 1851, when negotiations were again resumed, silk had fallen in value, prices of foreign commodities had changed, and the former schedule of duties no longer represented the rate of 5 per cent ad valorem.

In 1858, China concluded what was known as the Tientsin Treaties with the United States, Russia, Great Britain, and France.

The British treaty, which was the most conprehensive, being completed by an agreement as to the tariff and rules of trade, was signed at Shanghai on November 8, 1858. By this agreement a schedule of duties was provided to take the place of the schedule previously in force. Most of the duties were specific calculated on the basis of 5 per cent of the then prevailing values of articles.

The tariff schedule thus adopted in 1858 underwent no revision, except in reference to opium, until 1902.

The beginning of foreign administrative supervision of the Chinese maritime customs dates back to the time of the Taiping Rebellion, when, in September, 1853, the city of Shanghai was captured by the Taiping rebels. As a consequence the Chinese customs was closed and foreign merchants had no offices to collect customs duties.

In order to meet the emergency, the foreign consuls collected the duties until June 29, 1854, when an agreement was entered into with the British, American, and French consuls for the establishment of a foreign board of inspectors. Under this agreement a board of foreign inspectors was appointed, and continued in office until 1858, when the tariff commission met and agreed to rules of trade, of which Article X provided that a uniform customs system should be enforced at every port, and that a high officer should be appointed by the Chinese Government to superintend the foreign trade, and that this officer might select any British subject whom he might see fit to aid him in the administration of the customs revenue, and in a number of other matters connected with commerce and navigation. In 1914, just as the Great War was breaking, there were 1357 foreigners in the Chinese customs service, representing 20 nationalities among a total of 7441 employees.

It is appropriate to observe that the present administrative system has given very great satisfaction in the matter of its efficiency and its fairness to the interests of all concerned, and in that connection I desire to say that, when the consideration of this tariff treaty was before the sub-committee that prepared it, there was a general, and, I may say, universal sentiment about the table from the delegates representing the nine Powers, that on account of the disturbed conditions in China to-day, unsettled governmental conditions, it was desirable, if it met with the approval of China, that there should be no disturbance at this time of the present administration of the customs system. In response to that sentiment, which was discussed at the table, Dr. Koo, speaking for the Chinese Government, made a statement which I have been directed by the full committee to report to this plenary session, which is as follows:

" The Chinese Delegation has the honor to inform the Committee on the Far Eastern Questions of the Conference on the Limitation of Armament that the Chinese Government have no intention to effect any change which may disturb the present administration of the Chinese maritime customs."

Speaking only for myself, I hope that the day may not be far distant when China will have established a parliamentary government representing her people, and that thus an opportunity will be given her to exercise in every respect her full sovereignty and regulate her own customs tariffs.

But for the present, on account of the disturbed conditions in China, it is manifest that there must be an agreement and understanding between China and the other nations involved in her trade, and I want to say that this agreement, as it is presented to the Conference to-day, meets the approbation of the representatives of the Chinese Government.

Between the period of 1869 and 1901 a series of agreements were entered into which established special tariff privileges with various Powers respecting movements of trade. This period culminated in a greatly involved state of affairs which led to the Boxer Revolution, out of which grew the doctrine of the open door.

In 1902, in accordance with the terms of the Boxer protocol, a commission met at Shanghai to revise the tariff schedule. This revision applied only to the import duties and to the free list. Most of the duties were specific in character, and the remainder were at 5 per cent ad valorem. Non-enumerated goods were to pay 5 per cent ad valorem. All the duties remained subject to the restrictions of the earlier treaties, and those of the export duties which are still in force are the specific duties contained in the schedule of 1858.

In 1902 a treaty was concluded between China and Great Britain which laid a basis for the subsequent treaties between China and the United States and China and Japan in 1903, along similar lines. In the preamble of the British treaty the Chinese Government undertakes to discard completely the system of levying likin and other dues on goods at the place of production, in transit, and at destination.

The British Government in turn consents to allow a surtax on foreign goods imported by British subjects, the amount of this surtax on imports not to exceed the equivalent of one and one-half times the existing import duty. The levy of this additional surtax being contingent upon the abolition of the likin has never gone into effect, but remains, nevertheless, the broad basis upon which the general schedules of Chinese tariff duties may be increased.

It is clear from the foregoing brief summary that two measures were necessary in dealing with the Chinese customs, the first being that of the revising of the tariff schedules, as they exist, so as to make them conform to the rate of 5 per cent effective, as provided by the treaty.

Second, to pave the way for the abolition of the likin, which constitutes the basis of higher rates. In the meantime, however, it is recognized that the Chinese Government requires additional revenue, and, in order that this may be supplied, a special conference is charged with the levying of a surtax of $2\frac{1}{2}$ per cent on ordinary duties, and a surtax of 5 per cent on the luxuries, in addition to the established rate of 5 per cent effective.

In 1896 an agreement was made between Russia and China for the construction of the Chinese Eastern Railway, and as a part of this agreement, merchandise entering China from Russia was allowed to pass the border at one-third less than the conventional customs duties. Afterwards, similar reductions were granted to France, Japan, and Great Britain, where the merchandise entered China across her land frontiers and not by sea.

This discrimination was unfair to the other nations, and not the least important paragraph in the proposed treaty is the one which abolishes this discrimination entirely.

Chinese Statements. After the proposed treaty had been read, Mr. Sze, in behalf of the Chinese Delegation, said:

As the views of the Chinese Delegation on the various aspects of this question have been fully set forth in the various statements made by my colleague, Dr. Koo, at several meetings of the Committee on Far Eastern Questions, I shall content myself, Mr. Chairman, with a request that the following statements be spread upon the records of this session, namely: the statement of January 5, 1922; the statement of January 16, 1922; and the statement of February 3, 1922.

Dr. Koo's statement of January 5 has been earlier quoted. His statement of January 16 was as follows:

I wish to add a few words concerning the actual situation in China with reference to the non-treaty Powers.

According to the draft resolution it was evident that many conditions were required to qualify a Power to participate in the proposed revision, and one of the conditions was that such a Power should have a treaty tariff with China on imports and exports. If a Power did not possess such a qualification then she would naturally be precluded from taking part in the revision. The Chinese Government had promulgated a national tariff for the non-treaty Powers. If the rates in the national tariff were lower than those prescribed in the treaty tariff, then all the treaty Powers could immediately enjoy the benefit of the lower rates through the operation of the most-favored-nation clause. Generally, however, the rates in the national tariff were higher than the rates in the treaty tariff. Therefore, the doctrine of the open door could not be invoked to reduce the application of the Chinese national tariff with reference to the non-treaty Powers.

Dr. Koo's statement for the Chinese Delegation, made in the Committee on Pacific and Far Eastern Questions on February 3, 1922 was with reference to the declaration by China that it had no intention of disturbing the present system of maritime customs administration. Dr. Koo said that this declaration was a voluntary declaration of policy on the part of the Chinese Government and his colleagues around the table would no doubt recall that when he had had the honor, on behalf of his delegation, to present the Chinese viewpoint on the tariff question, he had made that declaration without any suggestion or request from any quarter. He had made it because it represented the policy of the Chinese Government—as that policy had been pursued for many decades in the past; no departure from this policy was contemplated at the present time. So far as he was aware, there was no international treaty or convention in which this policy had been stipulated. It occurred only in two loan contracts which the Chinese Government had made in 1896 and in 1898, with two groups of foreign bankers. Of course, those contracts were still in force and their terms were still binding. He therefore desired to say that, when this subject had been brought up in the sub-committee, he did not recall that any question of signature had been raised. If he remembered correctly the form in which it was reported to this committee by the chairman of the sub-committee some time before was exactly the form which the members of the sub-committee had accepted. He felt certain that his colleagues around the table would not wish to make a treaty obligation, an international obligation, out of a matter which fell within the domestic policy of the Chinese Government. He felt certain that, thus explained, his colleagues would be perfectly satisfied with this declaration of policy, which was made voluntarily in the original instance and made in all good faith, and therefore he wished to say that, so far as the Chinese Delegation were concerned, they did not feel quite the necessity of putting it in just the form in which it had been suggested.

Mr. Koo said that he also wished to remind the members of the committee, who had sat on Senator Underwood's sub-committee on Chinese tariff, of the statement which he (Mr. Koo) had made in the sub-committee that that declaration of intention not to disturb the present administration could not be reasonably construed to preclude the Chinese people from realizing a legitimate aspiration to make the Chinese maritime customs service an institution more national in character. Though the present system of administration had been in existence for nearly 60 years, very few Chinese had been trained by that service. Out of 44 Commissioners of Customs, distributed among the treaty ports, he was not aware of a single post being at present occupied by a Chinese. He had no desire to make any particular comment on this state of affairs, but he merely wished to throw some light on the subject in order to make clear the point he had in mind. The services of the present maritime customs administration had been valuable and efficient, as had been often testified to by Chinese officials in many ways, but there was nevertheless a very general feeling on the part of the Chinese people that more Chinese should be trained to assume the functions of the more responsible posts in the service. Mr. Koo felt confident, however, that in suggesting to give the Declaration of the Chinese Delegation the solemnity of a public announcement at a plenary session of the Conference, his friend and colleague, Mr Balfour, had no desire to see the policy, embodied in the declaration, invested with the character of permanency. Senator Underwood's statement that the present customs treaty was drawn up to meet only the present temporary conditions in China coincided with the understanding of the Chinese Delegation and the aspirations of the Chinese people, who looked eagerly toward the earliest restoration of full tariff autonomy.

I may add [said Mr. Sze at the plenary session of the Conference on February 4] that the present seeming disarray and unrest in China is only a transition, unavoidable in the great change of a country from a despotic form of government to that of a democratic republic. This has been the experience of all the countries of the world. The Chinese people are fully convinced that, with their genius and their experience of four thousand years of government, they will be able to evolve at an early date, a united and strong China.

Upon being put to vote, the treaty relating to China's tariff was unanimously adopted by the Conference, and its official text, as signed by the nine Powers on February 6, 1922, will be found in the appendix to this volume.[7]

---

[7] It is possible that some misapprehension may arise from certain remarks made by Senator Underwood in the United States Senate at the time the Tariff Treaty was under consideration by that body. Senator Underwood at that time, defending the treaty, said that it has met the wishes of the Chinese Delegation. It is true that the Chinese Delegation preferred that the Conference should adopt the treaty rather than that no agreement should be reached and thus China obtain no relief whatever in the matter of its maritime customs. But, as the foregoing account has shown, the Chinese Delegation never departed from its desire that China should obtain complete tariff autonomy at as early a date as the Powers might be willing to agree to it.

CHAPTER VIII

Regarding Armed Forces In China

Resolution of the Powers Other Than China

Proposed Resolution. It has already been pointed out that the Powers represented in the Conference expressed some question as to whether China would benefit by its Government's deriving larger revenues from the maritime customs so long as there was a possibility or probability that increased sums of money would thus be made available for expenditure upon the military forces stationed throughout the country. At the seventeenth meeting of the Committee on Pacific and Far Eastern Questions, in reporting the conclusions of the sub-committee on Chinese Revenue, Senator Underwood called attention to the fact that the sub-committee had realized that the matter of supreme importance that had come before it was to secure to the Chinese Government sufficient revenues to maintain properly a stable and safe government, but that the committee had realized that the maintenance in China of large military forces was a serious drain on the finances of China and materially affected the question of raising revenues, and, also, that the continued maintenance of these forces was in contravention of the great principles of the Conference which looked to the disarmament of nations and the securing of the peace of the world. Senator Underwood thereupon read the following resolution which the sub-committee, the Chinese Delegate not voting, had adopted on January 3, 1922, as an annex to its report on Chinese revenue and tariff:

The members of the sub-committee in studying the question of increasing the customs tariff rates to meet the urgent needs of the Chinese Government have been deeply impressed with the severe drain on China's public revenue through the maintenance of excessive military forces in various parts of the country. Most of these forces are controlled by the military chiefs of the provinces, and their continued maintenance appears to be mainly responsible for China's present unsettled political conditions. It is felt that large and prompt reduction of these forces will not only advance the cause of China's political unity and economic development but hasten her financial rehabilitation. Therefore, without any intention to interfere in the internal problems of China, but animated by the sincere desire to see China develop and maintain for herself an effective and stable government, alike in her own interest and in the general interest of trade, and inspired by the spirit of this conference whose aim is to reduce through the limitation of armament "the enormous disbursements" which "manifestly constitute the greater part of the encumbrance upon enterprise and national prosperity," the sub-committee venture to suggest for the consideration of the committee the advisability of laying before the conference for its adoption a resolution expressing the earnest hope of the conference and embodying a friendly recommendation to China that immediate and effective steps be taken by the Chinese Government to reduce the aforesaid military forces and expenditure.

Chinese Statement. At the time this resolution had been adopted, by the sub-committee, Dr. Koo, in behalf of the Chinese Government, made the following statement:

The hope for effective reduction of military forces and expenditures in China as expressed by the Chairman coincides completely with the desire and determination of the Government and people of China. Knowing the profound sentiment of sympathy and disinterested friendship which the United States always entertains towards my country, and to which our Chairman has so frequently given expression in the deliberations of this body, and feeling confident that the suggestion is animated by the best of intentions, I do not hesitate to say that I have no objections to it [the resolution]; and though naturally I wish to abstain from voting on it myself, I nevertheless appreciate the spirit in which it is moved.[1]

On January 20, at its twenty-second meeting, the Resolution, redrafted, was approved by the Committee of the Whole on Pacific and Far Eastern Questions.

Statement by Sir Robert Borden. In support of its adoption, Sir Robert Borden said that its presentation was " inspired by a sincere and earnest wish to aid the purpose of the Chinese people in establishing stable government and in freeing the country from the incubus of excessive militarism." The existing situation, he said, though it had existed several years was wholly alien to the habits and traditions of the Chinese people. Continuing, Sir Robert said:

Up to the present there had been an unfortunate lack of such organizing capacity as would establish a strong and stable central Government and bring the country once more under its effective direction and control. For such a purpose the provision of great revenues or the placing of large funds at the disposal of a weak administration was not of itself effective. So long as the military governors retained their present dominating authority and influence such financial resources would probably be absorbed to a very

[1] There is some reason to believe that the Chinese Delegation was willing to accept the proposed resolution of the Powers because it forestalled any movement to create a commission to make a general inquiry into conditions of order in China.

great extent by these military chiefs instead of being employed to cut down their power.

Exact accuracy, Sir Robert Borden continued, in any statistics of military forces and expenditure in China at the present time could not be expected; but reasonable estimates placed the total number of men under arms at not less than one million; at least the payroll probably included that number. It was confidently asserted that more than half of the total revenues of the country were employed in the upkeep of these forces. They had not been raised for the defense of the country against outside aggression; on the contrary they were really maintained for the purpose of civil war and when on active service they were fighting against their own countrymen enlisted under the banner of some other military chieftain. However in one province, which was said to be exceptionally well governed by a man who devoted his whole attention to the welfare and prosperity of his district, a considerable military force maintained as a necessity to his prestige was made to do duty in the construction of excellent roads. In that province the progress and advancement of the people were said to be quite remarkable and they gave an illustration of what the Chinese people might accomplish under good government.

The forces enlisted under the various military chieftains were said to regard their military duties as entirely occupational and it was believed that they would be quite ready to accept employment in the construction of railways, highways, and otherwise, provided the arrears in their pay were made good.

The weakness, and indeed the impotency, of the central Government, so far as a great portion of the country is concerned, must necessarily be a matter of concern to the other powers. The Chinese people had developed a high civilization which, in some of its characteristics, afforded a notable lesson to the nations of the West. They had behind them centuries of splendid tradition, a great development of art and of literature. At present they were passing through a period of transition from the autocratic rule of an ancient dynasty to the development of advanced democratic institutions. There was no occasion for surprise that, under these circumstances, the conditions to which had been alluded to should have arisen. It might rather have been anticipated that the disorders and the instability would have been more pronounced. But among all the tumult and the fluctuations attending the development of democracy in China, the attachment of the people to the soil and their untiring industry had remained unchanged. One might adapt the words of a well-known quotation:

> They hear the legions thunder past,
> Then plunge in toil again.

Notwithstanding the present conditions, no one should fear for the future of the Chinese people. It had sometimes been thought that they would be absorbed by other nations. In his judgment, they were more likely to absorb than to be absorbed. The mere passive resistance of that vast nation of 400,000,000 was powerful to protect it. Out of the present disorders would eventually arise a permanent system of stable government and China would take her deserved and well-recognized place among the great powers of the world. This could not be accomplished for China by any other nation or group of nations. External beneficent influences might aid, but in the end the Chinese people must work out their own political salvation. There was abundant reason to believe that they could and would accomplish this. In the meantime, it was the duty of other nations—and that duty had been exemplified in the work of this conference—to lend a helping hand wherever that might be possible to remove hampering restrictions as soon as practicable and to give every assistance and encouragement for the political regeneration of this illustrious people.

Resolution Adopted. As finally embodied in the ninth of the Resolutions adopted by the Conference, at its fifth plenary session, this Resolution reads as follows:

Whereas the Powers attending this Conference have been deeply impressed with the severe drain on the public revenue of China through the maintenance in various parts of the country, of military forces, excessive in their number and controlled by the military chiefs of the provinces without coordination.

And whereas the continued maintenance of these forces appears to be mainly responsible for China's present unsettled political conditions,

And whereas it is felt that large and prompt reductions of these forces will not only advance the cause of China's political unity and economic development but will hasten her financial rehabilitation;

Therefore, without any intention to interfere in the internal problems of China, but animated by the sincere desire to see China develop and maintain for herself an effective and stable government alike in her own interest and in the general interest of trade;

And being inspired by the spirit of this Conference whose aim is to reduce, through the limitation of armament, the enormous disbursements which manifestly constitute the greater part of the encumbrance upon enterprise and national prosperity;

It is resolved: That this Conference express to China the earnest hope that immediate and effective steps may be taken by the Chinese Government to reduce the aforesaid military force and expenditures.

CHAPTER IX.

Extraterritoriality

Chinese Statement. China's wishes with regard to the modification and ultimate abolition of the extraterritorial rights of foreigners within her borders were presented by Dr. Wang to the Committee at its sixth meeting, held November 25.[1]

Extraterritoriality in China, said Dr. Wang, dated back almost to the beginning of China's treaty relations with foreign countries. It was clearly laid down in the treaty of 1844, between the United States and China, and similar provisions had since been inserted in treaties with other powers.

These extraterritorial rights were granted at a time when there were only five treaty ports—that is, places where foreigners could trade and reside. Now there are fifty such places and an equal number of places open to foreign trade on China's initiative. This meant an ever-increasing number of persons within China's territory over whom she was almost powerless. This anomalous condition had become a serious problem with which local administration was confronted; and if the impairment of the territorial and administrative integrity of China was not to be continued, the matter demanded immediate solution.

Dr. Wang said that he would point out some of the serious objections to the extraterritorial system:

(a) In the first place, it is in derogation of China's sovereign rights, and is regarded by the Chinese people as a national humiliation.

---

[1] What follows is quoted or paraphrased from U. S. Senate Document, No. 126, 67th Congress, 2d session, pp. 475 ff.

(b) There is a multiplicity of courts in one and the same locality, and the interrelation of such courts has given rise to a legal situation perplexing both to the trained lawyer and to the layman.

(c) Disadvantages arise from the uncertainty of the law. The general rule is, that the law to be applied in a given case is the law of the defendant's nationality, and so, in a commercial transaction between, say, X and Y of different nationalities, the rights and liabilities of the parties vary according as to whether X sued Y first, or Y sued X first.

(d) When causes of action, civil or criminal, arise in which foreigners are defendants, it is necessary for adjudication that they should be carried to the nearest consular court, which may be many miles away; and so it often happens that it is practically impossible to obtain the attendance of the necessary witnesses, or to produce other necessary evidence.

(e) Finally, it is a further disadvantage to the Chinese that foreigners in China, under cover of extraterritoriality, claim immunity from local taxes and excises which the Chinese themselves are required to pay. Sir Robert Hart, who worked and lived in China for many years, had said in his book, " These from the Land of Sinim ": " The extraterritoriality stipulation may have relieved the native official of some troublesome duties, but it has always been felt to be offensive and humiliating, and has ever a disintegrating effect, leading the people, on the one hand, to despise their own Government and officials, and, on the other, to envy and dislike the foreigner withdrawn from native control."

Until the system is abolished or substantially modified, Dr. Wang continued, it would be inexpedient for China to open her entire territory to foreign trade and commerce. The evils of the existing system had been so obvious that Great Britain in 1902, Japan and the United States in 1903, and Sweden in 1908 agreed, subject to certain conditions, to relinquish their extraterritorial rights. Twenty years had elapsed since the conclusion of these treaties, and while it is a matter of opinion as to whether or not the state of China's laws has attained the standard to which she is expected to conform, it is impossible to deny that she has made great progress on the path of legal reform. A few facts would suffice for the present. A law codification mission for the compilation and revision of laws has been sitting since 1904. Five codes have been prepared, some of which have already been put into force: (a) The Civil Code, still in course of revision; (b) the Criminal Code, in force since 1912; (c) the Code of Civil Procedure, and (d) the Code of Criminal Procedure, both of which have just been promulgated; and (e) the Commercial Code, part of which has been put into force.

These codes, Dr. Wang said, have been prepared with the assistance of foreign experts, and are based on the principles of modern jurisprudence. Among the numerous supplementary laws especial mention might be made of a law of 1918, called " Rules for the Application of Foreign Laws," which deals with matters relating to private international law. Under these rules, foreign law is given ample application. Then there is a new system of law courts established in 1910. The judges are all modern, trained lawyers, and no one can be appointed a judge unless he has attained the requisite legal training. These are some of the reforms which have been carried out in China.

Dr. Wang declared that the China of to-day was not the China of 20 years ago, when Great Britain encouraged her to reform her judicial system, and, a fortiori, she is not the China of 80 years ago, when extraterritorial rights were first granted to the treaty powers. Dr. Wang said he had made these observations, not for the purpose of asking for an immediate and complete abolition of extraterritoriality, but for the purpose of inviting the powers to cooperate with China in taking initial steps toward improving and eventually abolishing the existing system, which is admitted on all hands to be unsatisfactory both to foreigners and Chinese. It is gratifying to learn of the sympathetic attitude of the powers toward this question, as expressed by the various delegations at a previous meeting of this committee.

In concluding, Dr. Wang asked, in the name of the Chinese delegation, that the powers now represented to this conference agree to relinquish their extraterritorial rights in China at the end of a definite period. In the meanwhile, he proposed that the abovementioned powers should, at a date to be agreed upon, designate representatives to enter into negotiations with China for the adoption of a plan for a progressive modification and ultimate abolition of the system of extraterritoriality in China, the carrying out of which plan was to be distributed over the above-mentioned period.

The chairman, Secretary Hughes, said that certain treaties had been referred to by Dr. Wang. In order to bring these concretely before the delegates, he would like to read from the Treaty of 1903 between the United States and China:

"ART. XV.—Reform of judicial system—Extraterritoriality to terminate.—The Government of China having expressed a strong desire to reform its judicial system and to bring it into accord with that of western nations, the United States agrees to relinquish extraterritorial rights when satisfied that the state of the Chinese laws, the arrangements for their administration, and other considerations warrant it in so doing."

He understood that substantially the same statement was found in the other treaties with Great Britain in 1902 and with Japan in 1903. So far as the Government of the United States is concerned, it had already formulated an expression of its desire to give all possible assistance to China's project for reform, and he had no doubt that the other powers were equally in favor of furthering a more complete juridical integrity for China. The question, however, is one of treaty right—of fact, rather than of principle, for the principle had already been defined by the three Governments referred to by Dr. Wang. What is the state of the administration of justice in China? What are the laws? And how were they administered? The chairman said that extraterritoriality was designed for the protection of certain juridical rights, and though he agreed that the extraterritorial machinery left much to be desired, he felt that in determining what could be done to assist China in this matter, a very definite notion must be had of the administration of justice in that country before existing treaty rights should be abolished. Whatever steps were taken, they should be preceded by an inquiry into existing conditions, and this would be, as a matter of fact, a very difficult problem to deal with. The chairman repeated that some nations had already formulated an expression of principle; it is now a question of finding the best way of aiding China when she is ready.

Dr. Wang said that China was ready to give every facility to the powers for ascertaining what her laws are and how they are administered.

For the more particular consideration of the proposals thus presented by China, a sub-committee was appointed composed of one member nominated by each Delegation.[2]

Resolution Adopted. At the ninth meeting of the Committee of the Whole the sub-committee on Extraterritoriality submitted the following draft resolutions which were unanimously adopted by the Committee without further discussion, and later approved, also without further discussion, by the Conference at its fourth plenary session, held December 10, 1921:

The representatives of the Powers hereinafter named, participating in the discussion of Pacific and Far Eastern questions in the Conference on the Limitation of Armament—to wit, the United States of America, Belgium, the British Empire, France, Italy, Japan, the Netherlands and Portugal—

Having taken note of the fact that in the Treaty between Great Britain and China dated September 5, 1902, in the Treaty between the United States of America and China dated October 8, 1903, and in the Treaty between Japan and China dated October 8, 1903, these several Powers have agreed to give every assistance towards the attainment by the Chinese Government of its expressed desire to reform its judicial system and to bring it into accord with that of Western nations, and have declared that they are also " prepared

---

[2] The Sub-Committee on Extraterritoriality was composed of Senator Lodge, for the United States; Senator Pearce, for the British Empire; M. Sarraut, for France; Senator Ricci, for Italy; Mr. Hanihara, for Japan; Japan; Chevalier de Wouters, for Belgium; Dr. Wang Chang-hui, for China; Jonkheer van Karnebeek, for the Netherlands; and Captain Vasconcellos, for Portugal.

to relinquish extraterritorial rights when satisfied that the state of the Chinese laws, the arrangements for their administration, and other considerations warrant" them in so doing;

Being sympathetically disposed towards furthering in this regard the aspiration to which the Chinese Delegation gave expression on November 16, 1921, to the effect that "immediately, or as soon as circumstances will permit, existing limitations upon China's political, jurisdictional and administrative freedom of action are to be removed";

Considering that any determination in regard to such action as might be appropriate to this end must depend upon the ascertainment and appreciation of complicated states of fact in regard to the laws and the judicial system and the methods of judicial administration of China, which this Conference is not in a position to determine;

Have resolved—

That the Governments of the Powers above named shall establish a Commission (to which each of such Governments shall appoint one member) to inquire into the present practice of extraterritorial jurisdiction in China, and into the laws and the judicial system and the methods of judicial administration of China, with a view to reporting to the Governments of the several Powers above named their findings of fact in regard to these matters, and their recommendations as to such means as they may find suitable to improve the existing conditions of the administration of justice in China, and to assist and further the efforts of the Chinese Government to effect such legislation and judicial reforms as would warrant the several Powers in relinquishing, either progressively or otherwise, their respective rights of extraterritoriality;

That the Commission herein contemplated shall be constituted within three months after the adjournment of the Conference in accordance with detailed arrangements to be hereafter agreed upon by the Governments of the Powers above named, and shall be instructed to submit its report and recommendations within one year after the first meeting of the commission;

That each of the Powers above named shall be deemed free to accept or to reject all or any portion of the recommendations of the

Commission herein contemplated, but that in no case shall any of the said Powers make its acceptance of all or any portion of such recommendations either directly or indirectly dependent on the granting by China of any special concession, favor, benefit, or immunity, whether political or economic.

And the further resolution:

That the non-signatory Powers having by treaty extraterritorial rights in China may accede to the resolution affecting extraterritoriality and the administration of justice in China by depositing within three months after the adjournment of the Conference a written notice of accession with the Government of the United States for communication by it to each of the signatory Powers.

And the further resolution:

That China, having taken note of the resolutions affecting the establishment of a Commission to investigate and report upon extraterritoriality and the administration of justice in China, expresses its satisfaction with the sympathetic disposition of the Powers hereinbefore named in regard to the aspiration of the Chinese Government to secure the abolition of extraterritoriality in China, and declares its intention to appoint a representative who shall have the right to sit as a member of the said Commission, it being understood that China shall be deemed free to accept or to reject any or all of the recommendations of the Commission. Furthermore, China is prepared to cooperate in the work of this Commission and to afford to it every possible facility for the successful accomplishment of its tasks.

CHAPTER X

FOREIGN POST OFFICES IN CHINA

The matter of securing the removal from China of the post offices which foreign nations, without treaty right, had established upon Chinese soil was brought before the Committee of the Whole at its sixth meeting held November 25.

Chinese Statement. Mr. Sze, in behalf of the Chinese Delegation, made the following statement:

As Mr. Koo said the other day in his remarks before the committee, China has suffered and is now suffering not only from limitations upon her territorial and administrative integrity, to which she has been led to consent, but also from open violations of her rights as a territorial sovereign for which not even a vestige of contractual right can be claimed.

Among these violations are the stationing of foreign troops and railway guards at various points, the installation of wire and wireless telegraph communications, the maintenance of foreign post offices, and so-called "police boxes." I shall first speak of the foreign postal services maintained upon Chinese soil.

China requests that the powers assembled in the conference agree at once to abolish all postal services now maintained by them in China. She bases her request upon the following propositions:

1. China has organized and is now conducting a postal system covering the entire country, and maintaining relations with all foreign countries adequate to meet all requirements. The transmission of postal matter is a government monopoly, the first paragraph of the postal statutes of October 12, 1921, reading: "The postal business is exclusively conducted by the Government."

2. The existence of foreign post offices interferes with and makes more difficult the development of this system, and deprives it of a revenue which legally and equitably should belong to it.

3. The maintenance by foreign Governments of post offices in China is in direct violation of the latter's territorial and administrative integrity, and rests upon no treaty or other legal rights.

Early in the sixties of the last century foreign post offices began to open branches and agencies in the particular treaty ports of China. The opening of these offices was not based on any treaty provision or concession. Their existence and gradual increase was merely tolerated by the Chinese Government.

About the same time a regular service for the carriage of mails was established on foreign lines in connection with the customs, operating chiefly between the numerous ports on the coast of China and those far up the Yangtze River. This service continued to work and to improve its machinery year by year. By imperial decree of March 20, 1896, this system was developed into a distinct Chinese postal system and placed under the general direction of the inspector general of customs. Finally, by imperial decree of May 28, 1911, the system was taken from under the administration of the inspector general of customs and developed into an independent system operating directly under the minister of posts and communications. Since that date the system has operated wholly as one of the administrative services of the Chinese Government.

On March 1, 1914, China gave her adherence to the Universal Postal Convention, and since September 1 of that year she has continued as a member in good standing of the Universal Postal Union.

As the Universal Postal Union does not recognize the right of any country to maintain post offices in another country which is a member of the postal union, the Chinese delegation brought up the question of alien establishments in China at the Universal Postal Congress opened at Madrid, on October 1, 1920. The question of their withdrawal was regarded as within the purview of their respective foreign offices and no definite decision was reached. A measure was passed, however, to the effect that only such foreign postal agencies could be considered as within the union as were established in a foreign country not itself within the Universal Postal Union, of which China has been a member since September 1, 1914.

The Chinese post office maintains the cheapest general service in the world, and the following rates are in force:

	Chinese currency	United States currency
Letters (local)	$0.01	$0.00½
Letters (domestic)	.03	.01½
Post card (local)	.01	.00¼
Post card (domestic)	.01½	.00¾
Newspapers (local) per 100 grams	.00½	.00¼
Newspapers (domestic) per 50 grams	.00½	.00¼
Printed matter 100 grams rate graduated to	.01	.00½
Printed matter 1,500 grams for	.15	.07½
Unaddressed circulars	.001	.0005
Registration fee	.05	.02½
Express fee (special delivery)	.10	.05

In spite of these very cheap rates and the very high transportation costs in maintaining long courier lines where no modern facilities are available, the surplus of receipts over expenditures has been steadily increasing. All profits are being put into improvements in the service to the smaller villages inland. Its income in 1920 was $12,679,121.98 and its expenditures $10,467,053.07, thus leaving a surplus for the year's operation of $2,212,068.91.

Senders of registered articles, parcels, insured letters, and express articles are entitled to claim indemnity in case of loss by the post office. Although in 1920 over 37,000,000 such articles were posted, less than 400 claims for indemnity were made, the percentage being about 1 in 90,000.

There has been a decrease of 30 per cent in the number of insured letters posted in the past four years, though other mail matter has increased by 50 per cent in the same time. This is considered as indicating a growing public confidence in the other non-insured services.

The Chinese post office has over 3000 interpreter employees, and every office serving places of foreign residence in China is amply supplied from this large number of interpreters to cope with all foreign correspondence.

The efficiency of the Chinese postal service is further guaranteed by strictly civil service methods in appointments of staff. Employees enter only after a fair examination, both mental and physical. Postmasters, even in the larger cities, are selected from the most efficient of the employees; never from outside the service. The penalty for invoking political aid is dismissal, and in practice is never done.

The post office functions under the same central administration over the entire country. In time of local disturbance and revolution the revolutionists have recognized the post office as a necessity to the welfare of the community and have always permitted it to continue its functions without change of staff or control.

Notwithstanding the disturbed condition of affairs in China during recent years, the system has been steadily developed since it was placed wholly under the direction and control of Chinese authorities. Mail matter posted has increased approximately 300 per cent since 1911 (from 126,539,228 to 400,886,935 in 1920). Parcels posted have increased from 954,740 in 1911 to 4,216,200 in 1920, the increase being over 300 per cent.

There is now scarcely a Chinese village which is not served either by a post office, postal agency, or minor postal establishment. Major establishments (offices and agencies) have increased from 9103 in 1917 to 10,469 in 1920. Minor establishments (town box offices and rural stations) have increased from 4890 in 1917 to 20,806 in 1920. This makes a total of 31,275 places now provided with postal facilities, more than double the number of places served four years ago.

During and immediately following the war the Chinese post office transmitted through its money-order service over $10,000,000 for the British and French Governments, which were making payments to the families of over 100,000 Chinese laborers employed for work in connection with the war in France and Belgium. The Chinese post office was made use of by the Government bureaus concerned in tracing and locating relatives of deceased laborers and in determining the identity and other particulars of claimants. In this work the Chinese post office used its large force of very efficient inspectors, and made no charge for investigations and reports.

An international money-order department is now functioning, conventions for the exchange of money orders being in successful operation between China and Great Britain, the Dutch East Indies, and Hongkong. It is hoped that it may soon be extended to other countries.

That this system is giving efficient and satisfactory service has been abundantly attested to by foreign observers. To quote from the Commercial Hand-Book of China, published by the United States Department of Commerce in 1920 (vol. 2, p. 106):

"The Chinese postal service has extended its facilities to every district in the country, including in many of the outlying districts extensive courier lines. In spite of unsafe conditions that have prevailed in certain sections of the country during the past few years, and notwithstanding the great difficulty of transportation in other sections, the Chinese postal service has been remarkably efficient, and one hears but little criticism in connection with its organization and general work. It reports that very few complaints concerning loss of mail or stolen mail are made, and, on the whole, it is rendering a very satisfactory postal service."

Mr. Willoughby, in his careful study, "Foreign Rights and Interests in China," says, in speaking of this system:

"At the present time (1920) the postal service in China is one for which the Government deserves great credit. Generally speaking, the service is efficiently operated and with reasonable financial success, notwithstanding the fact that China has been obliged to acquiesce in the operation within her borders of some 60 or more foreign post offices."

Notwithstanding the fact that China now has an efficient postal system, certain foreign Governments continue to maintain post offices in China. At the present time Great Britain, France, America, and Japan are maintaining and operating offices of this kind at a large number of places. The alien postal establishments in China as they stand at present are as follows: Great Britain, 12; France, 13; Japan, 124; United States, 1.

The Japanese establishments are classed as follows: First-class offices, 7; second-class offices, 23; third-class offices, 4; unclassified offices, 10; sub-offices, 3; box offices, 1; agencies, 33; letter boxes, 33; field post offices, 10.

Those post offices have their own postage stamps, and operate in every respect in direct competition with the Chinese System. It is to be noted, moreover, that these foreign offices are located at the chief centers of population, industry, and commerce. They are thus in a position where they can, so to speak, skim the cream of the postal business, since they are under no obligation to maintain offices at unimportant points, and, in fact, do not do so.

Parcels and mail matter entering China from abroad should pass a customs examination. With the exception of parcels from Shanghai and one or two other ports, however, it is a notorious fact that but few parcels or other articles transmitted by foreign post offices are ever examined. Cooperation between foreign postal establishments and the Chinese customs is extremely difficult and in practice has proven almost impossible. Thus the customs revenues are very materially affected, and foreign post offices become an efficient aid to smugglers of contraband, particularly of morphia, cocaine, and opium. On the other hand, parcels handled by the Chinese post offices are subject to rigid customs examination, duties being collected, in most cases, by the post office on behalf of the customs administration. The Chinese post office is thus working under a handicap in competition with whose of other nations within its own territories.

It is submitted that if the necessity ever existed for the maintenance of foreign post offices in China, this necessity has now passed away. As early as April 20, 1902, the American minister at Peking reported to his Government (United States Foreign Rels., 1902, p. 225):

"I have given such investigation as I have been able, and report that, in my judgment, foreign post offices in China, except at Shanghai, are not a necessity, because the Chinese postal service, under the imperial maritime customs, is everywhere giving satisfactory service, and is rapidly and effectively increasing and extending into the interior."

More recently the Commercial Hand-Book of China, from which we have already quoted, says:

"The developments of the Chinese postal service during the past decade have been so extensive and so favorable that there is in reality no longer any need for a continuance of the foreign post offices operated in that country."

It is to be noted, moreover, that the maintenance of these foreign offices rests upon no treaty or other legal right. Regarding this point, the American minister, in his communication to his country, of April 20, 1902, to which reference has already been made, said:

"The foreign post offices are being established principally for political reasons, either in view of their future designs upon the Empire, to strengthen their own footing, or because jealous of that of others. They are not established with the consent of China, but in spite of her. They will not be profitable. Their establishment materially interferes with and embarrasses the development of the Chinese postal service, is an interference with China's sovereignty, is inconsistent with our well-known policy toward the Empire, and I can not find any good reason for their establishment by the United States."

That China has never recognized any such right is evidenced by a communication that her postmaster general addressed to the postal union on March 18, 1915. After referring to pertinent provisions of the Universal Postal Convention and of the Reglement d'Execution, the communication continued:

"Relying upon the principles inscribed in the Universal Postal Convention and in agreement on this point with the jurists in international law of all countries, China considers that by virtue of its entry into the union the offices maintained upon its territory by other countries of the union have ceased to have a legal existence. Although in consequence of the difficulties mentioned above and those that have their origin in the present events of the war, China has found herself obligated, in order not to impede the transmission of its mails, to continue temporarily for the purpose of its relations with other countries to have recourse to the intermediation of certain of the foreign post offices established upon its territory, or to accept this intermediation, it must declare that this course of action implies no recognition on its part of the legality of these offices, and, furthermore, that no status, in that respect, can be created by the written communications that have been or that may hereafter be exchanged in regard to them, either with those offices or with the administration to which they belong. China protests against the maintenance, by the majority of the foreign post offices operating upon its territory, of tariffs lower than those fixed by article 5, of the Rome convention, for the payment of postage upon mails exchanged by those offices, either between themselves or with the countries to which they respectively belong.

"China, having adhered as from September 1 last to the Rome convention concerning the exchange of parcels post, must declare that what has been said above, in regard to the temporary continuation, necessitated by circumstances, of the intermediation of foreign post offices established upon its territory, applied likewise to the parcels post service."

The following letter of the American representative at the Madrid conference of the Universal Postal Union, to the Director General of the Chinese Post Office, speaks for itself:

MADRID, 27 November, 1920.

"MR. LIOU FOU TCHENG,
 "Director General of the Chinese Posts, Madrid.

"DEAR SIR.—With regard to the conversation which we last had concerning the postal service of China, permit me again to assure you of the high appreciation of the American postal administration of the efficiency and excellence of the postal service of the Chinese Government.

"I am authorized by my Government to express to you the sympathy of the United States with the desire of the Chinese Government that all of the foreign post offices should be withdrawn from its territory and the United States will be willing to participate in a unanimous movement of all the foreign Powers for the cessation of postal operations carried on by the other nations in the territory of China.

"The Postal Administration of your country has the right to the approbation and respect of the entire world with regard to the efficiency of your postal operations.

"Please accept, sir, the assurance of my high consideration.
 "(Signed) OTTO PRAGER,
  "Sub-Assistant Postmaster General."

In conclusion, China wishes to point out that, wholly apart from the financial loss suffered by her as a result of the existence of foreign post offices on her soil, and the obstacles placed thereby in the way of the development of her own postal system, the maintenance of such offices represents a most direct violation of her territorial and administrative integrity. It is one, moreover, that is peculiarly objectionable, since it is a constant, visible reminder to the Chinese people that they are not accorded the consideration given to other peoples. This necessarily has a tendency to lower the prestige of the Chinese Government in the eyes of her people, and to make more difficult the already difficult problem of maintaining a government that will command the respect and ready obedience of her population. From whatever standpoint it is viewed, the continuance of these foreign post offices upon Chinese soil should, therefore, be condemned.

Discussion. At the seventh meeting of the Committee, held November 26, a discussion was had of Mr. Sze's statement.

The Chairman, Secretary Hughes, said that the United States was ready to give up its only post office in China, that at Shanghai, if the other governments maintaining postal establishments in China were willing to take similar action. The information possessed by the American Delegation, he said, was in accordance with the Chinese claims as to the efficiency of China's postal service.

Mr. Sze, supplementing his previous statement, said that China's postal service had not been disturbed by the Revolution of 1911, but that upon the contrary, since that time, its efficiency had steadily increased.

Mr. Balfour suggested that the Chinese system had probably owed a good deal of its efficiency to the aid of the Frenchman who, as co-director general of the posts, had been at its head, and asked if it was the intention of China to continue to make use of his services.

M. Viviani said that France was willing to accede to China's desires if the other Powers would do the same, if the present co-director were retained, and if the efficiency of the service were maintained.

Mr. Sze said that China had no intention of making any immediate radical changes in her postal administration.

Mr. Harihara said that Japan had no desire to perpetuate the existing system of foreign post offices, but that actual conditions and necessities should be taken into consideration. "Information received by the Japanese Delegation," he said, "had convinced it that safety of communications in China was not assured, and on this ground there was some reason why the foreign post offices should not be withdrawn; as a practical measure it would be difficult to withdraw at once. The plain fact was that there were more Japanese in China, either as residents or travellers, than there were nationals of any other Power—possibly thirty or fifty times as many—and their activities were more varied. Japan had no objection to the withdrawal of the foreign post offices under the guarantees suggested by Mr. Balfour and M. Viviani (which the Japanese Delegation considered very necessary), but Japan asked that she be given time in order that it might be seen that no necessity or justification existed for the continued maintenance of the system; as it became evident that conditions warranted, Japan would be prepared to withdraw her post offices."

Mr. Sze asked of Mr. Hanihara whether he had in mind any period of time within which his country would withdraw its post offices, and if he had any suggestions to make as to the manner in which the Chinese postal service might be improved. As to his statement regarding the number of Japanese in China, Mr. Sze said that he knew of no principle of international law that recognized such a fact as a sufficient justification for the maintenance by one country of postal agencies upon the soil of another country without that country's consent. He called attention to the fact that there were Chinese post-offices at all the places where foreign offices were maintained.

To this Mr. Hanihara replied that he had not intended to state a principle but only a fact. He suggested that the whole matter be referred for discussion to the Ministers of the various interested Powers at Peking who would be in a position to know when a withdrawal of the foreign post offices should be effected. This suggestion was not accepted by the Committee, and a sub-committee was appointed to draft resolution for withdrawal in accordance with the conditions which had been spoken of.[1]

Resolutions. At the fifteenth meeting of the Committee of the Whole, held December 12, this sub-committee reported the following resolution as having been agreed upon:

A. Recognizing the justice of the desire expressed by the Chinese Government to secure the abolition of foreign postal agencies in

[1] The membership of this sub-committee was as follows: Senator Lodge (Chairman), for the United States; Sir Auckland Geddes, for the British Empire; M. Viviani, for France; Mr. Sze, for China; and Mr. Hanihara, for Japan.

China, save or except in leased territories or as otherwise specifically provided by treaty, it is resolved:

(1) The four powers having such postal agencies agree to their abandonment subject to the following conditions:

(a) That an efficient Chinese postal service is maintained;

(b) That an assurance is given by the Chinese Government that they contemplate no change in the present postal administration so far as the status of the foreign co-director general is concerned.

(2) To enable China and the powers concerned to make the necessary dispositions, this arrangement shall come into force and effect not later than ——

B. Pending the complete withdrawal of foreign postal agencies, the four powers concerned severally undertake to afford full facilities to the Chinese customs authorities to examine in those agencies all postal matter (excepting ordinary letters, whether registered or not, which upon external examination appear plainly to contain only written matter) passing through them, with a view to ascertaining whether they contain articles which are dutiable or contraband or which otherwise contravene the customs regulations or laws of China.

Japanese Statement. Senator Lodge stated that the above resolution had been read, amended, and approved in the full committee, but the date had been left open for consideration by the Japanese Delegates; and that he had since received a letter from Mr. Hanihara which he would now read:

December 9, 1921.

DEAR SIR: With regard to the proposed abolition of foreign postal agencies, I am happy to inform you that my Government have no objection to the initiation of the arrangement as from the date in the draft resolution—that is, not later than January 1, 1923.

In announcing this agreement of my Government, I am instructed to state before the committee their desire concerning the maintenance of efficient Chinese postal service substantially to the following effect:

Taking into account the fact that the proposed change in the postal régime in China can not fail practically to affect the Japanese to a much greater extent than any other nationals, the Japanese Government wish to place on record their desire that a suitable number of experienced Japanese postal officers be engaged by China, to promote the efficiency of the Chinese postal administration. The reasonableness of this desire will readily be appreciated, when it is considered that the Powers concerned have recognized the need of effective foreign assistance in the Chinese postal administration, and that no less than seventy British subjects and twenty Frenchmen are in that service, while Japan is there represented by only two experts.

(Signed) MR. HANIHARA.

The resolution reported by the sub-committee with the insertion of the date January 1, 1923, was thereupon put to vote and unanimously approved.

The resolution, as approved by the Committee of the Whole was reported to the Conference in plenary session at the fifth session, held February 1, 1922, and adopted without amendment or debate.

Chinese Statement. At the fifteenth meeting of the Committee, held December 12, Mr. Sze, in behalf of the Chinese Delegation, made the following statement which he asked to be recorded:

Since the establishment of her national postal service, China has at all times handled with efficiency all foreign mail. She appreciates that, with the withdrawal of foreign post offices from her soil, the amount of foreign mail to be handled by her own postal system will be increased. This increase she undertakes to handle with the same efficiency by making such additions to the personnel and equipment of her postal service as will be required. As soon as the Siberian route is re-opened for the transportation of foreign mail matter between Asia and Europe, steps will be taken to make arrangements for the transportation of such mail matter as was formerly transported by this route. As regards actual railway transportation of such mail China will hold herself responsible for uninterrupted service upon those railways or sections of railways within her jurisdiction which are under her own control and operation.

With reference to the maintenance of foreign post-offices in China it is worthy of note that, in the sub-committee dealing with the subject, the British representative, Sir Auckland Geddes, said that he understood that the proposed agreement would have no effect upon foreign post offices which were established in leased areas. The French representative said that this was a matter to be considered in connection with the more important question of "leased areas." The Japanese representative, Mr. Hanihara, said that he did not wish to see railway zones or leased areas included within the application of the proposed resolution. Sir Auckland, who had drafted the resolution, said that it had not been his intention to have it apply to leased areas. Mr. Hanihara said that, according to his interpretation of the treaties between China and Japan, Japan had the right to establish post-offices in the railway zones which were under her control. Asked by Mr. Sze as to the treaty provisions to which he had reference, Mr. Hanihara said that the right was given by the Portsmouth Treaty of 1905 according to which Japan succeeded to the rights of Russia in the railway zones in South Manchuria, and that, both in the leased area and railway zones, Japan had every kind of authority including that of taxation and postal administration.

This discussion led to the insertion in the first paragraph of the Resolution of the words "save or except in leased territories or as otherwise specifically provided by treaty." It was, however, apparent in the discussion that was had that Japan received no support from the other Powers for the proposition that her rights of administration in the zones of the railways controlled by her carried with them the right to maintain in them post offices or indeed to exercise any other than ordinary powers of railway operation. Then again there is the fact that the resolution as finally framed excepted from its scope only rights " specifically " provided by treaty, and there is admittedly no specific right granted to Japan by the Portsmouth Treaty to establish post offices in her railway areas. It may be added that, at this time, it was expected that the rights of Japan within railway zones would receive further discussion when the subject of railways in China was taken up by the Conference—an expectation that was not realized.

CHAPTER XI

Foreign Troops and Police in China

Chinese Statement. At the eighth meeting of the Committee of the Whole, held November 28, Mr. Sze, in behalf of the Chinese Delegation, made the following statement:

At the session held on November 21, the Conference declared that it was the firm intention of the Powers represented to respect the sovereignty, the independence, and the territorial and administrative integrity of China; and to provide the fullest and most unembarrassed opportunity to China to develop and maintain for herself an effective and stable government.

It will have already appeared that, in application of these two principles, China is asking not merely that existing treaty or conventional limitations upon the autonomous and unembarrassed exercise by her or her territorial and administrative powers, should be removed as rapidly and as completely as circumstances will justify, but that conditions shall be corrected which now constitute a continuing violation of her rights as an independent State. The proposition that these limitations upon the exercise of her sovereign powers should be progressively removed was stated in principle No. 5 which the Chinese Delegation presented to the Conference on November 16, and applications of it are seen in the propositions that have been made to the Conference with reference to extraterritorial rights and to tariff autonomy.

A specific illustration of a *violation* of China's sovereignty and territorial and administrative integrity, as distinguished from *limitations* based upon agreements to which China has been a party, was presented to the Conference for correction last week and had to do with the maintenance of foreign postal services upon Chinese soil.

This morning it is the desire of the Chinese Delegation to bring before you, for correction in accordance with the controlling Principles which you have already affirmed, several other instances of subsisting violations of China's sovereignty, and territorial and administrative integrity. These relate to the maintenance upon the Chinese territory without China's consent and against her protests, of foreign troops, railway guards, police boxes and electrical wire and wireless communication installations.

I shall not exhaust your patience by enumerating all of the specific instances of these violations, for I shall not ask merely that each of these violations be specifically discountenanced, for this would not give complete relief to China since it would not prevent other similar violations in the future. In behalf of the Chinese Government I therefore ask that this Conference declare, as a comprehensive proposition, that no one of the Powers here represented—China of course not included—shall maintain electrical communication installations, or troops, or railway guards, or police boxes upon Chinese soil, except in those specific cases in which the Powers desiring to do so may be able to show, by affirmative and preponderant evidence and argument that it has a right so to do such as can be defended upon the basis of accepted principles of international law and practice and with the consent of the Chinese Government.

No argument by me is needed to show that this Conference stands committed to the declaration which I now ask, by the Principles which were adopted on November 21. Should any one of you consider the possibility of foreign troops or railway guards, or police boxes, or electrical communication installations being maintained upon the soil of your own country without the consent of the government which you represent, your feelings of justice and your sense of the dignity due to your own State, would make evident to you the propriety of the joint declaration which China now asks you to make in her behalf. The proposition surely stands self-evident that, if a nation asserts a right to maintain troops, or guards, or police, or to erect and operate systems of communication upon the soil of another State, whose sovereignty and independence and territorial and administrative integrity it has just solemnly affirmed and obligated itself to respect, upon that State should lie a heavy burden of proof to justify so grievous an infringement of the rights of exclusive territorial jurisdiction which international law as well as a general sense of international comity and justice, recognize as attaching to the status of sovereignty and independence.

In behalf of my Government and the people whom I represent, I therefore ask that the Conference give its approval to the following proposition:

"Each of the Powers attending this Conference hereinafter mentioned, to wit, the United States of America, Belgium, the British Empire, France, Italy, Japan, the Netherlands, and Portugal, severally declare that, without the consent of the Government of China, expressly and specifically given in each case, it will not station troops, or railway guards or establish and maintain police boxes, or erect or operate electrical communication installations, upon the soil of China; and that if there now exist upon the soil of China such troops or railway guards or police boxes or electrical installations without China's express consent, they will be at once withdrawn."

Upon request of the Committee, the Chinese Delegation, at the ninth meeting, held November 29, submitted a Memorandum showing, according to its information, the foreign troops, police, "railway guards" and electrical installations upon the soil of China without the consent of the Chinese Government.

This information (the Memorandum declared) is furnished simply in order to show the extent to which China's territorial and administrative integrity is now being violated, and not as implying that the Chinese Government will be contented with the abatement of these specific violations of her sovereign rights; for China, as declared in the resolution which it has proposed, desires that there should be a general or comprehensive declaration upon the part of the powers represented in this conference that, without China's consent, expressly and specifically given in each case, they will not maintain troops or police boxes, or railway guards or electrical installations upon China's soil, with the result that upon the powers will lie the burden of establishing their right to do so in each case in which they may assert a right or claim to maintain upon China's soil such troops, police boxes, railway guards, or electrical installations.

The resolution proposed by the Chinese delegation will not affect the rights of the powers obtained under the protocol agreement of 1901, nor their right to maintain police forces in their various municipal settlements and concessions. If, as to these matters, any revision should be desired, separate discussion or negotiation may be had.[1]

Japanese Statement. In rejoinder to this statement upon the part of the Chinese Delegation, the Japanese Delegation submitted a rejoinder in which it was said that the draft resolution which the Chinese had proposed was, in effect, embodied in the first of the Root Resolutions that had already been adopted, and therefore, that its adoption would be repetitious. The Japanese Delegation, the statement said " is further persuaded that the withdrawal or abolition of the foregoing troops, railway guards, police stations, and telegraph and wireless installations should not be immediately decided simply because the Chinese authorities have not given them their express consents. There are specific reasons for the existence of such institutions in each special case. We are prepared to explain these specific reasons which have brought about the existing conditions in the cases in which Japan is concerned."

Mr. Sze replying, in behalf of the Chinese Delegation, said that No. 5 of the Chinese Ten Points had used the term " immediately " as well as the phrase " as soon as circumstances will permit," and that the

[1] The matter of electrical installations will be separately considered in the next chapter.

matters of troops, railway guards, etc., furnished instances in which immediate relief was properly demandable, and, therefore, that the Chinese had asked that they be at once withdrawn. He added that the Chinese Delegation would be glad to have the Japanese Delegation furnish the data which it claimed to have in substantiation of its view that immediate withdrawal should not be provided for. Mr. Hanihara, of the Japanese Delegation, then read the following statement:

The Japanese Delegation wishes to explain, as succinctly as possible, why and how the Japanese garrisons in various parts of China have come to be stationed there. At the outset, however, I desire to disclaim most emphatically that Japan has ever entertained any aggressive purposes or any desire to encroach illegitimately upon Chinese sovereignty in sending or maintaining these garrisons in China.

(1) Japanese railway guards are actually maintained along the South Manchuria Railway and the Shantung Railway.

With regard to the Shantung Railway guards, Japan believes that she has on more than one occasion made her position sufficiently clear. She has declared and now reaffirms her intention of withdrawing such guards as soon as China shall have notified her that a Chinese police force has been duly organized and is ready to take over the charge of the railway protection.

The maintenance of troops along the South Manchuria Railway stands on a different footing. This is conceded and recognized by China under the Treaty of Peking of 1905. (Additional Agreement, Art. II.) It is a measure of absolute necessity under the existing state of affairs in Manchuria—a region which has been made notorious by the activity of mounted bandits. Even in the presence of Japanese troops, those bandits have made repeated attempts to raid the railway zone. In a large number of cases they have cut telegraph lines and committed other acts of ravage. Their lawless activity on an extended scale has, however, been effectively checked by Japanese railway guards, and general security has been maintained for civilian residents in and around the railway zone. The efficiency of such guards will be made all the more significant by a comparison of the conditions prevailing in the railway zone with those prevailing in the districts remote from the railway. The withdrawal of railway guards from the zone of the South Manchuria Railway will no doubt leave those districts at the mercy of bandits, and the same conditions of unrest will there prevail as in remote corners of Manchuria. In such a situation it is not possible for Japan to forego the right, or rather the duty, of maintaining railway guards in Manchuria, whose presence is duly recognized by treaty.

(2) Towards the end of 1911 the first Revolution broke out in China, and there was complete disorder in the Hupeh district which formed the base of the revolutionary operations. As the lives and property of foreigners were exposed to danger, Japan together with Great Britain, Russia, Germany, and other principal Powers, dispatched troops to Hankow for the protection of her people. This is how a small number of troops have come to be stationed at Hankow. The region has since been the scene of frequent disturbances; there were recently a clash between the North and South at Changsha, pillage by troops at Ichang, and a mutiny of soldiers at Hankow. Such conditions of unrest have naturally retarded the withdrawal of Japanese troops from Hankow.

It has never been intended that these troops should remain permanently at Hankow, and the Japanese Government have been looking forward to an early opportunity of effecting complete withdrawal of the Hankow garrison. They must be assured, however, that China will immediately take effective measures for the maintenance of peace and order and for the protection of foreigners, and that she will fully assume the responsibility for the damage that may be or may have been done to foreigners.

(3) The stationing of the garrisons of foreign countries in North China is recognized by the Chinese Government under the protocol relating to the Boxer revolution of 1900. Provided there is no objection from the other countries concerned, Japan will be ready, acting in unison with them, to withdraw her garrison as soon as the actual conditions warrant it.

(4) The Japanese troops scattered along the lines of the Chinese Eastern Railway have been stationed in connection with an interallied agreement concluded at Vladivostok in 1919. Their duties are to establish communication between the Japanese contingents in Siberia and South Manchuria. It goes without saying, therefore, that these troops will be withdrawn as soon as the evacuation of Siberia by the Japanese troops is effected.

The Chairman of the Committee, Secretary Hughes, asked Mr. Hanihara if his Delegation relied upon Article II of the Additional Agreement to the Sino-Japanese of December 22, 1905. Mr. Hanihara said that it did.[2]

With regard to Police or "Police Boxes," as distinguished from Troops, Mr. Hanihara, in behalf of the Japanese Delegation, made the following statements:

In considering the question of Japanese consular police in China, two points must be taken in account.

(1) Such police do not interfere with Chinese or other foreign nationals. Their functions are strictly confined to the protection and control of Japanese subjects.

(2) The most important duties with which the Japanese police are charged are, first, to prevent the commission of crimes by Japanese, and second, to find and prosecute Japanese criminals when crimes are committed.

---

[2] This Article is as follows:

"Article II. In view of the earnest desire expressed by the Imperial Chinese Government to have the Japanese and Russian troops and railway guards in Manchuria withdrawn as soon as possible, and in order to meet this desire, the Imperial Japanese Government, in the event of Russia agreeing to the withdrawal of her railway guards, or in case other proper measures are agreed to between China and Russia, consent to take similar steps accordingly. When tranquillity shall have been reestablished in Manchuria, and China shall have become herself capable of affording full protection to the lives and property of foreigners, Japan will withdraw her railway guards simultaneously with Russia."

In view of the geographical proximity of the two countries, it is natural that certain disorderly elements in Japan should move to China, and, taking advantage of the present conditions in that country, should there undertake unlawful activities. When these lawless persons are caught in the act of crime by the Chinese police, it is not difficult for that police force to deal with the case. The culprits are handed over as early as possible to the Japanese authorities for prosecution and trial. But when the criminals flee from the scene of their acts, it is in many cases hard to discover who committed the crimes and what were the causes and circumstances that led up to their commission. This is more difficult for the Chinese authorities, as they have no power to make domiciliary visits to the homes of foreigners, who enjoy extraterritorial rights, or to obtain judicial testimony in due form from such foreigners:

Without the full cooperation of the Japanese police, therefore, the punishment of crime is, in a great many cases, an impossibility, and those who are responsible for lawbreaking escape trial and punishment.

This tendency is especially evident in Manchuria in which region hundreds of thousands of Japanese are resident. In places where the Japanese police are stationed, there are far fewer criminal cases among Japanese than in places without Japanese police. Lawless elements constantly move to districts beyond the reach of Japanese police supervision.

Apart from the theoretical side of the question, it will thus be observed that the stationing of Japanese police in the interior of China has proved to be of much practical usefulness in the prevention of crimes among Japanese residents, without interfering with the daily life of Chinese or of other foreign nationals. The Japanese policing provides a protection for the Chinese communities which at present their own organization fails to provide.

The Japanese delegation is in possession of knowledge and information as to the actual conditions prevailing in China and especially in Manchuria. However, it is unnecessary to go into details at the present stage.

Chinese Rejoinder. Mr. Sze stated that both of these matters were serious infringements of China's sovereignty and integrity, and that there was nothing in international law permitting one country to station troops or police upon the soil of another, especially over the protest of the latter. While expressing admiration for the efficiency of the Japanese police system and thanking Mr. Hanihara for his explanation of conditions, he could not accept that as justifying the presence of Japanese police, and he hoped that Japan would be able to check Japanese law-breakers at the source and to prevent their coming to China. In conclusion, while reserving the right to reply further after study, he observed that the Chinese nation could not look upon the presence of these troops and police without concern.

At the tenth meeting of the Committee, held December 2, the Chinese Delegation submitted an elaborate statement, which, except as to an introductory paragraph, is here reproduced.

> The Chinese Delegation wishes to make it clear that its proposal is advanced not only because China has not given its consent to these breaches of its sovereign rights, but also because the breaches were deliberately made and insistently continued even in the face of the formal protests of the Chinese Government and the unanimous opposition of the Chinese people. In view of the fact that the infringements in question are of many years standing, it is believed the Conference will agree that China has not unduly pressed for the termination of them.
>
> As to the withdrawal of Japanese troops from the Shantung Railway, the Japanese delegation states that "she has on more than one occasion made her position sufficiently clear. She has declared and now reaffirms her intention of withdrawing such guards as soon as China shall have notified her that a Chinese police force has been duly organized and is ready to take over the charge of the railway protection."

It should be noted that China has repeatedly sent notice to Japan that her police forces are well organized and prepared to assume the protection of the railway; and the Chinese delegation, on behalf of the Chinese Government, hereby again offers to take charge of the Shantung Railway with a well organized police force of its own and to protect the same.

As to the grounds for stationing Japanese troops along the South Manchuria Railway, Japan appears to rely on the additional agreement to the treaty of December 22, 1905, between Japan and China, and on the disturbed conditions in Manchuria. The treaty of December 22, 1905, provides:

"ARTICLE I. The Imperial Chinese Government consents to all the transfers and assignments made by Russia to Japan by Articles V and VI of the treaty of peace above mentioned." The pertinent article of the treaty of peace of September 5, 1905, between Russia and Japan, is Article VI which provides for the transfer by Russia to Japan, with the consent of China (which was procured as above stated), of the South Manchurian Railway, "together with all rights, privileges and properties appertaining thereto in that region."

Article III of the same treaty provides:

"1. To evacuate completely and simultaneously Manchuria except the territory affected by the lease of the Liao-tung Peninsula, in conformity with provisions of additional Article I, annexed to this treaty; and

"2. To restore entirely and completely to the exclusive administration of China all portions of Manchuria now in occupation or under the control of the Japanese or Russian troops, with the exception of the territory above mentioned.

"The Imperial Government of Russia declares that they have not in Manchuria any territorial advantages or preferential or exclusive concessions in impairment of Chinese sovereignty or inconsistent with the principle of equal opportunity."

Article II of the additional agreement referred to provides:

"ARTICLE II. In view of the earnest desire expressed by the Imperial Chinese Government to have the Japanese and Russian troops and railway guards in Manchuria withdrawn as soon as possible, and in order to meet this desire, the Imperial Japanese Government, in the event of Russia's agreeing to the withdrawal of her railway guards, or in case other proper measures are agreed to between China and Russia, consent to take similar steps. Accordingly, when tranquillity shall have been reestablished in Manchuria and China shall have become herself capable of affording full protection to the lives and property of foreigners, Japan will withdraw her railway guards simultaneously with Russia."

Russia has withdrawn her troops from Manchuria, but Japan has retained hers, as she states, under Article II of the additional agreement quoted. China has time and again offered to take over the protection of the South Manchuria Railway and requested Japan to withdraw her troops. If Japan continues to maintain that the alleged existing state of banditry in Manchuria requires the presence of Japanese troops as a "measure of absolute necessity," China may never have an opportunity to show that she is capable of affording protection to the lives and property of foreigners. Moreover, the mere presence of Japanese troops themselves makes for friction with the natives and arouses rather than allays disorders throughout the adjacent districts. The Japanese delegation refers to a "large number of cases" of cutting "telegraph lines" and committing "other acts of ravage." These cases do not appear to be serious ones. Similar cases occur every day even in the best regulated States. But in China especially many cases of disturbance may be traced directly to the presence or activities of Japanese troops along the railway.

Consequently China asks to be given an opportunity to show that she can maintain order along the South Manchuria Railway. The opportunity can only be granted if Japan will withdraw her forces, which China asks be done for the reasons given. The present conditions of Japanese military control have continued for over 15 years and on the present contentions of the Japanese delegation may be prolonged indefinitely at the will of Japan. China can not continue to submit to these infractions of its territorial and administrative integrity and asks the conference to take definite measures to bring these irritating controversies to a close.

The Japanese delegation refers to the presence of Japanese troops at Hankow and gives as a reason the revolution of 1911 and subsequent disorders. It should be pointed out, however, that Great

Britain, Russia, Germany, and the other powers forthwith withdrew their troops and that Japan is the only country that insists on their continuance. This insistence is based on continued disorders, but it will be noted that the other powers have not felt constrained to again introduce troops into that region. The disorders, therefore, must be of minor importance, as compared with those of 1911, which caused the entry of foreign military forces. The only special reason that Japan can advance therefor is the presence of larger numbers of Japanese in that region than subjects of any other power. But this has never been a valid reason for quartering troops on the soil of a friendly country for an indefinite period. It is said that at Hankow the Japanese forces have erected substantial barracks of a more or less permanent character.

The Japanese delegation declares that Japan is looking forward to an early opportunity of effecting the complete withdrawal of the Hankow garrison. China now offers Japan this opportunity by undertaking to maintain peace and order and the protection of foreigners.

Japan further asks that China will fully assume the responsibility for damage that may be or may have been done to foreigners. This is an unusual condition and one which it is believed no sovereign power would give in advance. The question of damages already sustained, if any, by Japanese subjects is a matter which may readily be settled by a mixed board or commission and need not, therefore, be made a condition for the withdrawal of Japanese troops. No government can absolutely guarantee the protection of foreigners any more than it can absolutely guarantee the protection of its own nationals. Moreover, every violation of that degree of protection which international law assumes that a government shall give is not a ground for military intervention or the dispatching of troops to the district in disorder. If the rule were the contrary every country would have garrisons of foreign troops stationed at various quarters within its territory. The normal procedure is for a foreign government, whose nationals are threatened on account of disorders in a friendly country, to call upon the government of that country to accord them adequate protection. If, nevertheless, loss of life or damages to property is sustained, the usual course is to have an investigation of the facts, and, if they warrant it, to request amends by way of pecuniary compensation. It is well known that the Chinese Government has in the past made every effort to satisfy such demands in the most liberal manner.

As to the stationing of garrison of foreign countries in North China, under the protocol of 1901, China admits that such troops are quartered in China with her express and formal approval. While China is desirous eventually of having these troops removed, it wishes to defer the consideration of this question at the present conference, limiting itself now to the request for the cessation of violations of its territorial and administrative integrity which have taken place without her free consent.

It is said that Japanese troops along the Chinese Eastern Railway are maintained in connection with an interallied agreement concluded in Vladivostok in 1919, and for the purpose of establishing communication between the Japanese contingents in Siberia and South Manchuria.

The interallied agreement of 1919 was concluded as a result of negotiations extending through the summer and autumn of 1918 with reference to the allied military control of the Trans-Siberian Railway, and this agreement, approved by all of the allied representatives at Vladivostok and by certain Russian authorities, expressly provided for supervision by international or Russian control and not by any one power. Moreover, the purpose of this agreement was to keep the Siberian Railway opened as a line of communication for the Czecho-Slovak troops which were operating in Siberia. The object of interallied control of the railroad was to avoid control by a single country which might arouse suspicion as to the political intentions of any such country. However, it appears that under this agreement Japan sent such a large number of troops as to indicate a departure on its part from the purposes of the agreement. As the objects and purposes of the allied agreement have long since disappeared, the other allied troops have long ago been withdrawn from Siberia and the Chinese Eastern Railway, but the Japanese troops still remain in both localities without any apparent vestige of authority. As to the necessity for maintaining troops along the Chinese Eastern Railway to establish communication between the

Japanese contingents in Siberia and South Manchuria, it need only be pointed out that this argument might be made the excuse for placing additional troops in Chinese territory in order to establish communication with garrisons already quartered at various points. As the general question of the Chinese Eastern Railway is a special subject on the American agenda, it is thought fit to postpone further discussion of matters relating to it until that point of the agenda is taken up.

To endeavor to defend the maintenance of Japanese police in Manchuria by saying that they do not interfere with Chinese or other foreign nationals, that their functions are restricted to the protection and control of Japanese subjects, and that their duties are to prevent the commissions of crime by Japanese and to apprehend Japanese criminals is to lead the conference far afield from the point at issue, namely, the illegal and unwarranted infraction of Chinese territorial and administrative integrity. The reasons advanced have never been regarded in international law and practice as sufficient to justify the institution of police administration in a foreign friendly country.

The Chinese delegation questions the statement that the Japanese police do not interfere with Chinese. It can present numerous instances in which Japanese police have arrested Chinese and otherwise molested them on Chinese soil. The argument that under the system of extraterritoriality inconveniences occur in the arrest of Japanese offenders or in procuring evidence for use in trial are only arguments in favor of the surrender of extraterritorial rights. Other powers enjoying these rights in China do not pretend that they carry with them the right of police. The ground of extraterritoriality being disposed of, it may be said that mere numbers of Japanese residents in Manchuria is not a sufficient or proper ground for the establishment of a police administration.

In conclusion it may be pointed out that the extension of Japanese military or police control over Chinese districts has been gradually expanding from very small beginnings in about 1900 and spreading out in various directions wherever an opportunity offered itself. China asks the conference to take appropriate measures to prevent further aggressions of this character and to relieve

China of these impositions under which it is laboring to maintain its independence and integrity.

Japanese Reply. At the thirteenth meeting of the Committee of the Whole, Mr. Hanihara, in behalf of the Japanese Delegation, submitted a reply to the Chinese statement that has been given. The essential portions of this reply were as follows:

With reference to the Shantung Railway Guards, China has declared her intention to send a suitable force of Chinese police for the protection of the Railway. She has, however, so far failed to send any such police force to whom the Japanese troops can actually hand over the duties.

The fact pointed out by the Chinese Delegation that Russia has withdrawn her troops from Manchuria apparently refers to the condition of things created by the existing anomalous situation in Russia. It does not prove that Russia has definitely agreed to the withdrawal of her troops as is contemplated in the Sino-Japanese Agreement of 1905.

That Agreement also provides that when tranquillity shall have been re-established in Manchuria and when China shall have become herself capable of affording full protection to the lives and property of foreigners, Japan will withdraw her railway guards simultaneously with Russia. Referring to that provision I would like to invite the attention of the Committee to the actual conditions described in the written statement which I shall presently lay before you.

As for the contention that China should be given an opportunity of proving her ability to maintain peace and order in Manchuria, the reply is obvious: Japanese interests and Japanese security are matters of such importance that she cannot afford to take obvious risks.

With regard to the stationing of Japanese troops at Hankow, I believe that I have made our position sufficiently clear at a previous meeting of the Committee, and I shall not attempt to repeat it. I would only add that in many cases of local disturbances in and around Hankow, the menace to the security of foreign communities in general assumed so serious a proportion that those various communities organized volunteer corps for their self-protection, and that the Japanese garrison was called upon to extend active assistance and cooperation to the foreign volunteer corps.

In connection with the subject of Japanese troops stationed along the Chinese Eastern Railway, criticisms have been made by the Chinese Delegation on the continued presence of Japanese expeditionary forces in Siberia. The Japanese Delegation desires to reserve the discussion of this question for a suitable opportunity which will later on be afforded by the Conference. For the present, I shall content myself by pointing out that the stationing of Japanese troops along the Chinese Eastern Railway is due to the Inter-Allied Agreement of 1918, in which China participated, and that those troops will be withdrawn immediately upon the evacuation of Maritime Province by Japanese forces.

In connection with this reply, Mr. Hanihara filed with the Committee Appendices giving, facts as the Japanese Delegation conceived them to be, regarding conditions of law and order or disorder in Manchuria and elsewhere in China.[3]

Commission of Inquiry Proposed. In the discussion which followed the presentation of these statements M. Viviani suggested that, since a commission of jurists had already been provided for, charged with the function of investigating upon the spot the question of extraterritoriality, it should also be

[3] The Chinese Delegation was rather surprised to find these appendices published in the report of the Conference (Senate Document No. 126), since these documents, while circulated by the Japanese Delegation, were never discussed in the Conference or, as the Chinese Delegation supposed, released for publication. The Chinese Delegation itself circulated statements of facts showing the extent to which the Japanese troops in China had caused, rather than prevented, disorder, and that, indeed, in a considerable number of cases, they had even cooperated, under the direction of the Japanese General Staff, with lawless elements in China.

authorized to examine as to the necessity for the continued maintenance of foreign troops upon Chinese soil.

Mr. Sze said that his Delegation did not deem it wise that a commission of inquiry of such a nature should be sent to China; that there was no analogy between the question of foreign troops in China which was based upon no treaty right, and the maintenance of extraterritorial jurisdiction which was supported by treaties to which China was a party. He feared that the sending of such a commission would tend to aggravate rather than to relieve, the feeling which the Chinese had upon the subject.

After some further discussion it was agreed that the whole matter should be referred to the Drafting Committee.

Chinese Objection. In this Committee, considerable discussion was had as to the agency through which an inquiry was to be made as to whether conditions in China were such as to justify the continued stationing of foreign troops in China. That respect for China's sovereignty required that these troops should be removed as soon as conditions would possibly justify was conceded by the representatives of all the Powers. At the same time it developed that the Chinese Delegation was unwilling, and quite properly so, that, without the consent and cooperation of the Chinese Government, the foreign Powers should assume and exercise the function of making an inquiry into China's domestic affairs. At the fifth meeting of the Committee Dr. Koo made the following statement:

Whatever may be the practice of nations under international law as to the sending of troops into a foreign state for the protection of their nationals, it is recognized by the civilized world that the sending of such troops is, and rightfully can be, only a temporary measure in order to meet emergencies that threaten imminent danger to the lives and property of the nationals of the state taking such action, and, upon the passing of such emergency, the troops sent should be immediately withdrawn. It is furthermore recognized that the obligation to make such withdrawal should not, as a general principle, be made dependent upon an inquiry into the domestic conditions of the country into which such troops are sent, but, in every case, their retention should depend upon clearly evident conditions of disorder in the localities where such troops are stationed such as to make demonstrable the inability or indisposition of the local territorial sovereignty to afford adequate protection to the lives and property of the nationals of the State sending troops.

Resolution Adopted. The following resolution, adopted by the Drafting Committee on January 3, was reported to the Committee of the Whole at its seventeenth session, held January 5:

Whereas the powers have from time to time stationed armed forces, including police, in China to protect the lives and property of foreigners lawfully in China;

And whereas it appears that certain of these armed forces are maintained in China without the authority of any treaty or agreement;

And whereas the powers have declared their intention to withdraw their armed forces now on duty in China without the authority of any treaty or agreement, whenever China shall assure the protection of the lives and property of foreigners in China;

And whereas China has declared her intention and capacity to assure the protection of the lives and property of foreigners in China;

Now to the end that there may be a clear understanding of the conditions upon which in each case the practical execution of those intentions must depend;

It is resolved that the diplomatic representatives in Peking of the powers now in conference at Washington, to wit: the United States of America, Belgium, the British Empire, France, Italy, Japan, the Netherlands, and Portugal, will be instructed by their respective Governments, whenever China shall so request, to associate themselves with three representatives of the Chinese Government to conduct collectively a full and impartial inquiry into the issues raised by the foregoing declarations of intention made by the powers and by China and shall thereafter prepare a full and comprehensive report setting out without reservation their findings of fact and their opinions with regard to the matter hereby referred for inquiry, and shall furnish a copy of their report to each of the nine Governments concerned which shall severally make public the report with such comment as each may deem appropriate. The representatives of any of the powers may make or join in minority reports stating their differences, if any, from the majority report.

That each of the powers above named shall be deemed free to accept or reject all or any of the findings of fact or opinions expressed in the report, but that in no case shall any of the said powers make its acceptance of all or any of the findings of fact or opinions either directly or indirectly dependent on the granting by China of any special concession, favor, benefit, or immunity, whether political or economic.

Chinese Statement. Mr. Sze at this time, in behalf of the Chinese Delegation, made the following statement which was later repeated in the fifth plenary session of the Conference:

The Chinese Delegation takes note of the Resolution with regard to the withdrawal of foreign troops from China and expresses its appreciation of the offer of the eight Powers approving this Resolution to instruct their respective diplomatic representatives at Peking to associate themselves with representatives of the Chinese Government, when that Government shall so request, in order to conduct collectively a full and impartial inquiry as to the necessity for continuing to maintain foreign armed forces in China. The Chinese

Delegation will assume, unless now notified to the contrary, that, should their Government at any future time desire to avail itself of the foregoing offer inquiries and resulting recommendations may be asked for with reference to the presence of foreign armed forces at particular places or in particular localities in China.

The Chinese Delegation desires further to say with reference to the general matter of maintaining armed forces by a nation or nations within the borders of other states which have not given their express consent thereto, that it is its understanding that, according to accepted principles of international law, the sending or stationing of such forces can rightfully be only a temporary measure in order to meet emergencies that threaten imminent danger to the lives and property of the nationals of the States taking such action, and that, upon the passing of such emergency, the forces sent should be immediately withdrawn. It is also the understanding of the Chinese Delegation that the obligation to make such withdrawal cannot, as a general principle, be rightfully postponed until the Government of the State where they are located has consented to an inquiry by the representatives of other Powers into its own domestic conditions as regards the maintenance of law and order, and a report has been made declaring that there is no necessity for the presence of such foreign armed force. In other words, it is the understanding of the Chinese Delegation that accepted international law recognizes the basic right of every sovereign state to refuse its consent to the sending into or the stationing within its borders of armed forces, and that while it may, by the exercise of its own will, consent that an inquiry shall be made as to the necessity in fact of the continuance within its borders of such foreign armed forces as may be therein, such action upon its part, or a Resolution by other Powers offering their cooperation in such an inquiry, is not to be deemed in derogation or limitation of the inherent right of a sovereign state to refuse entrance to, or further continuance within its borders, of foreign armed forces.

Mr. Sze asked whether " railway guards " were included within the armed forces referred to in the resolution. Mr. Root said that they should be included and therefore asked that the first paragraph of the resolution be amended by inserting the words " and railway guards " after the words " including police." As to this, he said " it was not a matter of terms. It was not a question of the name that happened to be given to the person who was employed in a public capacity with arms to preserve order. He might be called a policeman, or he might be called a guard, or what not."

These amendments were accepted, and, as thus amended, the resolution was unanimously adopted (China not voting) by the Committee, and, later approved by the Conference in its fifth plenary session, held February 1, 1922.

CHAPTER XII

WIRELESS AND OTHER ELECTRICAL COMMUNICATIONS INSTALLATIONS IN CHINA

The matter of the existence of radio stations upon China's soil without the consent of her Government became connected with the general topic of "Electrical Communications" that appeared upon the Agenda of the Conference for the consideration of Pacific and Far Eastern Questions, and gave rise to considerable discussion which finally led to no very definite results.

Chinese Statement. In the Committee of the Whole, Mr. Sze asked that the Conference should take action that would lead to the immediate abolition or surrender to the Chinese Government of all electrical means of communication, including wireless stations, maintained on Chinese soil without the consent of the Chinese Government, and submitted tentative lists of them. In this statement he said:

All of the arguments that have been presented in favor of the immediate abolition of foreign postal stations apply with equal force to the abolition or surrender to the Chinese Government of these foreign electrical means of communication. Just as China has built up a highly efficient postal system capable of transporting with speed and safety written communications between China and foreign countries and between important points within China so she has developed a system of telegraph stations adequate for the transmission of communications by wire, or between different parts of China, and has entered into contracts for the installation of high powered wireless apparatus which will put her into communication with other countries. She already has a number of lower-powered wireless stations for wireless communication between points within China. There is thus no need for the maintenance in China by other countries of wire or wireless installations. Their operation not only seriously interferes with the continued development of the Chinese system by diverting from it business properly belonging to it but represents an indefensible infringement of China's territorial and administrative integrity. To the foreign powers maintaining them they can have no significance except as they may seem to serve their purely political aims. Since these powers have now affirmed their intention of doing nothing that will infringe upon the political, territorial, or administrative integrity of China, it is to be expected that they will discontinue the maintenance of the stations to which China has not given her consent.

Since certain of these stations represent the investment of considerable sums of money, China, though recognizing no legal obligation to do so, is willing to pay to the foreign governments owning them the fair value of such stations as are of such a character or are so located that they can be made effective parts of her own systems of electrical communications.

In the discussion which followed Secretary Hughes called attention to the stations maintained under the Boxer Protocol of 1901: Mr. Balfour said that he understood that the British Government had in China only one wireless station, namely, that at Kashgar, in Turkestan, which had been erected during the war for the purpose of obtaining information in regard to the Bolshevists: M. Viviani raised, rather unnecessarily, the question as to the control of wave lengths which different stations should be permitted to use, and suggested the organization of a committee to investigate the technical sides of wireless telegraphy. It was then decided to refer the whole matter to the Drafting Committee.

Draft Resolution by Mr. Root. At the first meeting of this committee its Chairman, Mr. Root, submitted the following resolution:

AGREED: 1. That all radio-stations in China maintained under the provisions of the protocol of September 7, 1901, for the settlement of the disturbances of the year 1900 or in the grounds of any of the foreign legations in China shall be limited in their use to sending and receiving government messages and shall not receive or send commercial or personal and unofficial messages; Provided, however, that in case all other telegraphic communication is interrupted then, upon official notification accompanied by proof of such interruption to the Chinese Ministry of Posts and Communications, such stations may afford temporary facilities for commercial and personal messages until the Chinese Government has given notice of the termination of the interruption.

2. All radio-stations operated within the territory of China by foreign governments or their citizens under treaties or concessions of the Government of China, are to limit the messages sent and received by the terms of the treaties or concessions under which the respective stations are maintained.

3. In case there be any radio-station maintained in the territory of China by a foreign government or citizens or subjects thereof without the authority of the Chinese Government, such station and all the plant apparatus and material thereof shall be transferred to and taken over by the Government of China, to be operated under the Chinese Ministry of Posts and Communications, upon fair and full compensation to the owners for the value of the installation, as soon as the Chinese Ministry of Posts and Communications is prepared to operate the same effectively for the general public benefit.

4. The owners or managers of all radio-stations maintained in the territory of China by foreign Powers or citizens or subjects thereof are to confer with the Chinese Ministry of Posts and Communications for the purpose of seeking a common arrangement to

avoid intereference in the use of wave lengths by wireless stations in China, subject to such general arrangements as may be made by a general international conference for the revision of the rules established by the International Radio Telegraph Convention signed at London, July 5, 1912.

Discussion. With reference to this draft resolution, the French representative said that France had established a radio-station in the French Concession in Shanghai and one in the leased territory of Kwangchow-wan. These stations, he said, France had the right to establish by virtue of its concessional rights at Shanghai and as lessee of Kwangchow-wan, and therefore, they should be excluded from the operation of the Resolution. The British representative said that the radio station in the Kowloon leased area should receive separate consideration, and the one at Kashgar was there with China's consent.[1] The

[1] In a letter from the British Empire Delegation, dated December 28, 1921, to the Chinese Delegation the following statement was made regarding the British radio station at Kashgar: "During the summer of 1918, the position in Hsinkiang gave rise to anxiety owing to the activities of Bolsheviks, and especially to the fact that enemy prisoners of war were being armed by the Russians and sent as garrison troops to the Russian Pamirs. Great Britain notified China of her wish to send some intelligence officers into Hsinkiang, and a guard of some 30 men to the Consulate-General at Kashgar. On August 19, 1918, the Chinese Government replied that they had telegraphed instructions to the Governor of Hsinkiang pointing out that Great Britain and China stood together as Allies and it was the duty of each to render assistance to the other when occasions arose, and that the guard should therefore be allowed to enter Hsinkiang for the purpose of guarding the Consulate.

"On October 26, 1918, Sir J. Jordan, then His Majesty's Minister at Peking, wrote to the Wai Chiao Pu stating that the operations of our intelligence officers in Hsinkiang had been greatly hampered by the difficulty of communicating with the British authorities in India. It was accordingly proposed to send to Kashgar a small wireless telegraphy receiving set which would enable the Consulate to receive messages trans-

Japanese representative contended that the Japanese radio stations in the South Manchuria Railway zones were there by treaty right, that is, as ancillary to Japan's rights of railway control and operation. The station at Hankow, he said, would be withdrawn when the Japanese troops were withdrawn from that place and would be used only for military purposes; the stations at Tsingtao and Tsinan would be disposed of simultaneously with the settlement of the Shantung question.

In the Drafting Committee. Dr. Koo, in behalf of the Chinese Delegation, denied that the right to establish radio stations in the leased areas was included within the rights granted by China to the lessee states. He took the same position as to the maintenance of radio stations, without China's consent, in municipal " settlements " or " concessions " and within railway zones. The British representative agreed with Dr. Koo that the rights which foreign powers have in municipal concessions or settlements in China do not

---

mitted from India. Owing to the difficult nature of the frontier roads, it has been found impossible to send a transmitter set, and messages from Kashgar would have to be sent as before by post or by the Chinese land lines, until the new Marconi installation at Kashgar should be set up. His Majesty's Government offered to use the Kashgar receiving installation for Chinese official messages, should the Chinese Government so desire; and they undertook to remove the installation so soon as the Chinese Government's own wireless station had been erected.

"On November 7, 1918, Sir John Jordan telegraphed that the Chinese government had sent instructions to the Governor of Hsinkiang that the party in charge of the wireless installation were to be admitted.

"From the above I think you will agree that it is evident that the wireless receiving set at his Majesty's Consulate-General at Kashgar is there with the concurrence of the Chinese Government."

include, without specific consent of China, the rights of erecting and operating radio stations.

After some further discussion, Dr. Koo said that he understood the position of the French Delegation to be that a "concession" did not, as a matter of principle, carry with it the right to install a radio station, but that there was, in fact, such a station in the French settlement at Shanghai, and that its continuance there would be a matter for discussion between the French and Chinese Governments.

The Japanese representative said that the Japanese wireless station at Hankow was in the Japanese garrison there and was needed for military purposes; also that the stations within the railway zones were for the use of the railway guards. Dr. Koo again affirmed that, in the railway zones, Japan had by treaty only ordinary business administrative rights for the operation of the railway, and that while Japan might have the right to erect and operate such telegraph lines as might be required for the working of the railway, this did not carry with it the right to erect and operate radio stations. As to wireless stations, without China's consent in leased areas, he would make a reservation in behalf of his Government.

Resolution of December 7. As finally agreed to by the Drafting Committee and reported to, and adopted by the Committee of the Whole, at its thirteenth meeting, held December 7, the resolution ran as follows:

1. That all radio-stations in China, whether maintained under the provisions of the international protocol of September 7, 1901,

or in fact maintained in the grounds of any of the foreign Legations in China, shall be limited in their use to sending and receiving government messages and shall not receive or send commercial or personal or unofficial messages, including press matter: Provided, however, that in case all other telegraphic communication is interrupted then, upon official notification accompanied by proof of such interruption to the Chinese Ministry of Posts and Communications, such stations may afford temporary facilities for commercial and personal messages until the Chinese Government has given notice of the termination of the interruption.

2. All radio-stations operated within the territory of China by foreign governments or their citizens under treaties or concessions of the Government of China, shall limit the messages sent and received by the terms of the treaties or concessions under which the respective stations are maintained.

3. In case there be any radio-station maintained in the territory of China by a foreign government or citizens or subjects thereof without the authority of the Chinese Government, such station and all the plant, apparatus and material thereof shall be transferred to and taken over by the Government of China, to be operated under the direction of the Chinese Ministry of Posts and Communications, upon fair and full compensation to the owners for the value of the installation, so soon as the Chinese Ministry of Posts and Communications is prepared to operate the same effectively for the general public benefit.

4. If any question shall arise as to radio-stations in the leased territories, South Manchurian railway zones, and the French Concession in Shanghai, it is agreed that these shall be matters for discussion between the Chinese Government and the Governments concerned.

5. The owners or managers of all rado-stations maintained in the territory of China by foreign powers or citizens or subjects thereof shall confer with the Chinese Ministry of Posts and Communications for the purpose of seeking a common arrangement to avoid interference in the use of wave-lengths by wireless stations in China, subject to such general arrangements as may be made by a general international conference for the revision of the rules established by

the International Radio Telegraph Convention signed at London, July 5, 1912.

Viviani Resolution. At the fifteenth meeting of the Committee of the Whole, held December 12, a draft of a motion (dated December 7) was submitted by M. Viviani which was as follows:

Whereas competition in the establishment and operation of wireless stations in China, far from bringing about the creation of the necessary radio communications between China and the other countries, has on the contrary, produced results the reverse of those aimed at, the powers represented at the Washington conference consider that this competition should give way to co-operation under the control of the Government of China.

Therefore, it is decided that a committee shall be formed, including representatives of the interested countries and of China, to draw up practical recommendations in accordance with which this co-operation shall be accomplished in conformity with the following principles:

(1) The purpose of the co-operation should not be to favor certain interest at the expense of others but to enable China to obtain radio communications established and operated as much in its own interests as in that of the public of all countries and to avoid the waste of capital, of staff, of material, and of wave lengths.

(2) To this end China should be enabled to possess, as soon as possible, radio stations with all the latest technical improvements that can be contributed by the various companies of the countries which are concerned in the improvement of radio communications with China.

(3) Radio communications within the Chinese territory shall be subject to the Chinese laws and the external radio communications (between China and other countries) shall be regulated by the international conventions governing such matters.

(4) The Governments of the powers mentioned in the preamble shall give no support to any company or any person who does not conform to the above principles as well as to the practical rules prescribed in accordance with the recommendations of the committee.

Supplementary Suggestion

(5) The rates charged for radio communications shall never be higher than the rates for communications by wire or by cable for equivalent distances, and Government and press messages shall benefit by a reduction of at least 50 per cent.

In explanation of this motion, Mr. Viviani said that its aim was to save China from being invaded by a swarm of little competing radio companies by strengthening the present companies and enabling them to render efficient service. Its aim was not, however, to establish a monopoly in China upon the part of the existing companies.

Mr. Balfour thought that it was proper that the Conference should seek to bring present and future radio concessions in China into harmony with one another and without infringement of China's sovereignty, and that Mr. Viviani's proposals might be taken as a starting point for that purpose. He was inclined to the opinion that future radio rights in China should be arranged upon the consortium principle.

No action upon Mr. Viviani's proposals was taken at that time but the matter postponed so that the Delegations could have opportunity to consult their experts upon it. The matter of radio stations in China was not again brought up for discussion until the twenty-fifth meeting of the Committee of the Whole, held January 24, 1922. At that meeting Mr. Root said that while he was, upon the whole, in agreement with the purposes of the motion of Mr. Viviani, the matter was " a grave question of policy which primarily and fundamentally should be determined by the Government of China. . . . . The question lay between building up an electrical wireless system in China upon the principle of free competition, or building it up upon the principle of co-operation or consortium. . . . . One method, that of competition, was the method that existed in the United States today; another method, that of controlled cooperation, was the method that existed in many other countries. China ought to determine which she would follow; then the powers represented ought to help her in that course, but he did not think that the committee was in a position to decide now. With that end in view he had prepared for submission to the Drafting Sub-Committee a resolution which corresponded to Mr. Viviani's motion for the appointment of a committee or commission, but which, instead of undertaking to decide the fundamental question of policy in advance of the consideration of the commission, left that to be one of the things to be determined from the report of the commission.''

Chinese Statement. At the twenty-sixth meeting of the Committee of the Whole, held January 25, Mr. Sze, in behalf of the Delegation, made the following statement with reference to the policy of the Chinese Government regarding wireless communication:

I hope I have made it clear on a previous occasion that wireless stations not owned and operated by the Chinese Government, at present found in China, should, at the earliest possible moment, by negotiation with owners, be handed over to the operation and control of the Chinese Government. To state it clearly, I may say that the continuance of such radio stations under foreign operation as now exist in China, without its express consent, is only a matter of sufferance upon the part of China, and that their existence and continuance can be legalized only when the foreign nations concerned have obtained from the Chinese Government its formal consent thereto.

It is known to the world that in China wire telegraphy is a Government monopoly, and it will be a logical development to this Government monopoly that the Government should establish and maintain all wireless communications within the territory of China as a Government monopoly. The two systems of communication must cooperate, and in order that this cooperation may be harmonious, and efficient, it is necessary that both should be owned, controlled and operated by the Government.

The nature of international wireless communication makes international cooperation highly desirable. This cooperation is needed in order that several stations of different nationality may not interfere with each other's wave lengths, and that unnecessary high powered stations may not be established, or at improper places, and that suitable arrangements may be made for the distribution by wire telegraph or otherwise within the individual states of the wireless messages when received. Therefore, this important subject of international wireless communication is a matter which should be the subject of discussion looking toward cooperation between all stations concerned. While I do not pretend to be an expert on wireless communications, it seems to me that so important an international question should be dealt with as a whole, and not by taking China as a single unit for international discussion. As this Conference has been called—and its work has proved—for the purpose of assisting China by the removal of existing limitations on her sovereign rights, I am inclined to think that the public might have misapprehension should any such commission be appointed to deal with, even if only to discuss and report on, such a subject, which is manifestly China's own and sole problem. My honored friend, Senator Root, has truly remarked that it is a " grave question of policy, which primarily and fundamentally should be determined by the Government of China." Senator Root also remarked yesterday that the questions of competition or controlled cooperation are not uniform in practice in all countries. In view of this fact, and the importance of the whole subject of wireless communications, China, while determining for herself, wishes to have time to consider carefully the practices of other countries, before deciding for herself which course to follow.

The Chinese Government will be glad to cooperate with other Powers with a view to arriving at common policies applicable to all Governments and mutually beneficial to all, with regard to radio communications between herself and those Powers, and, for this purpose, to participate in a conference or other joint action for the determination of general principles and methods to be recommended to all the Governments concerned whereby this general matter may be mutually regulated in a manner similar to that by which international postal interests are harmonized and promoted.[2]

Revised Root Resolution. Following this statement by Mr. Sze, Mr. Root submitted a revision of the resolutions which he had submitted the day before, and which was as follows:

The United States of America, Belgium, the British Empire, China, France, Italy, Japan, the Netherlands, and Portugal, desiring to avoid controversies regarding electrical communication facilities and services in China, and between China and other countries, and particularly over concessions or contracts in China relating thereto, and desiring to promote the further development of the internal and external electrical communication facilities and services of China, and taking note of the general policy of the Government of China to own and operate electrical communication services within its territory, have agreed:

(1) That the provisions set forth in the resolution concerning the open door shall apply to electrical communications in China and between China and other countries.

(2) That in any case where, in the general interest, the rescission of an existing monopoly or preferential privilege in respect to electrical communications in China, or between China and other countries, is deemed desirable, the powers whose interests are affected

---

[2] This statement was again read in the fifth plenary session of the Conference.

stand ready to use their good offices, if requested by China, to bring about such rescission.

(3) That no radio stations shall be erected or operated on Chinese territory without the authorization of the Government of China, and, as to any existing unauthorized station, the right of the Government of China either to order its removal or to take it over upon payment of fair and reasonable compensation is expressly recognized.

(4) That without the express consent of the Government of China no additional radio stations shall be erected in the legation quarter at Peking, in settlements, in concessions, in leased territories, in railway areas or in other special areas; nor shall the power of existing stations in any such areas be increased; nor shall such stations carry on ordinary commercial working.

(5) That such radio stations as are authorized by the Government of China, whether by treaty or concession, shall comply with the terms of such authorization, and with the provisions of the International Radio-Telegraph Convention or any modification thereof, and, where the stations are authorized to conduct commercial services, such services shall be available on like terms to the nationals of every country.

(6) That any power or the nationals of any power operating radio stations in the territory of China, or in the special areas indicated heretofore, shall confer with the Government of China for the purpose of seeking a common understanding with a view to avoiding interference, subject to any general international arrangement which may hereafter be agreed to.

(7) That the electrical communication services between China and other countries may develop in a proper and orderly manner and in accord with the policy of China, the powers stand ready to exchange views, either generally or severally, as occasion may arise.

Discussion. Senator Underwood, as reported in the Minutes, spoke as follows:

First, to refer to what he had said the other day about China, he had come to this conference in the utmost good faith to try to help the Chinese people establish and maintain a sovereign government and their territorial integrity, and, so far as he was concerned, he was unwilling to take any step that did not recognize that principle of the future sovereignty and integrity of China. He knew, as they all did, that China was torn to pieces at the present time by dissensions at home; but every country represented at the conference table, at some time in its history had met a like fate. The same difficulties had been experienced in the United States, and because China was disturbed by internal differences at the present time was no reason to believe that, within the next decade, she would not have established a sound parliamentary government that would efficiently represent her people and protect the rights of foreigners dwelling within her territory. To help establish such a government was undoubtedly one of the high purposes of the conference, and he thought the conference should hesitate to take any step themselves that, for one minute, would recognize an invasion of that great principle of the sovereignty of China.

In the main he did not object to these resolutions; he thought they were a recital of what had been done before. But, as he understood the position of the radio question in China, China had made certain concessions in reference to the legations, legation rights in China, and communication between Peking and the sea. That had already been covered by the resolution that had already been passed. Outside of that, if he understood it rightly, there were no treaty rights that tied the hands of China in reference to radio communications. She had made some concessions, but those concessions, as a sovereign Government, were like a concession that the Government of the United States would make, or that of Japan would make; it was still within the power of her sovereignty, because it had not been made to a Government, but had been made to nationals of other countries, who, in taking it, had to conform to the laws of China properly administered.

His main objection to the resolution was to clause 5: "That such radio stations as are authorized by the Government of China, whether by treaty or concession, shall comply with the terms of such authorization. . . . ." So far so good; but the clause continued: ". . . . and with the provisions of the International Radio-Telegraph Convention or any modification thereof." In other words, if China granted the right to nationals of the Government of the United

States to establish a radio station in China, that radio station had to first comply with the regulations in China as far as it could; but, in addition to that, China had to recognize—and China became a party to this, if she entered into a treaty—that the radio station had to comply with the International-Telegraph Convention or any modification thereof; that was to say, any modification thereof as passed in a future convention; and that future convention might adopt regulations in reference to radio in China that would not be satisfactory to the Chinese Government; and yet, in such a case, China was to surrender her sovereignty, not to governments or representatives of governments, but, in reference to the regulation of those radio stations, to the representatives of corporations or individuals who controlled the International Radio-Telegraph Conventions.

He did not think the committee ought to ask China to do that. He thought it might not be a serious point; but, from his viewpoint, it was asking China to surrender her sovereignty in the control of this question to nationals or committees or organizations entirely outside of China; and he was not willing, occupying the position he did in reference to the sovereignty of China, and with his desire to see it established and maintained, to attempt to defend a proposition of that kind.

Mr. Root suggested that he thought perhaps Senator Underwood's point might be covered by inserting (in paragraph 5) after the words "with the provisions of the International Radio-Telegraph Convention or any modification thereof" the words "to which China shall consent."

The chairman, after some discussion, said that if there was no objection, the resolution proposed by Mr. Root would contain the amendment "to which China shall consent," at the place stated.

Mr. Sze asked whether that meant that China would be obliged to consent.

The chairman replied that it did not; that the phrase simply implied futurity. He thought the words in question indicate that there was no intent to have it mandatory.

An extended discussion then followed and additional resolutions were offered with the result that the subject under consideration became so complicated that it was finally decided to reconsider the resolutions of December 7 and again to refer the matter to the Committee on Drafting.

Resolution of December 7 Finally Approved. That committee, as a result of two sessions of discussion, decided to report back to the Committee of the Whole, without alteration, the resolutions originally adopted by the Committee of the Whole on December 7. Mr. Sze took occasion again to state that it was the position of the Chinese Government that radio stations installed in the special regions designated in the fourth Article of the resolutions of December 7, were installed and maintained only on sufferance so far as China was concerned, and that China had not surrendered and would not surrender her right to demand their removal or transfer to herself. The following motion was put to a vote and adopted:

> The undersigned powers declare that nothing in paragraphs 3 and 4 of the Resolution of 7th December, 1921, is to be deemed to be an expression of opinion by the Conference as to whether the stations referred to therein are or are not authorized by China.
>
> They further give notice that the result of any discussion arising under paragraph 4 must, if it is not to be subject to objection by them, conform with the principle of the open door or equal opportunity approved by the Conference.

The Committee of the Whole at twenty-seventh meeting, held January 27, upon receiving this report accompanied by the foregoing declarations, again adopted the Resolutions which had been approved on December 7.

Mr. Sze made the following statement:

The Chinese Delegation takes this occasion formally to declare that the Chinese Government does not recognize or concede the right of any foreign power or of the nationals thereof to install or operate, without its express consent, radio stations in legation grounds, settlements, concessions, leased territories, railway areas or other similar areas.

The radio resolution was reported to the Conference at its fifth plenary session, held February 1, and unanimously approved without discussion or amendment.

CHAPTER XIII

Spheres of Interest

Chinese Statement. In a statement made in behalf of the Chinese Delegation, at the fifteenth meeting of the Committee of the Whole, held December 12, Dr. Wang said:

The phrase "sphere of interest," or "sphere of influence" as it is sometimes called, is a more or less vague term which implies that the powers making such claims in China are entitled within their respective "spheres" to enjoy reserved, preferential, exclusive, or special rights and privileges of trade, investment and for other purposes.

Germany was the first to claim a sphere of influence or of interest in its crystallized form over the Province of Shantung; later the other powers made similar claims over other portions of the territory of China.

These claims are either based on agreements between the powers themselves to which China is not a party, such as the agreement of September 2, 1898, relative to railway construction concluded between British and German banking groups and sanctioned by their respective Governments, or based on treaties or agreements made with China under circumstances precluding the free exercise of her will, such as the convention with Germany for a lease of Kiaochow of March 6, 1898, and the treaties and notes of May 25, 1915, made with Japan in consequence of the latter's 21 demands on China.

A tentative list of the various treaties relating to this matter and to the so-called spheres of interest of the various powers has already been circulated for your information. I need not, therefore, enter into a detailed examination of them at present.

That China should have been thus divided into different spheres of interest is a most unfortunate state of affairs. In the first place, these spheres of interest seriously hamper the economic development of China. The powers claiming these spheres seem to take the view that certain portions of China's territory are reserved for their exclusive exploitation without regard to the economic needs of the Chinese people. There have been instances where a nation is unwilling or unable to finance a particular enterprise and yet refuses to allow it to be financed or carried out by other nations.

In the second place, the whole system is contrary to the policy of equal opportunity for the commerce and industry of all nations—a policy which, so far as the common interests of the powers are concerned, is fair and equitable and which has been adopted by this committee.

A further objection to the spheres of interest is that there has been a tendency, under cover of economic claims, to further political ends, thus threatening the political integrity of China and giving rise to international jealousy or friction.

It is gratifying to know that the United States and Great Britain have placed themselves strongly upon record as opposed to the continuance of spheres of interest in China. At the last meeting Mr. Balfour was good enough to say that a sphere of interest in China is a thing of the past.

The claims by the powers to spheres of interest have given rise to much misunderstandings and misgivings on the part of the Chinese people, and in view of the considerations which I have just advanced, the Chinese delegation asks that the powers represented in this Conference disavow all claims to a sphere or spheres of interest or of influence or any special interests within the territory of China.

Status of Question. The way for this formal disavowal by the Powers of Spheres of Interest in China had been prepared by the correspondence between the United States, Great Britain and Japan leading up to the creation, in 1920, of the International Banking Consortium, as well as by certain statements that had earlier been made in the Conference itself.

That one of the primary purposes which the United States and Great Britain had had in promoting the establishment of the Banking Consortium was the abolition of claims upon the part of the Powers to Spheres of Interest in China is certain. Mr. Lamont, the spokesman for the American banking interests, which had the support of the American Government, in his Preliminary Report on the Consortium had said: " Certainly if the principle laid down for its organization is carried out we shall see no more ' spheres of interest ' set up in China." In its Memorandum of August 11, 1919, submitted to the Japanese Government, the British Government said: " One of the fundamental objects of the American proposals as accepted by the British, Japanese and French Governments, is to eliminate claims in particular spheres of interest and to throw open the whole of China without reserve to the combined activities of an International Consortium. This object cannot be achieved unless all the parties to the scheme agree to sacrifice all claim to enjoy any industrial preference within the boundaries of every political sphere of influence." And again, in its Memorandum of November 20, 1919, the British Government declared that the " fundamental idea underlying the creation of the Consortium " is " to abolish spheres of interest and throw open the whole of China to the activities of an international financial combination." The American correspondence was equally emphatic upon this point.

Statements in the Conference. In the fourteenth meeting of the Committee of the Whole of the Washington Conference, Mr. Balfour, replying to a statement by Dr. Koo with reference to Inter-Power Agreements relating to China, called attention to the fact that one of the most important passages of Dr. Koo's speech had reference to spheres of influence, and said:

So far as Great Britain is concerned, spheres of interest are things of the past. The British Government has not the slightest wish to prolong a situation which, so far as they are concerned, has been abandoned. A better way of dealing with the matter is to make clear what had already been implicitly, if not explicitly, indicated, namely, to declare that no one wishes to perpetuate either the system of spheres of interest or the international understandings on which they depend.[1]

At this same meeting of the Committee, Mr. Root said that he believed that Mr. Balfour's statement that morning had created a new situation in regard to spheres of influence; it was, he said the most public open, positive declaration that had come to his notice; he recalled correspondence between the United States and Great Britain a few years ago when Mr. Balfour himself, as Minister for Foreign Affairs, had taken

---

[1] In the discussion had in the eighteenth meeting of the Committee of the Whole, when the matter of the Open Door was under consideration, Mr. Balfour said:

"The British Empire Delegation understood that there was no representative of any Power around the table who thought that the old practice of 'spheres of influence' was either advocated by any Government or would be tolerable to this Conference. So far as the British Government was concerned, they had, in the most formal manner, publicly announced that they regarded this practice as utterly inappropriate to the existing situation."

the position that Great Britain could not give up certain exclusive rights, confirmed by agreements with China, in what was then known as the British sphere, in the valley of the Yangtze, because other nations held rights to their spheres, and as long as British subjects were excluded from them Great Britain could not surrender her own rights; that stage had now been passed, and an endeavor should be made to define and make clear the new position.

Mr. Balfour said he did not wish to discuss then the correspondence of 1917, to which Mr. Root had referred, as it was of very little immediate relevancy to the question. It was, however, worth while for him to state, in order that it might appear on the records of the committee, that on October 31, 1921, the parliamentary undersecretary of the foreign office had made the following declaration in the House of Commons:

> The policy of spheres of influence in China has been superseded by one of international cooperation, and the further development of this policy will no doubt form one of the subjects of discussion at Washington.

Commenting upon the statement which Dr. Wang had made at the fifteenth meeting of the Committee, Mr. Root said that, as he understood it, China asked to be released from the effect of certain restrictions and stipulations that were collateral to certain grants or negative stipulations (undertakings given to particular powers not to alienate or lease specific portions of her territory).

This, it is to be observed, was not exactly what Dr. Wang had asked for. However, upon being requested to do so, he furnished the Committee at its sixteenth meeting a list of so-called "restrictive stipulations," which included not only China's non-alienation agreements, and the various agreements that had been entered into by the Powers relating to China but to which she was not a party, but also the group of treaties and exchange of notes of May 25, 1915, that had resulted from the Twenty-One Demands that Japan, in that year, had made upon China.

Resolution Adopted. No formal or definitive action was taken by the Committee of the Whole or by the Conference in plenary session with reference to the various restrictive stipulations, the list of which Dr. Wang submitted. However, at the twenty-third meeting of the Committee, held January 21, a resolution was unanimously adopted which was later approved by the Conference in plenary session and embodied, with unimportant verbal changes, as Article IV, in the final Nine Power Treaty Relating to Principles and Policies to be followed in Matters Concerning China, signed February 6, 1922. This Article IV reads:

> The Contracting Powers agree not to support any agreements by their respective nationals with each other designed to create Spheres of Influence or to provide for the enjoyment of mutually exclusive opportunities in designated parts of Chinese territory.[2]

---

[2] This resolution originated in connection with the matter of listing by the Powers the commitments claimed by them to have been made by China to them or to their nationals and will again be referred to in the chapter dealing with that subject.

It will be observed that this agreement upon the part of the Powers has only a prospective and not a retrospective operation. At the same time, when regard is had to the other declarations made by the Powers at the Conference and to the other Principles and Policies to which they have committed themselves, especially with reference to the Open Door, it may fairly be said that, if these Policies and Principles are faithfully followed, there will be little opportunity in the future for any Power to claim, within any particular region of China, upon the basis of any agreements it already has with that country, such preferential or exclusive rights as will amount to a claim, within that region of what, in the past, has been known as a Sphere of Interest or of Influence.[3]

---

[3] Article III, paragraph designated (a) of the Nine Powers Treaty Relating to Principles and Policies to be Followed in Matters Concerning China provides that the Power will not seek nor support their nationals in seeking "any arrangement which might purport to establish in favor of their interests any general superiority of rights with respect to commercial or economic development *in any designated region of China.*"

CHAPTER XIV

LEASED AREAS

That China should desire to obtain an abandonment of the leases held by certain of the Powers of important portions of her territory was but a natural result of her general effort to free herself from the various limitations upon her sovereign freedom of action. Relief in this specific matter was brought before the Conference by Dr. Koo, of the Chinese Delegation, at the twelfth meeting of the Committee of the Whole, held December 3. Dr. Koo, as reported in the minutes of that meeting, made the following statement:

The existence of the leased territories in China was due in the original instance to the aggressions of Germany, whose forcible occupation of part of Shantung Province constrained the Chinese Government on March 6, 1898, to grant a lease for 99 years of the Bay of Kiaochow in the Shantung Province. This was closely followed, on March 27, 1898, by a demand on the part of Russia for the lease of the Liaotung Peninsula, in which are found the ports of Port Arthur and Dalny, along with the demand for the right of building a railway to be guarded by Russian soldiers traversing the Manchurian Provinces from Port Arthur and Dalny to join the Trans-Siberian Railway and Vladivostok. This was later the cause of the Russo-Japanese war which resulted in 1905 in the transfer of those territories to Japan with the consent of China. Following the lease of Kiaochow Bay to Germany and that of Port Arthur and Dalny to Russia, France obtained from China on April 22, 1898, the lease of Kwangchow-wan on the coast of Kwangtung Province for 99 years. Great Britain on June 9, 1898, secured the lease, also for 99 years, of an extension of Kowloon and the adjoining territory and waters close to Hongkong, and on July 1, 1898, the lease " for so long a period as Port Arthur should remain in the occupation of Russia " of the Port of Weihaiwei on the coast of Shantung. Both Great Britain and France based their claims for the leases on the ground of the necessity of preserving the balance of power in the Far East.

While the measures and extent of control by the lessee powers over the leased territories varied in different cases, the leases themselves were all limited to a fixed period of years. Expressly or impliedly they were not transferable to a third power without the consent of China. Though the exercise of administrative rights over the territories leased was relinquished by China to the lessee power during the period of the lease, the sovereignty of China over them had been reserved in all cases. The leases were all creatures of compact, different from cessions both in fact and in law. As stated in the beginning, these leaseholds were granted by China with the sole purpose of maintaining the balance of power in the Far East, not so much between China and the other powers, but between other powers themselves concerning China.

Twenty years had elapsed since then and conditions had entirely altered. With the elimination of German menace in particular, an important disturbing factor to the peace of the Far East had been removed. Russia had equally disappeared from the scene and it could be hoped with confidence that she would eventually return, not as the former aggressive power, but as a great democratic nation. The misrule of the Manchu dynasty which had aggravated the situation had also disappeared. The very fact that this conference was being held at Washington for the purpose of arriving at a mutual understanding on the part of the powers, provided an added reason for dispensing with the necessity of maintaining the balance of power in the Far East, which was the principal ground on which the original claims of the different powers were based. In the absence of that necessity the Chinese delegation believed that the time had come for the interested powers to relinquish their control over the territories leased to them.

The existence of such leased territories had greatly prejudiced China's territorial and administrative integrity, because they were all situated at the strategical points along the Chinese littoral. Furthermore these foreign leaseholds had hampered her work of national defense by constituting in China a virtual "imperium in imperio," i. e., an empire within the same empire. There was another reason which the Chinese delegation desired to point out. The shifting conflict of interests of the different lessee powers had involved China more than once in complications of their own. It would be sufficient to refer here to the Russo-Japanese war, which was caused by the Russian occupation of Port Arthur and Dalny. The Kiaochow leasehold brought upon the Far East the hostilities of the European war. Furthermore some of these territories were utilized with a view to economic domination over the vast adjoining regions, as points d'appui for developing spheres of interest to the detriment of the principle of equal opportunity for the commerce and industry of all nations in China. In the interest not only of China, but of all nations, and especially with a view to the peace of the Far East, the Chinese delegation asked for the annulment and an early termination of these leases. But pending their termination these areas should be demilitarized—that is, their fortifications dismantled—and it was hoped that the lessee nations would undertake not to make use of their several leased areas for military purposes, either for naval bases or for military operations of any kind whatsoever.

In concluding Mr. Koo observed that the Chinese Delegation was fully conscious of the obligations which China would assume after the termination of the leaseholds, and that the Chinese Government would be prepared to respect and safeguard the legitimately vested interests of the different powers within those territories.

Kwangchow-wan. M. Viviani made a formal declaration, in the following form:

The French delegation has heard the detailed statement of the Chinese claims and is ready to examine them in the most friendly spirit.

As Mr. Koo has just said, it was only after the other powers had obtained concessions of this sort that France requested the lease of Kwangchow-wan, in order that the equilibrium of the powers in the Far East should not be disturbed to her disadvantage.

We have developed the resources of the territory leased to us; we have brought the benefits of civilization to a country torn by piracy, we have established the reign of prosperity and peace to such a degree that the neighboring population seeks refuge on our territory in times of trouble. When China recovers Kwangchow-wan she will receive back a country of greater value than the territory she had leased.

These being the facts, I state that, since we have responded to the appeal of the American Government to perform a sincere and generous undertaking, we must pass from theory to action.

The French delegation, in so far as it is concerned, welcomes the claims of China with the greatest favor.

She must, however, add conditions to her acceptance: France can not be the only one of the powers to relinquish territory which has been leased to her; the settlement of the retrocession, on the other hand, should take place under suitable conditions and in accordance with the forms which govern such transfers, all private rights being respected.

Finally, it is thoroughly understood that China shall pledge herself not to alienate or to lease to any other power the territory thus restored to her.

In order to clearly define the position of the French Government, I have the honor to place in the hands of the chairman the statement which I am about to read:

"After having taken note of the request made by the Chinese delegation, December 1, 1921, the French delegation states that the Government of the Republic is ready to join in the collective restitution of territories leased to various powers in China, it being understood that this principle being once admitted and all private rights being safeguarded, the conditions and time limits of the restitution shall be determined by agreement between the Chinese Government and each of the Governments concerned."

Kiaochow and Kwantung District. Mr. Hanihara, on behalf of the Japanese delegation, submitted a statement in writing, as follows:

The leased territories held by Japan at present are Kiaochow and Kwantung Province, namely, Port Arthur and Dairen. It is characteristic of Japan's leased territories that she obtained them, not directly from China, but as successor to other powers at considerable sacrifice in men and treasure. She succeeded Russia in the leasehold of Kwantung Province with the express consent of China, and she succeeded Germany in the leasehold of Kiaochow under the Treaty of Versailles.

As to Kiaochow, the Japanese Government have already declared on several occasions that they would restore the leased territory to China. We are prepared to come to an agreement with China on this basis. In fact, there are now going on conversations between representatives of Japan and China regarding this question, initiated through the good offices of Mr. Hughes and Mr. Balfour, the result of which, it is hoped, will be a happy solution of the problem. Therefore, the question of the leased territory of Kiaochow is one which properly calls for separate treatment.

The only leased territory, therefore, which remains to be discussed at the conference so far as Japan is concerned is Kwantung Province, namely, Port Arthur and Dairen. As to that territory, the Japanese delegates desire to make it clear that Japan has no intention at present to relinquish the important rights she has lawfully acquired and at no small sacrifice. The territory in question forms a part of Manchuria—a region where, by reason of its close propinquity to Japan's territory more than anything else, she has vital interests in that which relates to her economic life and national safety. This fact was recognized and assurance was given by the American, British, and French Governments at the time of the formation of the international consortium, that these vital interests of Japan in the region in question shall be safeguarded.

In the leased territory of Kwantung Province there reside no less than 65,000 Japanese, and the commercial and industrial interests they have established there are of such importance and magnitude to Japan that they are regarded as an essential part of her economic life.

It is believed that this attitude of the Japanese delegation toward the leased territory of Kwantung is not against the principle of the resolution adopted on November 21.[1]

Kowloon.[2] Mr. Balfour pointed out that leased territories, though nominally all described under the same title, were held under very different and varying circumstances. The Japanese delegation had already indicated that Shantung and Manchuria, respectively, were held on entirely different bases and must be considered from different points of view. Great Britain had two different kinds of leases, and these, as he thought the Chinese delegation itself would admit, must be held to stand on a different footing one from the other.

Mr. Balfour referred first to the leased territory of Kowloon extension. Why, he asked, was it considered necessary that the leased territory of Kowloon should come under the same administration as Hongkong? The reason was that, without the leased territory, Hongkong was perfectly indefensible and would be at the mercy of any enemy possessing modern artillery. He hoped that he would carry the conference with him when he asserted that the safeguarding of the position of Hongkong was not merely a British interest but one in which the whole world was concerned. He was informed that Hongkong was

[1] For the Chinese rejoinder to this statement of the Japanese Delegation regarding Manchuria, see the next chapter entitled "Japan's Claim to 'Special Interests' in China."

[2] The following remarks of Mr. Balfour are as reported in the official minutes.

easily first among the ports of the world, exceeding in this respect Hamburg before the war, Antwerp, and New York. Mr. Balfour then read the following extract from " The United States Government Commercial Handbook of China."

The position of the British colony of Hongkong in the world's trade is unique and without parallel. It is a free port except for a duty on wine and spirits; it has relatively few industries; it is one of the greatest shipping centers in the world; it is the distributing point for all the enormous trade of South China and about 30 per cent of the entire foreign commerce of China. The conditions of Hongkong in its relations to commerce are in every way excellent, and the Government centers all its efforts on fostering trade, while the future is being anticipated by increased dock facilities, the dredging of the fairways, and other improvements. The merchants, both native and foreign, give special attention to the assembling and transshipping of merchandise to and from all the ports of the world, and with the world-wide steamship connection at Hongkong the necessity of retransshipment at other ports is reduced to a minimum. Hongkong is the financial center of the East.

Mr. Balfour said he could not add anything to this perfectly impartial testimony to the conditions of absolute equality of nations under which the affairs of Hongkong were administered and the motives on which they were conducted. The lease of the Kowloon extension had been obtained for no other reason except to give security to the port of Hongkong, and it would be a great misfortune if anything should occur which was calculated to shake the confidence of the nations, using this great open port, in its security. He hoped he need say no more to explain that Kowloon extension was in a different category and must be dealt with in a different spirit from those leased territories which had been acquired for totally different motives.

Dr. Koo at the thirteenth meeting of the Committee of the Whole, replying to the statement which Mr. Hanihara had made with reference to Leased Areas, declared as follows concerning Kowloon:

"As to the leased territory of Kowloon, leased to Great Britain, much is to be said for the importance of Hongkong to the trade of nations, and for the way in which its facilities are made accessible to the traders of the world, and while there may be a necessity to provide for the protection of the Hongkong Harbor in the interests of such trade, the retention of Kowloon may not necessarily be, in the view of the Chinese delegation, the sole solution of this problem."

In making the foregoing statement, however, the Chinese delegation have desired only to make its position clear and they wish to reserve further observations on the question of the leased territories till a later opportunity, if the committee is not prepared to continue discussion at this meeting.

Weihaiwei. Mr. Balfour then passed to the question of Weihaiwei. The acquisition by Great Britain of this lease had been part of the general movement for obtaining leased territories in 1898, in which Russia, Germany, and France, as well as Great Britain, had been concerned. The motive which had animated the Germans in acquiring Kiaochow had been largely to secure economic domination. The motive of the British Government, on the other hand, in acquiring the lease of Weihaiwei had been connected with resistance to the economic domination of China by any other powers; in fact, it had been based on a desire for the maintenance of the balance of power in the Far East with a view to the maintenance of the policy of the open door, and had been intended as a check to the predatory action of Germany and Russia. Mr. Balfour laid emphasis on the fact that the convention of July 1, 1898, confirming the lease, gave no economic rights or advantages to Great Britain. There had been no question of its being a privileged port of entry for British commerce, nor for the establishment of British commercial rights to the exclusion or diminution of the rights of any other power. In fact, on April 20, 1898, Great Britain had announced that "England will not construct any railroads or communication from Weihaiwei and the district leased therewith into the interior of the Province of Shantung." As regards the attitude of the British Government to the request of the Chinese delegation for an abrogation of those leases, Mr. Balfour stated that he had very little to add to, and he did not wish to qualify, the conditions contained in the statement just made by M. Viviani, which represented very much the spirit in which the British Government approached the question. The British Government would be perfectly ready to return Weihaiwei to China as a part of a general arrangement intended to confirm the sovereignty of China and to give effect to the principle of the "open door." This surrender, however, could only be undertaken as part of some general arrangement, and he spoke with his Government behind him when he said that on these conditions he was prepared to give up the rights which Great Britain had acquired at Weihaiwei.

Mr. Balfour, also with reference to Weihaiwei, stated specifically that it was the policy of the British Government to make use of the surrender of that area in aid of a settlement of the Shantung question,—that if an agreement could be reached between Japan and China upon that question, Great Britain would not hesitate to do its best to promote a general settlement by restoring Weihaiwei to the Central Government of China.

Summarizing the statements that had been made, the Chairman of the Committee, Secretary Hughes, said it appeared that there were five special situations, two relating to Shantung, one to Kwantung, one to Kowloon, and one to Kwangchow-wan: the proposal by France and the British offer with reference to Weihaiwei were important forward steps; but that he did not see what the Committee could do further in the matter since the question was not one of general policy.

Dr. Koo thanked the British and French Delegations for their offers, but expressed great disappointment at the statement by the Japanese Delegate that Japan had no intention of surrendering her Kwantung lease.

Chinese Statement. At the next meeting (the thirteenth) of the Committee, held December 7, Dr. Koo made a statement by way of rejoinder to the statement made by Mr. Hanihara at the twelfth meeting, in which he noted the fact, mentioned by Mr. Hanihara, that Japan had obtained her leased territories in China not directly from China but from other Powers at considerable sacrifice of men and treasure. This, said Dr. Koo, confirmed the view of the Chinese Delegation that the maintenance of foreign leased areas in China jeopardized the peace in the Far East.

Dr. Koo recalled the fact that Russia's possession of Port Arthur and Dalny and Germany's possession of Kiaochow had brought on two wars on Chinese territory and resulted in the installation of Japan herself in those leased areas. "As to the leased territory of Kwantung Province, namely Port Arthur and Dalny," he said, "its original term will expire in 1925, and while an extension to 99 years was obtained by Japan in 1915 it was obtained in such circumstances that the dispute about its validity remains one of the most grave outstanding questions between China and Japan."

Dr. Koo then went on to discuss the implications of Mr. Hanihara's remarks as to the relationship between the Port Arthur and Dalny lease and the Japanese interests in Manchuria. This portion of Dr. Koo's remarks can best be presented in the next chapter, which deals with Japan's claims to "Special Interests" in China.

Weihaiwei. At the fifth plenary session of the Conference, held February 1, 1922, at which the Shantung Agreement between China and Japan was reported, Mr. Balfour, in fulfillment of the undertaking which he had previously made, announced that the British Government was ready to surrender the lease of Weihaiwei under suitable conditions similar to those that had been agreed upon with reference to the leased area of Kiaochow. "When this is accomplished," he said, "this great Province of China (Shantung) will again be what every Chinese citizen must desire that it should be, in the fullest sense an integral part of that great Empire."

Kwangchow-wan. The next day, at the thirtieth meeting of the Committee of the Whole, Mr. Sze, in behalf of the Chinese Delegation, said that he had understood that the French Delegation would make a further statement with regard to its lease of Kwangchow-wan. M. Sarraut, replying to this suggestion, repeated merely what M. Viviani had said at the meeting of December 4, namely, that France was ready to surrender her lease *pari passu* with the surrender of their respective leases by all the other Powers, but that, even if this surrender could not be secured, France would be willing to arrange directly with the Chinese Government the conditions under which, and the time when, the restitution of Kwangchow-wan should become effective.

CHAPTER XV

JAPAN'S CLAIM TO "SPECIAL INTERESTS" IN CHINA

Lansing-Ishii Agreement. That Japan has claimed " Special Interests " in China, that is to say, interests somewhat different to and somewhat greater than those claimed by the other Powers, has been known for a considerable number of years, a claim which found declaration, if not definition, in a number of treaties or understandings which she has had with other Powers, notably in the Anglo-Japanese Alliance agreements of 1902, 1905 and 1911, in the Franco-Japanese Arrangement of 1907, and in the so-called Lansing-Ishii Agreement of November 2, 1917. How significant to the other Powers and serious to China were her desires or claims under this title or designation was made known to the world when Secretary Lansing, in August, 1918, gave to the Committee on Foreign Relations of the United States Senate a statement of the conversations between himself and Viscount Ishii leading up to the agreement which has since borne their joint names.

The divergence between the Japanese and American Governments as to the significance to be attached to the recognition by the United States, and the assertion by Japan, that " territorial propinquity creates special relations between countries," and, consequently that " Japan has special interests in China, particularly in the part to which her possessions are contiguous," was disclosed in letters of the Russian Ambassador to his Government which reported statements made to him by the Japanese Minister for Foreign Affairs.[1]

Consortium. Still more significant becomes Japan's claim to special rights or interests in China, and especially in South Manchuria and Eastern Inner Mongolia, when one reads the correspondence leading up to the establishment, in 1920, of the International Banking Consortium.

In that correspondence the Japanese Government made strenuous efforts to have Japan's railway and other activities in Manchuria and Mongolia, past and prospective, excluded from the operations of the Consortium.

Japan in her Memorandum of March 2, 1920, supplied to the American and British Governments, asked those Governments to accept a Formula according to which " in matters .... relating to loans affecting South Manchuria and Eastern Inner Mongolia, which in their opinion are calculated to create a serious impediment to the security of the economic life and national defense of Japan, the Japanese Government reserve the right to take the necessary steps to guarantee such security."

Both of the Governments addressed found this Formula unsatisfactory. The British Government in its Memorandum of March 19, 1920, declared that

---

[1] For general discussion of Japan's claim to "Special Interests" in China, see Chapter XVI of Willoughby's *Foreign Rights and Interests in China*.

it was " so ambiguous and general in character that it might be held to indicate on the part of the Japanese Government a continued desire to exclude the cooperation of the other three banking groups from participating in the development, for China's benefit, of important parts of the Chinese Republic and therefore creates the impression that the Japanese reservation cannot be reconciled with the principle of the independence and the realization of the integrity of China." The American Government, in its Memorandum of March 16, 1920, expressed its " grave disappointment " that the Japanese Memorandum should be in terms so "exceedingly ambiguous and in character so irrevocable " as to indicate a continued desire upon the part of the Japanese Government " to exclude American, British and French banking interests from participation in the developments, for the benefit of China, of important parts of that Republic—a construction which could not be reconciled with the principle of the independence and territorial integrity of China." The American Memorandum continued:

The Government of the United States is not unsympathetic with the professed objects of the principle embodied in the Japanese formula: it considers, on the other hand, first, that the right of national self-preservation is one of universal acceptance in the relations between states, and therefore would not require specific formulation as to its application in any particular instance; and, second, that the recognition of that principle is implicit in the terms of the notes exchanged between Secretary Lansing and Viscount Ishii on November 2, 1917. This Government therefore considers that by reason of the particular relationships of understanding thus existing between the United States and Japan, and those which, it is understood, similarly exist between Japan and the other Powers proposed to be associated with it in the Consortium, there would appear to be no occasion to apprehend on the part of the Consortium any activities directed against the economic life or national defense of Japan. It is therefore felt that Japan could with entire assurance rely upon the good faith of the United States and of the other two Powers associated in the Consortium to refuse their countenance to any operation inimical to the vital interests of Japan; and that Japan's insistence that the other three Powers join with it in the proposed formula as a condition precedent would only create misapprehension. It is felt, moreover, that such a formula would not only be unnecessary, but would lend itself to misconstruction for the reason that it apparently differentiates between the status of South Manchuria and Eastern Inner Mongolia and that of other Chinese territory. The mere fact of differentiation would, it is apprehended, give rise to questions which would tend still further to unsettle the already complex situation in China. This Government is therefore hopeful that the Japanese Government may, in view of its several existing relationships of understanding with the United States and the other two Powers, be persuaded to rely upon their good faith in this matter and forego its proposal to require explicit guarantees, the mere statement of which opens the way for possible misconstruction and misapprehension in the future.

Replying to these Memoranda from the American and British Governments, the Japanese Government abandoned its request for the acceptance of its formula, in view of the assurance which it had received (to quote the words of the reply) " that the right of national self-preservation, which forms the basis of the guarantee required by Japan in order to assure the security of her national defense and the economic existence of her people, not only are of universal acceptance but one of which the recognition is implied in the terms of the notes exchanged between

Secretary Lansing and Viscount Ishii, so that the new Consortium would in no case embark upon any activities against the national defense and the economic existence of Japan and so that the Powers associated in the Consortium would refuse their countenance to any enterprise inimical to the vital interests of Japan."[2]

From the foregoing one sees how far the American and British Governments were from giving approval to the statement made by Mr. Hanihara in the Committee of the Whole with reference to Japan's rights or interests in Manchuria. Secretary Hughes, in behalf of the American Delegation, contented himself with the statement that he assumed that, in the references which had been made to the Consortium, the representatives of Japan and China had no intention of referring to anything other than the actual texts of the correspondence, and, as that had been made public, he did not consider it necessary to add anything thereto.[3]

Manchuria. This Consortium correspondence and other declarations of the Japanese Government have tended to make plain that Japan, by reason of the considerable railway and other investments which her nationals have made in Manchuria and Mongolia, reinforced by the urgent need which her people and industries have for the food-stuffs and mineral resources which are available in China, has a keen

[2] One sees in this language a possible source of some of the words of the fourth Root Resolution adopted by the Conference.
[3] Thirteenth meeting of the Committee, Senate Document, No. 126, p. 552. 552.

desire to obtain, in some way, an assurance that these food-stuffs and natural resources of China shall be made available to her people. The same desire serves to explain her recent policies in Eastern Siberia. It is equally plain that, had she been able to do so, she would have liked to obtain from the other Powers a recognition that these economic needs of her people, taken together with the concessions already obtained in China, and especially Manchuria, were sufficient to create a right upon her part that should be internationally recognized. At the same time it is important to note that, at the second meeting of the Committee of the Whole, held November 19, Baron Kato, speaking for the Japanese Delegation, said:

> We adhere without condition or reservation to the principle of the open door or equal opportunity in China. We look to China in particular for the supply of raw materials essential to our industrial life, and for foodstuffs as well. In the purchase of such materials from China, as well as in all our trade relations with that country, we do not claim any special rights or privileges, and we welcome fair and honest competition with all nations.

As has been already said, Dr. Koo, at the thirteenth meeting of the Committee, made a reply to Mr. Hanihara's statement regarding leased areas. As to Mr. Hanihara's assertions regarding Japan's interests in Manchuria, Dr. Koo said:

> Both Port Arthur and Dalny are situated in Manchuria, which is an important part of Chinese territory. Not only does the national safety of China rely upon the safeguarding of Manchuria as an integral portion of the Chinese Republic, because these three eastern Provinces, as the Chinese people call Manchuria, have been the historic road of invasion into China throughout the past centuries, but also the security of the economic life of the Chinese people

JAPAN'S SPECIAL INTERESTS

depends in a very vital measure upon the conservation and development with the surplus capital of the world of the natural and agricultural resources in Manchuria—a region where to-day an abundance of raw material and food supplies are already accessible to all nations, on fair terms and through the normal operation of the economic law of supply and demand. However, Manchuria is an important outlet for the surplus population from the congested provinces in other parts of China.

In view of the foregoing facts, it is clear that China has such truly vital interests in Manchuria that the interests of any foreign power therein, however important they may be in themselves, can not compare with them. The fact of close propinquity of Manchuria to Korea, if it justifies any claim to consideration, can be equitably appealed to only on the condition of reciprocity.

As to the statement that assurance was given by the American, British, and French Governments at the time of the formation of the international consortium, that the vital interests of Japan in Manchuria shall be safeguarded, the Chinese delegation do not feel in a position, since China was not consulted at the time, to express an opinion as to the question of its accuracy. Should such assurance have been given, they could not, however, conceal their feeling that it can not be reconciled with the principle which was adopted by the conference on November 21 of respect for the sovereignty, the independence and the territorial and administrative integrity of China.

Also, upon another occasion, Dr. Koo took pains to refer to Japan's claims to interests in China based upon its propinquity to that country. In his statement made at the fourteenth meeting of the Committee of the Whole, with reference to the Inter-Power Agreements relating to China, he called attention to the fact that certain of these agreements had dealt with the safeguarding of special interests in the Far East or, specifically, in China. As to this he said:

The maintenance of the independence and territorial integrity of China touched the supreme rights of China. As to the recognition of propinquity as creating special interests in China, it was equally obvious that such recognition could not be valid, because special interests on Chinese territory could not be created without the consent of China, and China had always contested the soundness of the doctrine of propinquity.

At the twentieth meeting of the Committee of the Whole, when the matter of the Open Door was under discussion, the Japanese Delegation again returned to this subject, Baron Shidehara submitting the following formal statement:

The Japanese Delegation understands that one of the primary objects which the present Conference on Far Eastern Questions has in view is to promote the general welfare of the Chinese people and, at the same time, of all nations interested in China. For the realization of that desirable end, nothing is of greater importance than the development and utilization of the unlimited natural resources of China.

It is agreed on all sides that China is a country with immense potentialities. She is richly endowed by nature with arable soil, with mines and with raw materials of various kinds. But those natural resources are of little practical value, so long as they remain undeveloped and unutilized. In order to make full use of them, it seems essential that China shall open her own door to foreign capital and to foreign trade and enterprise.

Touching on this subject, Dr. Sze, on behalf of the Chinese Delegation, made an important statement at the Full Committee on November 16, declaring that " China wishes to make her vast natural resources available to all people who need them." That statement evidently represents the wisdom and foresight of China, and the Japanese Delegation is confident that the principle which it enunciates will be carried out to its full extent.

It is to be hoped that, in the application of that principle, China may be disposed to extend to foreigners, as far as possible, the opportunity of cooperation in the development and utilization of China's natural resources.

Any spontaneous declaration by China of her policy in that direction will be received with much gratification by Japan and also, no doubt, by all other nations interested in China. Resolutions which have hitherto been adopted by this Committee have been uniformly guided by the spirit of self-denial and self-sacrifice on the part of foreign Powers in favor of China. The Japanese Delegation trusts that China, on her part, will not be unwilling to formulate a policy which will prove of considerable benefit, no less to China herself, than to all nations.

The Chinese Delegation did not make a reply to this statement until the thirtieth meeting of the Committee, held February 2, when Mr. Sze made the following statement:

At the meeting of this Committee on January 18th, Baron Shidehara on behalf of the Japanese Delegation, expressed a hope that China might be disposed to extend to foreigners, as far as possible, the opportunity of cooperation in the development and utilization of China's natural resources, and added that any spontaneous declaration of her policy in that direction would be received with much gratification.

The Chinese Government, conscious of the mutual advantage which foreign trade brings, has hitherto pursued an established policy to promote its development. Of this trade, products of nature of course form an important part. In view of this fact, as well as of the requirements of her large and increasing population, and the growing needs of her industries, China, on her part, has been steadily encouraging the development of her natural resources, not only by permitting, under her laws, the participation of foreign capital, but also by other practical means at her disposal. Thus in affording facilities and fixing rates for the transportation on all her railways of such products of nature as well as of other articles of merchandise, she has always followed and observed the principle of strict equality of treatment between all foreign shippers. Thanks to this liberal policy, raw material and food supplies in China—as my colleague

Dr. Koo stated before this Committee on a previous occasion with reference to Manchuria, and it is equally true of other parts of China—are today accessible to all nations, on fair terms and through the normal operation of the economic law of supply and demand.

The Chinese Government does not at present contemplate any departure from this mutually beneficial course of action. Consistent with the vital interests of the Chinese nation and the security of its economic life, China will continue, on her own accord, to invite cooperation of foreign capital and skill in the development of her natural resources.

The Chinese Delegation, animated by the same spirit of self-denial and self-sacrifice which Baron Shidehara was good enough to assure the Chinese Deelgation had uniformly guided the foreign Powers here represented in the Resolutions hitherto adopted by the Committee in favor of China, has no hesitation to make the foregoing statement. It is all the more glad to make it, because it feels confident that the Japanese Delegation, in expressing the hope for a voluntary declaration of policy on China's part in regard to the development and utilization of her natural resources, was not seeking any special consideration for Japan on this subject or for the foreign Powers as a whole, but merely wished to be assured that China was disposed to extend the opportunity of cooperation to foreigners on the same terms as are accorded by nations of the world equally favored by nature in the possession of rich natural resources.

Mining Code. In connection with Baron Shidehara's statement, and the reply of the Chinese Delegation thereto, Sir Auckland Geddes referred to an undertaking entered into by China in 1902 and again in 1903, in Anglo-Chinese and Sino-American treaties of those years with reference to a mining code.

Article IX of the Anglo-Chinese treaty provided that

The Chinese Government, recognizing that it is advantageous for the country to develop its mineral resources, and that it is desirable to attract foreign as well as Chinese capital to embark in mining enterprises, agree within one year from the signing of this treaty to initiate and conclude the revision of the existing mining regulations. China will, with all expedition and earnestness, go into the whole question of mining rules and, selecting from the rules of Great Britain, India, and other countries, regulations which seem applicable to the condition of China, she will recast her present mining rules in such a way as, while promoting the interests of Chinese subjects and not injuring in any way the sovereign rights of China, shall offer no impediment to the attraction of foreign capital or place foreign capitalists at a greater disadvantage than they would be under generally accepted foreign regulations.

Any mining concession granted after the publication of these new rules shall be subject to their provisions.

This undertaking, said Sir Auckland, corresponded verbally very closely to one portion of the statement that the Chinese Delegation had made, and he was interested to know if China hoped soon to promulgate such a code as has been promised.

To this inquiry Mr. Sze responded that the Chinese Delegation did not have at hand the information which would enable it to give a satisfactory answer. He would, however, refer to the fact that there was in operation in China a law which permitted the investment in Chinese mines of foreign capital to an amount as large as fifty per cent, and that, under that law, several British enterprises, in conjunction with Chinese capital, had profitably invested large sums. As one instance of this he could cite the Chinese Engineering and Mining Company which had, in 1919, made a profit so large that, as he had been told, it had paid to the British Treasury income and super-taxes amounting to over £1,000,000.

Sir Auckland said that he had been under the impression that that company had operated under a special charter, and, further, that he was not sure that the satisfactory profits had been due to the mining code rather than to the richness of the mine that had been operated.

CHAPTER XVI

The Open Door

In its statement of the Ten Points or Principles which the Chinese Delegation had made to the Conference on November 16, the following declaration was made:

> China, being in full accord with the principle of the so-called open-door or equal opportunity for the commerce and industry of all nations having treaty relations with China, is prepared to accept and apply it in all parts of the Chinese Republic without exception.

Upon a number of occasions in the past the Chinese Government in its communications with foreign Powers had made approving reference to the Open Door doctrine as applied to herself, but this declaration to the Conference, which has been quoted, was the first formal statement in behalf of the Chinese Government that it was prepared itself to accept and abide by this doctrine in its dealings with the treaty Powers or their nationals.[1]

As for the Powers themselves, they gave a renewed adherence to the doctrine in the third of the "Root Resolutions," adopted November 21, which declares their firm intention

---

[1] For instances in which China had referred with approval to the Open Door doctrine, see her reply of November 9, 1917, to the American Government's notification of the Lansing-Ishii Agreement; her communication of July 21, 1910, to the Treaty Powers with reference to the Russo-Japanese Convention of July 4, 1910; and her statement to the Powers giving reasons why she had signed the Treaties and Agreements of May 25, 1915.

To safeguard for the world, so far as within their [our] power, the principle of equal opportunity for the commerce and industry of all nations throughout the territory of China.

The difficult matter still remained, however, of giving to the Open Door doctrine a more precise and mutually agreed upon definition than it had previously received, and, possibly, of indicating certain specific applications to be made of it as thus defined.

Open Door Defined. At the eighteenth meeting of the Committee of the Whole, held January 16, the Chairman, Secretary Hughes, after quoting the third of the Root Resolutions, said that " it was manifest that the granting of special concessions of a monopolistic or preferential character, or which secured a general superiority of rights for one power to the exclusion of equal opportunity for other powers, was in opposition to the maintenance and application of this principle of equal opportunity." In order, then, he continued, that the Committee might discuss the principle more concretely, he would submit for adoption the following draft resolution:

With a view to applying more effectually the principle of the open door or equality of opportunity for the trade and industry of all nations, the powers represented in this conference agree not to seek or support their nationals in asserting any arrangement which might purport to establish in favor of their interests any general superiority of rights with respect to commercial or economic development in any designated region of the territories of China, or which might seek to create any such monopoly or preference as would exclude other nationals from undertaking any legitimate trade or industry or from participating with the Chinese Government in any category of public enterprise, it being understood that this agreement is not to be so construed as to prohibit the acquisition of such properties or rights as may be necessary to the conduct of a particular commercial or industrial undertaking.²

Sir Auckland Geddes, commenting upon this proposal, raised the points: (1) whether it would not be well to make provision for some simple machinery, in the nature of a court of reference, to which differences of opinion with regard to matters embraced within the resolution might be referred; and (2) whether specific provision should not be made for the recognition and protection of such things as patent rights, trade-marks, copyrights, mining permits and the like.

Secretary Hughes, in further explanation of his resolution, said that it was not the intention " to

² In connection with definition of the Open Door it is important to consider the American declaration contained in the note of July 1, 1921, of Secretary Hughes to Mr. Sze, the Chinese Minister at Washington—a note arising out of protests made by several Powers against a wireless concession granted by the Chinese Government to an American corporation. Secretary Hughes then said:

"Your reference to the principle of the Open-Door affords me the opportunity to assure you of this Government's continuance in its wholehearted support of that principle, which it has traditionally regarded as fundamental both to the interests of China itself and to the common interests of all powers in China, and indispensable to the free and peaceful development of their commerce on the Pacific Ocean. The Government of the United States never has associated itself with any arrangement which sought to establish any special rights in China which would abridge the rights of the subjects or citizens of other friendly states; and I am happy to assure you that it is the purpose of this Government neither to participate in nor to acquiesce in any arrangement which might purport to establish in favor of foreign interests a superiority of rights with respect to commercial and economic development in designated regions of the territories of China, or which might seek to create any such monopoly or preference as would exclude other nationals from undertaking any legitimate trade or industry or from participating with the Chinese Government in any category of public enterprise."

interfere with the appropriate relations between China and her own nationals," and that, therefore the phrase "other than China" might well be inserted in the draft. He agreed that, before the labors of the Conference were completed, it might be well to provide some sort of machinery for dealing with questions which might arise with reference to the application of the principles to which the Powers might give their adherence. Regarding the last clause of this resolution he said that there was a great difference between a particular enterprise or undertaking of commerce and industry, and the assertion of, or the endeavor to obtain, a position from which it could be asserted that one Power or its nationals had a general superiority of right in any region of China.

"The distinction between a general superiority of rights," he said, "and the right to conduct a particular enterprise and to have the rights and properties which were essential to the conduct of a particular enterprise was, he thought, quite apparent." He continued:

With regard to the point that patents, trade-marks, copyrights, and mining permits represented a phase of monopolistic endeavor, quo ad hoc, was of course well taken; but he assumed that it was certainly within the intention and, he would suppose, within the form of expression, that those particular rights would be embraced in the particular commercial or industrial undertaking with which it was not the purpose of this agreement to interfere. For example, if it were proposed that there should be an opportunity to obtain patent rights or copyrights such as inventors or authors enjoyed in this country or other countries, the fact that any inventor or author had that opportunity and when he made use of it according to the law obtained to that extent a monopoly was not in any true sense an exclusion of anybody else who had the same opportunity with respect to the same sort of enterprise under the same rules which were generally applicable. But if it were said that in any particular Province or region of China no one should obtain patents except the nationals of a particular power or that no one should enjoy the opportunity to have this or that sort of enterprise save one power or its nationals, then a situation would be created involving an assertion of an economic preference or superiority of privilege which would be utterly inconsistent with the open-door principle. He granted the difficulty of stating that precisely. Any improvement that could be suggested would be welcome. The main point was that, when it came to dealing with this question of concessions and monopolies and preferential economic privileges, a clear understanding should, if possible, be arrived at by this conference which would promote the friendly relations which existed between the powers represented and the spirit of friendly cooperation which had so happily been in evidence.

Mr. Balfour, after commenting favorably upon the fact that the language of the resolution involved the absolute repudiation of spheres of influence, went on to speak of the last clause of the resolution. As concerned most industrial enterprises, he said, there would be no difficulty in applying the rule, but that there were kinds of undertakings—railways and telephone or telegraph systems for example—which inevitably involved a monopolistic flavor. With these, as he understood them, the last words of the resolution were intended to deal.

In order to meet the foregoing comments, especially those of Sir Auckland Geddes, Secretary Hughes, at the next (nineteenth) meeting of the Committee introduced the following revised draft resolution:

I. With a view to applying more effectually the principle of the open door, or equality of opportunity, in China for the trade and industry of all nations, the powers other than China represented at this conference agree:

(a) Not to seek or to support their nationals in seeking any arrangement which might purport to establish in favor of their interests any general superiority of rights with respect to commercial or economic development in any designated region of China.

(b) Not to seek or to support their nationals in seeking any such monopoly or preference as would deprive other nationals of the right of undertaking any legitimate trade or industry in China or of participating with the Chinese Government or with any Provincial government in any category of public enterprise, or which by reason of its scope, duration or geographical extent is calculated to frustrate the practical application of the principle of equal opportunity.

It is understood that this agreement is not to be so construed as to prohibit the acquisition of such properties or rights as may be necessary to the conduct of a particular commercial, industrial, or financial undertaking, or to the encouragement of invention and research.

II. The Chinese Government takes note of the above agreement, and declares its intention of being guided by the same principles in dealing with applications for economic rights and privileges from Governments and nationals of all foreign countries whether parties to that agreement or not.

III. The powers including China represented at this conference agree in principle to the establishment in China of a board of reference, to which any question arising on the above agreement and declaration may be referred for investigation and report.

(A detailed scheme for the constitution of the board shall be framed by the special conference referred to in Article I of the convention of Chinese customs duties.)

IV. The powers including China represented at this conference agree that any provisions of an existing concession which appear inconsistent with those of another concession or with the principles of the above agreement or declaration may be submitted by the parties concerned to the board of reference when established for the purpose of endeavoring to arrive at a satisfactory adjustment on equitable terms.

As to the distinction between clauses (a) and (b) of Section I of the Resolution, Secretary Hughes gave an explanation, the following portions of which need to be quoted. He said:

The two clauses (a) and (b), were of course consistent. It was intended that they should be consistent and carry an application of the general principle. There was, however, a distinction between them. Clause (a) was not limited to the mere seeking of a concession which might be in the nature of a monopoly or preference with respect to a particular sphere of enterprise; it had a wider range. It took into account the facts with which all were familiar in connection with the recent history of China. It provided that the powers other than China represented at the conference should not seek, nor support their nationals in seeking, any arrangement which might purport to establish in favor of their interests any general superiority of rights with respect to commercial or economic development in any designated region of China. That was not limited to the question of a particular concession or enterprise, but it had the purpose of precluding the efforts by which, in a designated region, one power, or the nationals of that power, might have a superior position, broadly speaking, with respect to enterprises. It had direct relation to what had been known in the past as spheres of interest, which might be stated to be spheres of exclusion of other interests. In order words, it negatived the endeavor to secure not a particular concession or grant, or the facility for conducting a particular enterprise, whatever the scope of that enterprise might be, but a status with respect to a designated region which would give general superiority or opportunity, and thus conflict with the open-door principle.

Now, the second clause, paragraph (b), dealt with cases which did not rise to the dignity of an endeavor to obtain a general superiority of rights with respect to development in a designated region, but with the more limited, yet still objectionable, endeavor to obtain such a monopoly or preference as would deprive nationals of other powers of the right to undertake legitimate trade or industry with China or of participating with the Chinese Government or with any provincial government in any category of public enterprise which, by reason of its scope, duration, or geographical extent, was calculated to frustrate the practical application of the principle of equal opportunity.

That was to be read in connection with the concluding clause of the first section of the resolution, that it was not to be so construed as to prohibit the acquisition of such properties or rights as might be necessary to the conduct of a particular commercial, industrial, or financial undertaking or to the encouragement of invention and research. That was to say, paragraph (b) sought to preclude efforts by which monopolies or preferences would exclude other nationals from legitimate opportunity; it did not intend to prevent particular enterprises—commercial, industrial, or financial—which did not have that unfair exclusiveness which would make them inconsistent with the open-door principle.

It would therefore be seen, he thought, that there was a point in each of these paragraphs, the one relating to a general superiority of rights, with respect to development in designated regions, the other relating to particular concessions which had a monopolistic or preferential character which, by reason of that character, infringed the open-door principle. Neither of these provisions would be entirely satisfactory without the other as its complement. . . . .

In connection with paragraphs (a) and (b) it was deemed advisable to suggest as well as could be done by a general statement, the class of undertakings which it was not desired to exclude, which it was desired should be freely prosecuted, and at the same time to indicate the two classes of effort which it was designed so far as possible absolutely to prevent.

The first class included those which endeavored to establish over a designated region a superior privilege to the exclusion of powers or their nationals. The second was a monopoly or preference not inherent in a particular legitimate undertaking, but embodying the exclusion of powers or their nationals from fields of industry and economic development. There was in paragraph (b) the suggestion that the consideration of the scope, duration or geographical extent itself of an enterprise might be very important in determining its essential character in the light of the open-door principle.

And again, somewhat later, upon this same point, Secretary Hughes said that, as he understood it, the concluding paragraph of Article I of the resolution was intended to protect the particular commercial, industrial, or financial undertakings which might be prosecuted consistently with the maintenance of the general principle which was stated in paragraphs (a) and (b). Paragraph (b) referred to such undertakings which, by reason of their scope, duration, or geographical extent, were calculated to frustrate the practical application of the principles of equal opportunity.

As he had explained the day before, they were dealing with the open door, an avenue to opportunity, an avenue to legitimate enterprise—and not with obstacles to legitimate enterprise; and all that was embraced in the various undertakings which, to the extent of the particular right essential to their prosecution, of course monopolized a special line of endeavor in a concrete or particular case, were amply protected by the last clause of the first article. The purpose was, however, to safeguard the principle, so that under the guise of particular undertakings there should not be any assertion of a general superiority of right or a monopoly or preference which would be in conflict with the principles to which the powers represented on the committee adhered.

Regarding the scope of the Open Door as defined in the Resolution, Sir Auckland Geddes, in the twentieth meeting of the Committee, said that he thought it desirable to have it specifically stated that the activities of such a body as the International Consortium would not be excluded, and, therefore, he asked to have recorded in the minutes the following statement:

Of course it is clearly understood that there is nothing in this Resolution which affects, one way or the other, the existing International Consortium or any other form of voluntary cooperation among private financial or industrial groups of different countries which may join together in a manner not involving monopoly or infringement of the principles recognized by the Conference in order to furnish China with some essential service most efficiently and economically to be provided by united effort.

Secretary Hughes said that this statement was in full accord with the views which the American Delegation entertained: " The Resolution was not in any way intended to interfere with the operation of the Consortium, which in its provisions for cooperative effort would not in any way infringe the principles adopted by the Conference."

Reverting to the provisions of Section IV of the Resolution, Baron Shidehara, at the twentieth meeting of the Committee, raised the point that the Open Door was not a new doctrine; that it had been previously adopted and confirmed in various treaties and arrangements, but, since its original statement by Secretary of State Hay in 1899, it had undergone considerable changes in its application. He continued:

> It was then limited in its scope, both as concerning its subject matter and the area of Chinese territory to which it applied; it simply provided, in substance, that none of the powers having spheres of influence or leased territories in China should interfere with treaty ports or with vested rights or exercise any discrimination in the collection of customs duties or railroad or harbor charges. The principles formulated in the draft resolution was (*sic*) of an entirely different scope from the policy of " the open door " as conceived in 1898-99; the draft resolution gave, in a certain sense, a new definition to that policy. It seemed natural, therefore, that this new definition should not have any retroactive force.

Baron Shidehara therefore suggested that Section IV of the Resolution should be changed so as to read as follows:

> IV. The powers, including China, represented at this conference agree that if any provisions of a concession which may hereafter be granted by China appear inconsistent with those of another conces-

sion or with the principles of the above agreement or declaration they may be submitted by the parties concerned to the board of reference when established for the purpose of endeavoring to arrive at a satisfactory adjustment on equitable terms.

This led Secretary Hughes to present to the Committee a number of international documents including the Hay correspondence of 1899 and the Root-Takahira exchange of notes in 1908, in which the Open Door doctrine had found statement and application.

" In the light of these reiterated statements which could hardly be regarded as ambiguous," Secretary Hughes said that he " could not assume that the statement of principles recorded in the Resolution before the Committee was a new statement. He regarded it as a more definite and precise statement of the principle that had long been admitted, and to which the Powers concerned had given their unqualified adherence for twenty years."

Board of Reference. In the discussion which followed, it appeared that, especially as voiced by M. Sarraut, of the French Delegation, there was objection upon the part of some of the Powers to Section IV which provided that already existing concessions might be referred to the Board of Reference with a view to determining whether they were consistent with other concessions or with the principle of the Open Door as defined in the Resolution.

Baron de Cartier expressed the opinion that the reference in Section I to " provincial governments " might possibly be taken as a reflection upon the completeness of the authority of the central Government of China, and the term " local authorities " was substituted.

Regarding the Board of Reference provided for by Section III of the draft resolution presented by him to the Committee on January 17, Secretary Hughes said that " it did not constitute a board with authority to decide; it did not establish any instrumentality with anything in the nature of powers, the exercise of which would be in derogation of the sovereignty or the freedom of any State; but it did provide machinery for the examination of facts or, as the resolution said, for investigation and report."

At the twentieth meeting of the Committee, held January 18, Baron Shidehara raised the objection to the Board of Reference that it would be necessary for the Powers to appoint upon it their ablest jurists upon whose judgments the other interested Governments could rely, and that this would mean that these jurists would have to remain continuously and for an indefinite time in China. As a practical proposition, therefore, he queried whether the Governments would be willing to go to this expense, and whether they would be able to spare from their own countries such able and first-rate men.

Responding to this, Sir Auckland Geddes said that what the British Empire Delegation had in mind for the Board was that it would not be necessary for the representatives of all the Powers to attend all the meetings of the Board, but that each Power should nominate a panel of jurists from which two, three, four, or whatever number desired, could be drawn as required, to constitute the Board for the consideration of any special case that might be brought before it.

Secretary Hughes pointed out that the Resolution provided that the detailed scheme for the constitution of the Board was to be framed by the Special Conference referred to in Section I of the Resolution, and that, no doubt, that Conference would give due consideration to the points raised by Sir Auckland and Baron Shidehara.

Sir Robert Borden said that he was not of opinion that the Board should be composed of jurists. Rather, he thought, it should be composed of persons having a knowledge of economic conditions, a knowledge of the conditions of China and the trade of China. Sir Robert Borden observed that the principal difficulty in connection with the proposed Resolution had reference to Section IV. He, however, was of opinion that the Powers concerned could act with equal effect if that Section were omitted altogether. "Under that Article," he said, "there could be no effective action except with the consent of the parties concerned. If the fourth article were omitted it would still be open to the Powers, if they saw fit, to give the like consent and to utilize for the determination or investigation of any relevant question the Board of Reference to be established under Article III."

It appearing that several of the other Delegations supported this proposition of Sir Robert Borden, Secretary Hughes said that, in view of this fact, and of the fact that Article III gave full opportunity for dealing with all matters which might appropriately be the concern of the respective Governments, the American Delegation would withdraw Article IV from its draft Resolution.

Chinese Statement. Expressing the general attitude of the Chinese Delegation towards the proposed Resolution, Mr. Sze said:

He could do nothing better than to refer to the second of the proposals presented by the Chinese Delegation on November 16, namely: " China, being in full accord with the principle of the open door or equal opportunity for the commerce and industry of all nations having treaty relations with China, is prepared to accept and apply it in all parts of the Chinese Republic without exception." In this proposal the position of the Chinese delegation was put very simply and clearly, and he did not believe there was any use in his taking up the committee's time by offering any further explanation of it.

He desired, however, to say one word in regard to " the open door." The rendering of that expression into Chinese, some years ago, had given rise to some doubt in the minds of those who only read Chinese. He would, therefore, like to state that " the open door " did not mean the opening up of all parts of China to foreign trade, commerce, and industry; he only said this because of the misapprehension in the matter which had existed in China.

In regard to Article I b, his esteemed colleague, Baron de Cartier, had suggested on the previous day that the words " provincial government " be changed to " local authority." The procedure at present observed in China by the central Government with reference to concessions given by provincial authorities, he stated, would remain the same irrespective of which phrase was used, and this practice was too well known to need further elucidation.

In regard to Article III he wondered whether it would not be better to eliminate the words " in principle." If the committee reached an agreement it was probable that it would be on something definite. He only made this as a suggestion in the belief that it would make the paragraph more clear.

He had remarked a few minutes before on the great importance of the principle of "the open door," which had also been dealt with in the third of the "Root Resolutions" as follows:

"To use their influence for the purpose of effectually establishing and maintaining the principle of equal opportunity for the commerce and industry of all nations throughout the territory of China."

The committee would note that in this resolution—which had been accepted by all the powers represented at the table—that the words "establishing and maintaining" were used. His knowledge of English was limited, but he thought that the two words had different meanings—to establish, meaning to create, and to maintain, meaning to continue in operation; taken together, these two undertakings could mean nothing else than the bringing into existence of a régime under which the principles of the "open door" could be effectually applied. It therefore seemed that Section IV of the draft resolution could safely be adopted. Questions in regard to concessions had arisen in the past and would doubtless arise in the future. If questions should arise in the future it would be better, as the chairman had remarked, that the negotiations among the powers should not be confined to diplomatic notes; it would do no harm to either party in such a dispute to have it referred to a friendly body such as was provided for in Section IV for adjustment.

The Committee then unanimously approved the three articles of the Resolution in the following words, which later, with only the necessary verbal changes in order to put them in treaty form, were incorporated into the Nine Power Treaty Relating to the Principles and Policies to be Followed in Matters Concerning China, signed on February sixth:

I. With a view to applying more effectually the principle of the Open Door or equality of opportunity in China for the trade and industry of all nations, the Powers other than China represented at this Conference agree:

(a) Not to seek or to support their nationals in seeking any arrangement which might purport to establish in favor of their interests any general superiority of rights with respect to commercial or economic development in any designated region of China;

(b) Not to seek or to support their nationals in seeking any such monopoly or preference as would deprive other nationals of the right of undertaking any legitimate trade or industry in China, or of participating with the Chinese Government or with any local authority in any category of public enterprise, or which by reason of its scope, duration or geographical extent is calculated to frustrate the practical application of the principle of equal opportunity.

It is understood that this agreement is not to be so construed as to prohibit the acquisition of such properties or rights as may be necessary to the conduct of a particular commercial, industrial or financial undertaking or to the encouragement of invention and research.

II. The Chinese Government takes note of the above agreement and declares its intention of being guided by the same principles in dealing with applications for economic rights and privileges from governments and nationals of all foreign countries whether parties to that agreement or not.

III. The powers, including China, represented at this conference agree in principle to the establishment in China of a board of reference to which any question arising on the above agreement and declaration may be referred for investigation and report.

(A detailed scheme for the constitution of the board shall be framed by the special conference referred to in Article I of the Convention on Chinese Customs Duties.)

At the last (thirty-first) meeting of the Committee of the Whole at which the draft of the various treaties were given final consideration before being printed preparatory to their submission for formal approval by the Conference in plenary session, Dr. Koo said that he understood, and he was confirmed in his understanding by the Chairman, that the principle of equal opportunity as provided for in the contemplated treaty had reference to the Powers among themselves and not to China upon the one side and the Powers upon the other.

The relation of the Open Door to the Chinese Railways is discussed in the next chapter.[3]

---

[3] For purposes of convenience it will be appropriate to quote the following excerpts from the other agreements reached by the Conference in which the Open Door doctrine is expressly declared or applied:

Nine Power Treaty Relating to Principles and Policies to be Followed in Matters Concerning China. Article I, Section 3. " The Contracting Powers, other than China, agree .... To use their influence for the purpose of effectually establishing and maintaining the principle of equal opportunity for the commerce and industry of all nations throughout the territory of China."

Article V. " China agrees that, throughout the whole of the railways in China, she will not exercise or permit unfair discrimination of any kind. In particular there shall be no discrimination whatever, direct or indirect, in respect of charges or of facilities on the ground of the nationality of passengers or the countries from which or to which they are proceeding, or the origin or ownership of goods or the country from which or to which they are consigned, or the nationality or ownership of the ship or other means of conveying such passengers or goods before or after their transport on the Chinese Railways.

" The Contracting Powers, other than China, assume a corresponding obligation in respect of any of the aforesaid railways over which they or their nationals are in a position to exercise any control in virtue of any concession, special agreement or otherwise.

Nine Power Treaty Relating to Chinese Customs Tariff. Article V. " In all matters relating to customs duties there shall be effective equality of treatment and opportunity for all the Contracting Powers."

Resolution Regarding a Board of Reference. Preamble. [The Nine Powers] .... with reference to their general policy designed to stabilize conditions in the Far East, to safeguard the rights and interests of China, and to promote intercourse between China and the other Powers upon the basis of equality of opportunity " resolve, etc.

Declaration Concerning the Resolution on Radio Stations in China. The Powers other than China .... give notice that the result of any discussion arising under pargraph 4 must, if it is not to be subject to objection by them, conform with the principles of the open door or equality of opportunity approved by the Conference."

Statement of Chinese Delegation Regarding Chinese Railways. " .... It will be our policy to obtain such foreign financial and technical assistance as may be needed from the Powers in accordance with the principles of the Open Door or equal opportunity."

CHAPTER XVII

Chinese Railways and the Open Door

Unification of Railways. There had been some expectation that the Powers would discuss their future policies with regard generally to the railways of China, and especially as to the amount and character of the foreign control over their administration and operation that should be sanctioned. In fact, however, the only direct reference to this important subject was the resolution that Secretary Hughes presented to the Committee of the Whole at its twentieth meeting, and adopted at its twenty-first meeting. This resolution ran:

> The powers represented in this conference record their hope that to the utmost degree consistent with legitimate existing rights, the future development of railways in China shall be so conducted as to enable the Chinese Government to effect the unification of railways into a railway system under Chinese control, with such foreign financial and technical cooperation as may prove necessary in the interests of that system.[1]

Mr. Sze stated the position of the Chinese Delegation regarding this resolution as follows:

> The Chinese Delegation notes with sympathetic appreciation the expression of the hope of the Powers that the existing and future railways of China may be unified under the control and operation

---

[1] At Mr. Sze's suggestion the word "cooperation" in the last clause was changed to "assistance." This change Mr. Sze said, would facilitate the rendering of the resolution into the Chinese language.

of the Chinese Government with such financial and technical assistance as may be needed. It is our intention as speedily as possible to bring about this result. It is our purpose to develop existing and future railways in accordance with a general programme that will meet the economic, industrial and commercial requirements of China. It will be our policy to obtain such foreign financial and technical assistance as may be needed from the Powers in accordance with the principles of the Open Door or equal opportunity; and the friendly support of these Powers will be asked for the effort of the Chinese Government to bring all the railways of China, now existing or to be built, under its effective and unified control and operation.

The resolution was adopted by the Conference at its fifth plenary session, held February 1.

The Open Door and the Chinese Railways. The only other consideration given by the Conference to the Chinese Railways was with reference to the application to them of the principles of the Open Door which the Conference adopted.

At the twentieth meeting of the Committee of the Whole, when the matter of the Open Door was under discussion, Sir Auckland Geddes submitted a resolution which took the form of a statement which China was asked to make, and of an adhering or agreeing statement by the other Powers. This resolution, as later slightly amended by Sir Auckland, came up for discussion at the twenty-first meeting of the Committee in the following form:

The Chinese Government declares that throughout the whole of the railways in China it will not exercise or permit any unfair discrimination of any kind. In particular there shall be no discrimination whatever, direct or indirect, in respect of charges or of facilities on the ground of the nationality of passengers or the countries from which or to which they are proceeding, or the origin or ownership of goods or the country from which or to which they are consigned, or the nationality or ownership of the ship or other means of conveying such passengers or goods before or after their transport on the Chinese railways.

The other powers represented at this conference take note of the above declaration and make a corresponding declaration in respect of any of the aforesaid railways over which they or their nationals are in a position to exercise any control in virtue of any concession, special agreement, or otherwise.

Any question arising under this declaration may be referred by the powers concerned to the board of reference, when established for consideration and report.

In moving this resolution, Sir Auckland said that the British Delegation were animated by a desire to make the Open Door effective, but that there was no suggestion whatever that the past policy of the Government of China included any policy of discrimination on any ground. He wished to make that quite clear.

Mr. Sze, responding for the Chinese Delegation, said that "it had always been the policy of the Chinese Government—a policy that was well-known and the whole idea of which was to develop foreign trade—to welcome foreign shippers or passengers and to afford them equal treatment." He added that he had never heard of a complaint upon the part of any shipper of unfair or discriminating treatment. As to the third paragraph, he hoped that there would be no occasion to resort to it. In order to avoid any possible future misunderstandings he wished it to be noted that China, in giving her assent to the first paragraph, reserved to herself the right to classify the rates on any of her railways. Secretary Hughes said that he understood that there was nothing in the resolution that would limit this right, " subject simply to the qualification—with the explanation that it was not suggested on the basis that China had hitherto acted in a discriminating way—that there should be no unfair discrimination of any kind and particularly no discrimination on the basis stated in the resolution."

The resolution was then unanimously approved by the Committee with the single amendment (suggested by Mr. Sze) that the words " any of " should be inserted before the words " the powers " in the third paragraph.

At the fifth plenary session of the Conference at which this resolution was adopted, Mr. Sze repeated the statements which he had made in the Committee. He also added:

China took note but did not vote on the first article of the resolutions on Open Door adopted by the Committee on January 18, 1922, defining and declaring acceptance by the Powers of the principle of the Open Door, since the purpose of that article of the Resolution was to fix the policies of the Powers in their dealings with China or with each other with reference to China. That China was not intended to be included within the scope of the Resolution. It was not the purpose of that Resolution to interfere with the appropriate relations between the Chinese Government and its nationals, as was expressly indicated by the Chairman in replying to a question from Sir Auckland Geddes. However, as indicated by the second of the Ten Principles or Declarations which the Chinese Delegation had the honor to submit to this Conference on November 16, 1921, the Government of China is glad to give the assurance that, in the future, as it has consistently done in the past, it will make no discriminations in trade or industry between the Powers having treaty relations with China, or between their respective citizens or subjects because of their nationality.

CHAPTER XVIII

The Chinese Eastern Railway

Upon the Agenda of the Conference appeared the following item:

(c) Development of railways, including plans relating to Chinese Eastern Railway.

This topic was reached at the twentieth meeting of the Committee of the Whole, held January 18, and was introduced by the Chairman, Secretary Hughes, with the statement that he assumed that the Delegates had before them the documentary history of the Chinese Eastern Railway and that they were conversant with the problems relating to the proper and efficient management of that important line of communication. So far as the United States were concerned, he said, there was but one interest and that was that the railway should be maintained as an artery of commerce, with free opportunity to all and unfair discrimination against none. The United States Government had no interest whatever in the ownership of the road and had no desire to secure control. It wished, however, to do anything within its power to promote the proper conduct of the road as one of the greatest instrumentalities of commerce in the East.

Because of the complexity of the existing situation of the road, Secretary Hughes suggested that the matter be referred to a sub-committee of experts to be drawn from the technical advisers of the various Delegations. This suggestion was agreed to by the Committee.

Report of Technical Committee. The report of this Technical Sub-Committee is worthy of reproduction here since it sets forth the nature of the problems arising in connection with the Chinese Eastern Railway, as well as the recommendations that were made for their solution.

The Chinese Eastern Railway being an indispensable factor in the economic development of Siberia, as well as Northern Manchuria, and constituting an essential link in a trans-continental railway system of international importance, the nations represented at this Conference are interested in its preservation, its efficient operation, and its maintenance as a free avenue of commerce, open to the citizens of all countries without favor or discrimination.

The status of the Chinese Eastern Railway is determined by the contract concluded in 1896 between China and the Russo-Chinese (Russo-Asiatic) Bank and the contract concluded in 1898 between China and the Chinese Eastern Railway Company, and subsequent contracts between China and that company. The necessary funds for its construction were furnished by the Russian Government and it was built under the direction and supervision of that Government, acting through the Chinese Eastern Railway Company. The railway is in effect the property of the Russian Government. China has certain ultimate reversionary rights which are provided for in the original contract of 1896.

The absence of a recognized Russian Government since 1917 has made imperative for some time past certain measures providing for the preservation and continued operation of the railway. Early in 1919—as a consequence of assistance which had been given to Russia, at her request, in the operation of the entire trans-Siberian system, including the Chinese Eastern Railway—certain Powers, which are represented at this Conference, undertook to continue this assistance upon definite terms. An agreement was concluded in

January, 1919, between the United States and Japan, under the terms of which China, France, Great Britain and Italy subsequently cooperated. The fundamental purpose of the arrangement thus brought about was explicitly declared to be the temporary operation of the railways in question with a view to their ultimate return to those in interest without the impairing of any existing rights.

The trusteeship thus assumed continues in force. Changes which have intervened since 1919 render necessary readjustments in its mode of operation.

The three principal problems are: 1. Finance; 2. Operation; 3. Police.

1. As to the first, it is to be observed that funds will be obtainable from bankers and other outside sources only if suitable conditions are established for the economical operation of the railway and if the funds provided are to be expended under adequate supervision. A suitable manner of providing such supervision, in the opinion of the Committee, would be to establish at Harbin a Finance Committee, to consist of one representative of each of the Powers represented at the Conference (so far as they might care to participate.) This Committee would replace the so-called Interallied Committee now established at Vladivostok and the so-called Technical Board at Harbin. It should exercise general financial control and be entrusted with the exercise of the trusteeship which was assumed in 1919 and which cannot be discharged until the general recognition by the Powers of a Russian Government.

2. As to operation, in order to disturb as little as possible the normal situation, this should, in the opinion of the Committee, be left in the hands of the Chinese Eastern Railway Company, the Finance Committee not to interfere with the technical operation of the railway, except so far as may be necessary to meet the conditions stated in the first sentence of paragraph 1.

3. The protection of the railway property and the maintenance of public order within the railway zone are of fundamental importance. In order to assure these, it is necessary to provide a dependable and effective police force or gendarmerie. As the railway zone lies within Chinese territory, this could be made to consist, if China so desired, of Chinese; but it would be essential, in the opinion of the

Committee, that—as a temporary and exceptional measure, justified alike by existing conditions and the precedent of a Russian guard—this police or gendarmerie should be paid by and remain under the control of the Finance Committee, as this body would be responsible under the trusteeship for the preservation of the property of the railway and the maintenance of conditions suitable to unhampered operation.

Observations and Reservations Made by Dr. Hawkling Yen, Chinese Representative of the Sub-Committee on the Chinese Eastern Railway. In view of the great importance attached by the Chinese Government to the Chinese Eastern Railway and in view of some points in the Report in which he regretted that he was unable to concur, the Chinese Representative on this Sub-Committee was constrained, with the permission of the Chairman of the Sub-Committee, to make a few observations and reservations.

The construction of this Railway by the Russians was obviously for a strategic purpose and therefore political in nature. The very fact that this line runs through the Chinese territory gives to China additional interest peculiar to that country alone. For its construction the Chinese Government paid the sum of 5,000,000 Kuping taels to the Russo-Chinese Bank, and the Railway Company was to pay the Chinese Government a sum of 5,000,000 Kuping taels upon the completion of the Railway, which still remains unpaid.

The recent political disorder in Russia necessitated the conclusion of an agreement by which the Chinese Government for the time being undertook to assume the responsibilities on behalf of Russia respecting the Railway in the similar manner as the Chinese Government has done with respect to the Russian Concessions in Tientsin and Hankow. It should be understood that in doing so China did not intend to seek any undue advantage out of the present situation in Russia but rather to exercise the rights of a sovereign state within whose territory the Railway runs and also because of the deep interest in which she is involved.

It may also be observed that the Agreement made in 1919 among Six Powers referred to in the Report was expressly stated to be a temporary arrangement and was to come to an end when the foreign military forces were withdrawn from Siberia.

Of the three measures proposed in the Report, the Chinese Representative found it very difficult to agree to the measures 1 and 3. With respect to measure 1, in view of the existing administrative organization and operation, he felt that it would be very difficult for China to agree to the general financial control and the exercise of trusteeship as stated in the Report, and with respect to measure 3, he doubted the propriety, not to say the advisability, of putting Chinese police or gendarme under a mixed committee as proposed to be set up, as the police or gendarme is a State force. In this connection, it may also be pointed out that the precedent of a Russian guard has no legal ground as it was expressly stipulated in the Agreement of 1896 that it was the Chinese Government which was to take measures to assure the safety of the Railway and of the persons in its service. Under such circumstances, the Chinese Representative had to make reservations with respect to these two measures.

However, in making these remarks, the Chinese Representative does not wish to be understood that he is not aware of the fact there is room for improvement with respect to this Railway. He is of the opinion that the Chinese Government will welcome friendly assistance of foreign Powers and may be prepared to discuss matters regarding the technical and financial aspects of the Railway in so far as not inconsistent with the recognition of its political rights.

Resolution Adopted. Inasmuch as it appeared from this report that there were important points of disagreement between the technical experts upon the sub-committee, Secretary Hughes suggested that the Committee of the Whole appoint from among its own members a new sub-committee as delegates with the responsibility of plenipotentiary representatives of the Powers, to see if an agreement could not be reached. This suggestion was accepted by the Committee, and the new sub-committee created.

In the discussions of this committee it proved impossible to meet various points raised by the Japanese representative, Mr. Hanihara. While admitting that the Chinese Eastern Railway was a Chinese chartered corporation, he denied that the railway was Chinese property, and said that his Delegation could not discuss the question upon that basis. Furthermore, he questioned the right of the Conference to discuss and determine the treaty and other contractual rights involved, and contended that the whole situation could be considered only upon a *de facto* basis of expediency.

At the close of the first meeting of this Committee Dr. Koo and M. Kammerer were deputed to prepare, if possible, a report that would reconcile the various views that had been advanced. This report, which they made at the second meeting, after reciting certain facts by way of a preamble, went on to declare that it was desirable that the terms of the accord of January, 1919, should be amended, with the result that the Technical Commission should replace the instrumentalities instituted in 1919, and that it should also be authorized to counsel and aid the president and council of the directors of the Far Eastern Railway and of the Ussuri Railway respectively in the making of loans, and to supervise the expenditure of the funds thus obtained. By this proposed agreement, China was to furnish a sufficient force of gendarmerie, with modern equipment and instruction for the protection of the Chinese Eastern Railway, this force to be paid for by the Railway.

To these proposals Mr. Hanihara raised the objection that an amendment of the Inter Allied Accord could properly be effected only by the parties to that

Accord. He also insisted that, if the Technical Commission were to have financial powers, its name should be changed to Financial Commission. He concluded by saying that the subject was a complicated one and that he desired more time for consideration. It was then proposed by the chairman of the committee and agreed to, that Dr. Koo, M. Kammerer and Mr. Hanihara should constitute a sub-committee to see if a resolution could not be drafted to which a unanimous approval could be given and reported to the Conference.

This plan also proved futile. The Japanese representative remained unwilling that the Ussuri Railway should be included within the arrangement, and also that the Chairman of the Allied Board should be appointed instead of being elected.

In result the sub-committee was obliged to content itself with reporting the following resolution:

Resolved, That the preservation of the Chinese Eastern Railway for those in interest requires that better protection be given to the railway and the persons engaged in its operation and use; a more careful selection of personnel to secure efficiency of service, and a more economical use of funds to prevent waste of the property.

That the subject should immediately be dealt with through the proper diplomatic channels.

At the same time, the sub-committee reported that the Powers, other than China, had united in the following Reservation:

The Powers other than China in agreeing to the resolution regarding the Chinese Eastern Railway, reserve the right to insist hereafter upon the responsibility of China for the performance or non-performance of the obligations towards the foreign stockholders, bondholders, and creditors of the Chinese Eastern Railway Co. which the Powers deem to result from the contracts under which the railroad was built and the action of China thereunder and the obligations which they deem to be in the nature of a trust resulting from the exercise of power by the Chinese Government over the possession and administration of the railroad.

Dr. Koo, who represented the Chinese Delegation on the second sub-committee, speaking upon this report and proposed resolution, said that as the inter-allied agreement provided for the supervision of the whole Trans-Siberian system, including the Chinese Eastern Railway, it might give rise to misgivings in China if that particular railway should be singled out for separate treatment; and, furthermore, that any arrangement concerning that road would be of only limited value if it did not also include the Ussuri Railway which connected it with the sea at Vladivostok. In the third place, the Chinese Eastern Railway lay entirely within Chinese territory and that, therefore, the sovereign rights of China needed to be safeguarded.

The legal status of the railway, Dr. Koo pointed out, was expressly defined in the agreements between China and Russia and between China and the Railway Company and the Russo-Asiatic Bank, and that whatever changes might have taken place in the internal organization of the road had been effected by due process of law. As to this he had reference to the agreement of October 2, 1920, entered into between China and the Russo-Asiatic Bank. As to the extent of the trust that China had assumed, that applied only to the functions which had been exercised by the Russian Government under agreements with China and which China was now exercising as a provisional measure because of the absence, for the time being, of a recognized Russian Government: that the Chinese authorities had been handling the critical situation to the best of their abilities and if the protection afforded to the road and to those who used it had not been fully adequate that had been due more to the difficulties consequent upon the political disorganization in Russia than to any lack of determination on the part of China.

A vote upon the first resolution was thereupon taken to which all the Powers, including China, gave their assent.

At the sixth plenary session of the Conference, held February 4, 1922, the Resolution together with the Reservation to it by the Powers other than China, were unanimously approved.

CHAPTER XIX

INTER-POWER AGREEMENTS RELATING TO CHINA

The third of the Chinese "Ten Points" had declared as follows:

With a view to strengthening mutual confidence and maintaining peace in the Pacific and the Far East, the Powers agree not to conclude between themselves any treaty or agreement directly affecting China or the general peace in these regions without previously notifying China and giving to her an opportunity to participate.

Chinese Statement. This proposition was brought before the Committee of the Whole at its fourteenth meeting, held December 8, by Dr. Koo, who called attention to the fact that, in the past, agreements relating to the Far East generally and to China in particular, had been made by the Powers between themselves without notification to China that such agreements were in contemplation and, therefore, without giving to her an opportunity to participate therein should she desire to do so. Dr. Koo then continued:[1]

---

[1] What follows is from the official minutes of the meeting of the Committee. The Chinese Delegation submitted the following tentative list of Inter-Power Agreements that had, in the past, been entered into with reference to China:
  1. Franco-Japanese Agreement, June 10, 1907 (MacMurray 640).
  2. Anglo-Japanese Treaty, July 13, 1911 (MacMurray 900).
  3. Russo-Japanese Convention of July 30, 1907 (MacMurray 657).
  4. Russo-Japanese Secret Convention of July 30, 1907 (text not available).

These agreements, he said, fell roughly into two divisions, the one being in the nature of mutual engagements to abstain from certain action in special parts of China, the other being engagements for mutual assistance in support of the general interests of all foreign powers in China or of the special interests claimed by the parties to the agreement.

As to these treaties and agreements, Mr. Koo said he felt that they were all so well known to the members of the committee that the complete enumeration of them or specific illustrations would be unnecessary.

The first kind of agreements usually was in the nature of an engagement on the part of one contracting party not to seek any railway concessions in one part of China in return for a similar promise on the part of the other contracting parties not to seek railway concessions in another part of China.

As first it might seem as if a nation were within its rights in promising another to forego certain opportunities within a specific region. But any deeper examination of this matter would immediately show that there were a great many objections to such a method of arranging the action of one nation upon the territory of another. In the first place, it involved an incipient national monopoly or preference within the region affected, because the nation which had secured a promise of abstention from one power would then proceed with efforts to secure a similar promise from others.

    5. Russo-Japanese Convention of July 4, 1910 (MacMurray 803).
    6. Russo-Japanese Secret Convention of July 4, 1910 (text not available).
    7. Russo-Japanese Secret Convention of July 8, 1912 (text not available).
    8. Russo-Japanese Convention of July 3, 1916 (MacMurray 1327).
    9. Russo-Japanese Treaty of Alliance, of July 3, 1916 (MacMurray 1328).
    10. American-Japanese Exchange of Notes of November 30, 1908 (Root-Takahira Agreement) (MacMurray 769).
    11. American-Japanese Exchange of Notes of November 2, 1917 (Lansing-Ishii Agreement) (MacMurray 1394).
    12. Anglo-French Agreement of January 15, 1896, Article IV (MacMurray 54).
    13. Anglo-Russian Agreement, April 28, 1899 (MacMurray 204).
    14. Anglo-German Agreement, September 2, 1898 (MacMurray 266).

Thus by the making of only one agreement two nations would be backing a system of artificial limitation of economic activities.

The rights of China were involved both because she must wish that all the parts of her territory should be open on equal terms, or on such terms as she herself should determine, to foreign capitalists, merchants, and residents. As soon as such treaties as the above were made, without consultation with China, her territory was divided into distinct spheres for foreign enterprise. To this she could by no means be indifferent.

The other group of treaties dealt with the safeguarding and defending of territorial rights or special interests in the Far East, including or specially mentioning China.

These all had one or more of the following three features:

(1) A declaration that the contracting parties had a special interest in having order and a pacific state of things guaranteed in the regions of China adjacent to the territories where the contracting powers had rights of sovereignty, protection, or occupation, and an engagement to support each other for assuring peace and security in these regions; or

(2) A declaration to support the independence and integrity of China and the maintenance of the open door for foreign commerce and to aid each other for the defense of the contracting parties' special interests in said regions; or

(3) The recognition by one contracting power that, since propinquity creates special relations, the other contracting power had special interests in China.

It was clear that any one of the foregoing three features must be of vital interest to China. The assurance of peace and order in any part of Chinese territory was a matter of great concern to China herself. The maintenance of the independence and territorial integrity of China touched the supreme rights of China. As to the recognition of propinquity as creating special interests in China, it was equally obvious that such recognition could not be valid, because special interests on Chinese territory could not be created without the consent of China, and China had always contested the soundness of the doctrine of propinquity.

The effect of all such treaties and agreements had been to maintain in China conditions which intimately affected the rights, prospects, and liberty of action of China herself.

It appeared, therefore, that the Chinese Government had an equitable right to be consulted in all agreements which dealt with, or pretended to deal with, the general situation in the Far East, including China. Even if such treaties were animated by an entirely friendly spirit toward China, yet their bearing was such that they might involve consequences which would result in limitations on Chinese freedom of action; even such treaties, therefore, should not be made without consultation with China.

It might, of course, be said that China, not being a party to such treaties, need in no way recognize them nor consider herself bound by any of their provisions. That was legally true. But the political effect produced by a group of such treaties, just as in the case of spheres of influence, tended so to modify the political and economic situation in China that no efforts on the part of the Chinese Government would succeed in preserving its liberty of action. Should recognition be given to the practice that China need not be consulted, the total results of a group of such cases must be examined. In that case it was plain that vital interests of China would be affected, and that the nature of activities and interests within China would be determined entirely by the action of outside powers. The Chinese Government would then find itself obliged to move along grooves laid down by others without having once had an opportunity of insisting upon her own life needs as seen by herself.

It must therefore be concluded that though an individual agreement might, on the face of it, concern only the action of outside powers, if that action related to China, the Chinese Government could not remain indifferent to it, because of the effect which the continued practice of making agreements of this kind would have upon the liberty of movement and the development of the Chinese Government and the nation itself.

Discussion. Following upon this statement by Dr. Koo, there was an extended discussion in which the following objections to accepting, without qualification, the Chinese proposal were made.

Mr. Balfour thought that China could best be benefited, not by adopting the broad principle which her Delegation had proposed, but by dealing with her difficulties one by one, as the Conference had been doing, for example, with regard to spheres of interest, post offices, extraterritoriality and the like. "All that the Conference could do was to see that no undue limitations, no limitations which were not necessitated by the facts of the situation, were placed on China's sovereign independence, and to give all the help in its power toward the creation of a pure and vigorous administration." He also thought that the proposition put forward by Dr. Koo would, if accepted, involve a limitation of the treaty rights of the Powers. For example, if made of general international application, it would prevent France and Belgium from entering into a defensive treaty of any kind without consulting Germany. All agreed that the Powers had entered into treaties not only in regard to China but also as to other nations which reflected no credit on the parties to them, but the correction of this evil should be sought in publicity. Most of the nations represented at the Conference were members of the League of Nations and were bound by article XVIII of its covenant to publish their agreements. The United States, while not a member, was practically obligated by its Constitution to make its treaties public. He would ask the Chinese Delegation, therefore, not to press its proposition in the form in which it had been presented.

Secretary Hughes spoke somewhat along the same lines, stressing the four "Root Resolutions" that had been adopted by the Conference, and especially the one that provided that no advantage should be taken of China because of her present domestic difficulties, but that each Power should be left free to make agreements necessary for the preservation of its own proper interests, and that there should be no secret engagements.

Sir Auckland Geddes suggested that to the four Root Resolutions there might be added a fifth according to which the Powers would agree—

> To enter into no treaty, agreement, arrangement, or understanding, either with one another or individually or collectively, with any other Power or Powers which would infringe or impair the principles which they have herein declared.

Mr. Hanihara, speaking for the Japanese Delegation, expressed the view that this proposed resolution was practically included within the scope of the first of the Root Resolutions, and that to adopt it would have the effect of weakening that resolution; also that, if such proposed resolution were adopted, China herself should be brought within its application.

Resolution Adopted. As a result of these observations Sir Auckland's draft resolution was amended so as to read:

> That the powers attending this conference, hereinafter mentioned, to wit, the United States of America, Belgium, the British Empire, China, France, Italy, Japan, the Netherlands, and Portugal declare that it is their intention not to enter into any treaty, agreement, arrangement, or understanding, either with one another, or individually or collectively with any power or powers, which would in-

fringe or impair the principles which have been declared by the resolution adopted November 21 by this committee.

In this form the resolution was unanimously approved by the Committee and reported to the Conference which adopted it at its fourth plenary session, held December 10.

As it appears as Article II of the Nine Power Treaty Relating to Principles and policies to be Followed in Matters Concerning China, it reads:

> The Contracting Powers agree not to enter into any treaty, agreement, arrangement, or understanding, either with one another, or individually or collectively, with any Power or Powers, which would infringe or impair the principles stated in Article I [the four " Root Resolutions "].

CHAPTER XX

ARMS EMBARGO

As is well known the exportation of arms and ammunition to China by the Powers has, for a number of years, been a matter which has given concern to all the parties involved by reason of the fact that these arms and munitions have, to a considerable extent, found their way into the possession of bands of bandits operating in China, or have served to keep active the civil warfare which has prevailed in that country. In May, 1919, a diplomatic agreement, the purpose of which was to restrain this traffic, was arrived at but without completely satisfactory results.[1]

On January 22, 1922, a Resolution was approved by the President of the United States which had been adopted by Congress which provided that whenever the President should find that in any American country or in any country in which the United States exercised extraterritorial jurisdiction conditions of domestic violence existed which would be promoted by the use of arms and munitions if procured from the United States, he should make proclamation of

---

[1] It will be remembered that one of the Twenty-One Demands of 1915 by Japan upon China sought to impose upon China the obligation to purchase fifty per cent or more of her munitions from Japan, and that there should be established in China a jointly worked Sino-Japanese arsenal. It has also been supposed that a somewhat similar agreement was included in the secret Sino-Japanese Military Agreement of 1918.

the fact and declare it unlawful to export, except under such limitations as he might prescribe, any arms or munitions of war from the United States to that country.

That this Resolution had especial reference to China was made evident in a letter of Secretary of State Hughes to Senator Lodge of March 14, 1921.[2]

[2] This letter was as follows:
SIR: In view of the long continued civil strife in China, the powers allied and associated in the war, and also certain of the neutral powers, mutually agreed, through their diplomatic representatives in Peking, in May, 1919, to restrict shipments from their respective countries to China of arms and munitions of war, and material destined exclusively for their manufacture until the establishment of a government whose authority should be recognized throughout the whole country. The powers thus cooperating were the United States, Great Britain, France, Japan, Spain, Portugal, Russia, Brazil, the Netherlands, Denmark, Belgium, and Italy. The purport of this understanding was to put into effect internationally, as regards China, a policy identical with that which the United States has adopted in the past in connection with civil disturbances in countries in Latin America, as set forth in Public Resolution No. 22, of March 14, 1912 (37 Stat., p. 630). This Government was enabled to exercise the control over the export of arms and munitions to China, in pursuance of the policy thus adopted, on the basis of the provisions of the espionage act of June 15, 1917, as enforced by the War Trade Board.

By the joint resolution approved March 3, 1921, those provisions of the espionage act of June 15, 1917, providing for the control of exports were repealed. The Department of State was thus deprived of any legal authority by which it could control shipment of arms and thereby cooperate with the other interested powers in restricting shipments of arms used to promote and continue civil strife in China. It is believed that conditions in China do not at the present time warrant any change in this policy, and I therefore have the honor to renew the request contained in a letter addressed to you by Secretary Lansing under date of December 31, 1919, namely, that Public Resolution No. 22, of March 14, 1912 (37 Stat., p. 630), be amended by striking out the limiting word " American " in the first line, or by such other means as you in your discretion may consider adequate, to enable this Government to continue its cooperation with the other powers in a policy which it believes necessary under existing circumstances.

By proclamation, dated March 6, 1922, the President exercised the discretionary power granted him by this resolution and forbade the export to China from the United States of arms and munitions of war.

244   CHINA AT THE CONFERENCE

Draft Resolution. At the twenty-fifth meeting of the Committee of the Whole of the Washington Conference, held January 24, Mr. Balfour proposed for adoption the following resolution:

The United States of America, Belgium, the British Empire, France, Italy, Japan, the Netherlands, and Portugal affirm their intention to refrain themselves and to restrain their nationals from exporting to China arms, munitions of war, or material destined exclusively for their manufacture, until the establishment of a government whose authority is recognized throughout the whole country.

2. Each of the above powers will forthwith take such additional steps as may be necessary to make the above restrictions immediately binding upon all its nationals.

3. The scope of this resolution includes all concessions, settlements, and leased territories in China.

4. The United States of America will invite the adherence to this resolution of the other powers in treaty relations with China.

Discussion. Mr. Sze asked if he was right in assuming that the aim of this resolution was to help China—the same aim, in fact, as had animated the resolution that had earlier been reported from the sub-committee with regard to the revenues of China. He also observed that the importation into China of arms and material for their manufacture was not permitted by China except under licenses issued by the Chinese Government.

Mr. Balfour said that the sole motive of the British Empire Delegation in submitting the resolution was that thus China might be aided to obtain for herself a strong and stable government. He then quoted the following notification to the Chinese Government which, on May 5, 1919, the doyen of the diplomatic body had made, and which was almost identical in phraseology with the words of the first paragraph of the resolution:

> The Governments of Great Britain, Portugal, the United States, Russia, Brazil, France, and Japan have agreed effectively to restrain their subjects and citizens from exporting to or importing into China arms and munitions of war and material destined exclusively for their manufacture until the establishment of a government whose authority is recognized throughout the whole country, and also to prohibit, during the above period, delivery of arms and munitions for which contracts have already been made but not executed.[3]

Senator Schanzer said that while in sympathy with the resolution, the Italian Delegation was not ready to act upon it: he was not in a position to state whether the Italian Government, in the absence of an international agreement approved by the Italian Government, was allowed by existing legislation to impose the necessary restrictions upon this commerce. Upon his attention being called to the fact that Italy had joined in the resolution of May 5, 1919, Senator Schanzer referred to the reservation which Italy had at that time made according to which all contracts already concluded by Italians, or to be concluded by them before all the Powers should give their assent to the resolution, were to be excluded from its operation.

Jonkheer Beelaerts, of the Belgian Delegation, also thought that it would be necessary to consult his Government before giving assent to Mr. Balfour's resolution. He also called attention to the difference in wording between the Peking resolution, referring

---

[3] The Governments of the Netherlands, Denmark and Belgium subsequently adhered to this arrangement.

both to exportation from the various countries and importations into China, and the resolution then before the Committee which mentioned only exportation to China.

Baron Shidehara said that so long as Japan was in occupation of Port Arthur it would be impossible for her to undertake to restrict the dispatch of arms thither, but that Japan could easily take efficient measures to restrict re-exportation from her leased territory to other parts of China. He was assured by Mr. Balfour that it was not intended that a country should be restrained from sending arms and munitions to its own troops—that this would apply to British troops in Kowloon as well as to Japanese troops in the Liaotung leased area.

The United States Delegation said that, under its existing laws, its Government had no legal power to control importation into China; it could control only exportation from the United States.

Amended Resolution. As a result of this discussion and another brief one at the twenty-seventh meeting of the Committee, the Arms Embargo resolution was amended so as to read:

I. The United States of America, Belgium, the British Empire, France, Italy, Japan, the Netherlands, and Portugal affiirm their intention to refrain from exporting to China arms or munitions of war, whether complete or in parts and to prohibit such exportation from their territories or territories under their control, until the establishment of a Government whose authority is recognized throughout the whole of China.

II. Each of the above Powers will forthwith take such additional steps as may be necessary to make the above restrictions immediately binding.

III. The scope of this Resolution includes all Concessions and Settlements in China.

IV. The United States of America will invite the adherence to this Resolution of the other Powers in treaty relations with China.

The Netherlands, French and Italian Delegations announced that they had received instructions from their respective Governments which permitted them to agree to this resolution as amended.

Dr. Koo suggested that a time limit, say two years, should be placed upon the operation of the Resolution. To this Mr. Balfour rejoined that the resolution, by its terms, would cease to operate when China obtained a government whose authority was recognized throughout its area.

At the twenty-ninth meeting of the Committee, Mr. Hanihara said that if the Italian Government insisted upon maintaining its reservation of May, 1919, Japan would have to reserve the right to take such steps as might be necessary to prevent undue hardships upon Japanese nationals who had important unexecuted contracts for the delivery of arms and munitions to China—contracts that had been entered into during the period from July, 1918, to January, 1919. Since that time, he said, the Japanese Government had not allowed its nationals to enter into contracts for the sale of arms to China.

Resolution Withdrawn. At this point, somewhat to the surprise of the Committee, it developed that the Italian Delegation was unable to say whether, according to the instructions from its Government which were not explicit, by insisting upon its reservation of May, 1919, the Italian Government meant to save the right upon the part of its nationals to execute all contracts for the delivery of arms to China up to the present time, or whether only those contracts which had been entered into prior to May, 1919, were to be allowed to be executed. As there was then not time for the Italian Delegation again to communicate with its Government, and as it was agreed that it would not be feasible for the other Powers to restrict their freedom of action in the matter so long as one of the Powers remained practically unrestrained, it was agreed by the Committee that the Arms Embargo Resolution should be withdrawn.

CHAPTER XXI

THE TWENTY-ONE DEMANDS: TREATIES AND AGREEMENTS OF MAY 25, 1915

As has been earlier stated, the treaties and agreements of May 25, 1915, resulting from the Twenty-One Demands made in that year by Japan upon China, were presented to the Conference in Committee of the Whole by Dr. Wang on December 14, in connection with the request that China had made that the Powers disavow all claims to spheres of interest or of influence or any special interests within the territory of China. At this time Dr. Wang said that these agreements vitally affect the very existence, independence, and integrity of China and that " in the common interests of the Powers as well as of China, and in conformity with the principles relating to China already adopted by the Committee, the Chinese Delegation urged that the said treaties and exchange of notes be reconsidered and cancelled."

Mr. Hanihara, in behalf of the Japanese Delegation said that at that time he desired to reserve a reply until he could examine carefully the statement that Dr. Wang had made, but that if there was a question as to the validity or amendment or abrogation of the agreements he would announce that the Japanese Delegation could not agree that the matter should be made one for discussion at the Conference:

that the matter was one, if taken up at all, for discussion only between China and Japan.

At the eighteenth meeting of the Committee when this matter came up for consideration, Secretary Hughes suggested that inasmuch as this matter had a very close relationship to the other questions under consideration in the Shantung "Conversations" then in progress, it be passed over until the result of these Conversations could be learned. As it appeared that the other Delegations were in favor of this being done, Dr. Wang himself deemed it wise to offer no objection. The result was that the question of the continuing validity to be ascribed to the agreements of 1915 did not again come before the Conference until near its close, that is to say, until the thirtieth meeting of the Committee on February 2.

Japanese Statement. Baron Shidehara, in behalf of the Japanese Delegation, then read the following formal statement:

At a previous session of this committee, the Chinese delegation presented a statement urging that the Sino-Japanese treaties and notes of 1915 be reconsidered and cancelled. The Japanese delegation, while appreciating the difficult position of the Chinese delegation, does not feel at liberty to concur in the procedure now resorted to by China with a view to cancellation of international engagements which she entered into as a free sovereign nation.

It is presumed that the Chinese delegation has no intention of calling in question the legal validity of the compacts of 1915, which were formally signed and sealed by the duly authorized representatives of the two Governments, and for which the exchange of ratifications was effected in conformity with established international usages. The insistence by China on the cancellation of those instruments would in itself indicate that she shares the view that the compacts actually remain in force and will continue to be effective, unless and until they are cancelled.

It is evident that no nation can have given ready consent to cessions of its territorial or other rights of importance. If it should once be recognized that rights solemnly granted by treaty may be revoked at any time on the ground that they were conceded against the spontaneous will of the grantor, an exceedingly dangerous precedent will be established, with far-reaching consequences upon the stability of the existing international relations in Asia, in Europe and everywhere.

The statement of the Chinese delegation under review declares that China accepted the Japanese demands in 1915, hoping that a day would come when she should have the opportunity of bringing them up for reconsideration and cancellation. It is, however, difficult to understand the meaning of this assertion. It can not be the intention of the Chinese delegation to intimate that China may conclude a treaty, with the thought in mind of breaking it at the first opportunity.

The Chinese delegation maintains that the treaties and notes in question are derogatory to the principles adopted by the conference with regard to China's sovereignty and independence. It has, however, been held by the conference on more than one occasion that concessions made by China ex contractu, in the exercise of her own sovereign rights, can not be regarded as inconsistent with her sovereignty and independence.

It should also be pointed out that the term "twenty-one demands," often used to denote the treaties and notes of 1915, is inaccurate and grossly misleading.

It may give rise to an erroneous impression that the whole original proposals of Japan had been pressed by Japan and accepted in toto by China. As a matter of fact, not only "Group V," but also several other matters contained in Japan's first proposals were eliminated entirely or modified considerably, in deference to the wishes of the Chinese Government, when the final formula was presented to China for acceptance. Official records published by the two Governments relating to those negotiations will further show that the most important terms of the treaties and notes, as signed, had already been virtually agreed to by the Chinese negotiators before the delivery of the ultimatum, which then seemed to the Japanese Government the only way of bringing the protracted negotiations to a speedy close.

The Japanese delegation can not bring itself to the conclusion that any useful purpose will be served by research and reexamination at this conference of old grievances which one of the nations represented here may have against another. It will be more in line with the high aim of the conference to look forward to the future with hope and with confidence.

Having in view, however, the changes which have taken place in the situation since the conclusion of the Sino-Japanese treaties and notes of 1915, the Japanese delegation is happy to avail itself of the present occasion to make the following declaration:

1. Japan is ready to throw open to the joint activity of the international financial consortium recently organized, the right of option granted exclusively in favor of Japanese capital, with regard, first, to loans for the construction of railways in South Manchuria and Eastern Inner Mongolia, and, second, to loans to be secured on taxes in that region; it being understood that nothing in the present declaration shall be held to imply any modification or annulment of the understanding recorded in the officially announced notes and memoranda which were exchanged among the Governments of the countries represented in the consortium and also among the national financial groups composing the consortium, in relation to the scope of the joint activity of that organization.

2. Japan has no intention of insisting on her preferential right under the Sino-Japanese arrangements in question concerning the engagements by China of Japanese advisers or instructors on political, financial, military, or police matters in South Manchuria.

3. Japan is further ready to withdraw the reservation which she made, in proceeding to the signature of the Sino-Japanese treaties and notes of 1915, to the effect that Group V of the original proposals of the Japanese Government would be postponed for future negotiations.

It would be needless to add that all matters relating to Shantung contained in those treaties and notes have now been definitely adjusted and disposed of.

In coming to this decision, which I have had the honor to announce, Japan has been guided by a spirit of fairness and moderation, having always in view China's sovereign rights and the principle of equal opportunity.

Chinese Reply. Dr. Wang, replying to Baron Shidehara, said that it was not correct to say, as Baron Shidehara had said, that the mere fact that the Chinese had asked for an abrogation of the agreements of 1915 implied that they recognized their validity: that, as a matter of fact, the Chinese Government and the Chinese people had always regarded these agreements as peculiar in themselves by reason of the circumstances under which they had been negotiated, and that the conditions arising under them were only *de facto* and without any legal recognition upon the part of China. He said that he would make a detailed reply to Baron Shidehara's statement as soon as he had the time to prepare it. This reply, which he made at the last (thirty-first) meeting of the Committee, held February 3, was as follows:

The Chinese Delegation has taken note of the statement of Baron Shidehara made at yesterday's session of the Committee with reference to the Sino-Japanese Treaties and Notes of May 25, 1915.

The Chinese Delegation learns with satisfaction that Japan is now ready to throw open to the joint activity of the banking interests of other Powers the right of option granted exclusively in favor of Japanese capital with regard, first, to loans for the construction of railways in South Manchuria and Eastern Inner Mongolia, and, second, to loans secured on taxes in that region; and that Japan has no intention of insisting upon a preferential right concerning the engagement by China of Japanese advisers or instructors in political, financial, military or police matters in South Manchuria; also that Japan now withdraws the reservation which she made to the effect that Group V of her original demands upon China should be postponed for future negotiation.

The Chinese Delegation greatly regrets that the Government of Japan should not have been led to renounce the other claims predicated upon the Treaties and Notes of 1915.

The Japanese Delegation expressed the opinion that abrogation of these agreements would constitute "an exceedingly dangerous precedent," " with far-reaching consequences upon the stability of the existing international relations in Asia, in Europe and everywhere."

The Chinese Delegation has the honor to say that a still more dangerous precedent will be established with consequences upon the stability of international relations which can not be estimated, if, without rebuke or protest from other Powers, one nation can obtain from a friendly but, in a military sense, weaker neighbor, and under circumstances such as attended the negotiation and signing of the Treaties of 1915, valuable concessions which were not in satisfaction of pending controversies and for which no quid pro quo was offered. These treaties and notes stand out, indeed, unique in the annals of international relations. History records scarcely another instance in which demands of such a serious character as those which Japan presented to China in 1915, have, without even pretense of provocation, been suddenly presented by one nation to another nation with which it was at the time in friendly relations.

No apprehension need be entertained that the abrogation of the agreements of 1915 will serve as a precedent for the annulment of other agreements, since it is confidently hoped that the future will furnish no such similar occurrences.

So exceptional were the conditions under which the agreements of 1915 were negotiated, that the Government of the United States felt justified in referring to them in the identic note of May 13, 1915, which it sent to the Chinese and Japanese Governments. That note began with the statement that " in view of the circumstances of the negotiations which have taken place and which are now pending between the Government of China and the Government of Japan and of the agreements which have been reached as the result thereof, the Government of the United States has the honor to notify the Government of the Chinese Republic (Japan) that it can not recognize any agreement or undertaking which has been entered into between the

Governments of China and Japan impairing the treaty rights of the United States and its citizens in China, the political or territorial integrity of the Republic of China, or the international policy relative to China commonly known as the Open Door Policy."

Conscious of her obligations to the other Powers, the Chinese Government, immediately after signing the agreements, published a formal statement protesting against the agreements which she had been compelled to sign, and disclaiming responsibility for consequent violations of treaty rights of the other Powers. In the statement thus issued the Chinese Government declared that although they were "constrained to comply in full with the terms of the (Japanese) ultimatum" they nevertheless "disclaim any desire to associate themselves with any revision which may be thus effected, of the various conventions and agreements concluded between the other Powers in respect of the maintenance of China's territorial independence and integrity, the preservation of the status quo, and the principle of equal opportunity for the commerce and industry of all nations in China."

Because of the essential injustice of these provisions, the Chinese Delegation, acting in behalf of the Chinese Government and of the Chinese people, has felt itself in duty bound to present to this conference, representing the Powers with substantial interests in the Far East, the question as to the equity and justice of these agreements and therefore as to their fundamental validity.

If Japan is disposed to rely solely upon a claim as to the technical or juristic validity of the agreements of 1915, as having been actually signed in due form by the two Governments, it may be said that so far as this Conference is concerned the contention is largely irrelevant, for this gathering of the representatives of the nine Powers has not had for its purpose the maintenance of the legal status quo. Upon the contrary, the purpose has been, if possible, to bring about such changes in existing conditions upon the Pacific and in the Far East as might be expected to promote that enduring friendship among the nations of which the President of the United States spoke in his letter of invitation to the Powers to participate in this Conference.

For the following reasons, therefore, the Chinese Delegation is of the opinion that the Sino-Japanese Treaties and Exchange of

Notes of May 25, 1915, should form the subject of impartial examination with a view to their abrogation:

1. In exchange for the concessions demanded of China, Japan offered no quid pro quo. The benefits derived from the agreements were wholly unilateral.

2. The agreements, in important respects, are in violation of treaties between China and the other powers.

3. The agreements are inconsistent with the principles relating to China which have been adopted by the conference.

4. The agreements have engendered constant misunderstanding between China and Japan, and, if not abrogated, will necessarily tend, in the future, to disturb friendly relations between the two countries, and will thus constitute an obstacle in the way of realizing the purpose for the attainment of which this Conference was convened. As to this, the Chinese Delegation, by way of conclusion, can, perhaps, do no better than quote from a resolution introduced in the Japanese Parliament, in June, 1915, by Mr. Hara, later Premier of Japan, a resolution which received the support of some one hundred and thirty of the members of the parliament.

The resolution reads:

"*Resolved,* That the negotiations carried on with China by the present Government have been inappropriate in every respect; that they are detrimental to the amicable relationship between the two countries, and provocative of suspicions on the part of the Powers; that they have the effect of lowering the prestige of the Japanese Empire; and that, while far from capable of establishing the foundation of peace in the Far East, they will form the source of future trouble."

The foregoing declaration has been made in order that the Chinese Government may have upon record the view which it takes, and will continue to take, regarding the Sino-Japanese Treaties and Exchange of Notes of May 25, 1915.

Statement of the United States. Thereupon, on behalf of the American Government, Secretary Hughes stated that the position of the Government of the United States with reference to these agreements was as follows:

THE TWENTY-ONE DEMANDS

The important statement made by Baron Shidehara on behalf of the Japanese Government makes it appropriate that I should refer to the position of the Government of the United States as it was set forth in identical notes addressed by that Government to the Chinese Government and to the Japanese Government on May 13, 1915.

The note to the Chinese Government was as follows:

"In view of the circumstances of the negotiations which have taken place and which are now pending between the Government of China and the Government of Japan and of the agreements which have been reached as a result thereof, the Government of the United States has the honor to notify the Government of the Chinese Republic that it can not recognize any agreement or undertaking which has been entered into or which may be entered into between the Governments of China and Japan impairing the Treaty rights of the United States and its citizens in China, the political or territorial integrity of the Republic of China, or the international policy relative to China commonly known as the Open Door Policy.

"An identical note has been transmitted to the Imperial Japanese Government."

That statement was in accord with the historic policy of the United States in its relation to China, and its position as thus stated has been, and still is, consistently maintained.

It has been gratifying to learn that the matters concerning Shantung, which formed the substance of Group I of the original demands, and were the subject of the Treaty and exchange of notes with respect to the province of Shantung, have been settled to the mutual satisfaction of the two parties by negotiations conducted collaterally with this Conference, as reported to the Plenary Session on February 1st.

It is also gratifying to be advised by the statement made by Baron Shidehara on behalf of the Japanese Government that Japan is now ready to withdraw the reservation which she made, in proceeding to the signature of the treaties and notes of 1915, to the effect that Group 5 of the original proposals of the Japanese Government—namely, those concerning the employment of influential Japanese as political, financial, and military advisers; land for schools and hospitals; certain railways in South China; the supply of arms, and the right of preaching—would be postponed for future negotiations. This definite withdrawal of the outstanding questions under Group 5 removes what has been an occasion for considerable apprehension on the part alike of China and of foreign nations which felt that the renewal of these demands could not but prejudice the principles of the Integrity of China and of the Open Door.

With respect to the Treaty and the notes concerning South Manchuria and Eastern Inner Mongolia, Baron Shidehara has made the reassuring statement that Japan has no intention of insisting on a preferential right concerning the engagement by China of Japanese advisers or instructors on political, financial, military, or police matters in South Manchuria.

Baron Shidehara has likewise indicated the readiness of Japan not to insist upon the right of option granted exclusively in favor of Japanese capital with regard, first, to loans for the construction of railways in South Manchuria and Eastern Inner Mongolia; and, second, with regard to loans secured on the taxes of those regions; but that Japan will throw them open to the joint activity of the international financial Consortium recently organized.

As to this, I may say that it is doubtless the fact that any enterprise of the character contemplated, which may be undertaken in these regions by foreign capital, would in all probability be undertaken by the Consortium. But it should be observed that existing treaties would leave the opportunity for such enterprises open on terms of equality to the citizens of all nations. It can scarcely be assumed that this general right of the Treaty Powers of China can be effectively restricted to the nationals of those countries which are participants in the work of the Consortium, or that any of the Governments which have taken part in the organization of the Consortium would feel themselves to be in a position to deny all rights in the matter to any save the members of their respective national groups in that organization. I therefore trust that it is in this sense that we may properly interpret the Japanese Government's declaration of willingness to relinquish its claim under the 1915 treaties to any exclusive position with respect to railway construction and to financial operations secured upon local revenues, in South Manchuria and Eastern Inner Mongolia.

It is further to be pointed out that by Article II, III, and IV of the Treaty of May 25, 1915, with respect to South Manchuria and Eastern Inner Mongolia, the Chinese Government granted to Japanese subjects the right to lease land for building purposes, for trade and manufacture, and for agricultural purposes in South Manchuria, to reside and travel in South Manchuria, and to engage in any kind of business and manufacture there, and to enter into joint undertakings with Chinese citizens in agriculture and similar industries in Eastern Inner Mongolia.

With respect to this grant, the Government of the United States will, of course, regard it as not intended to be exclusive, and, as in the past, will claim from the Chinese Government for American citizens the benefits accruing to them by virtue of the most favored nation clauses in the treaties between the United States and China.

I may pause here to remark that the question of the validity of treaties as between Japan and China is distinct from the question of the treaty rights of the United States under its treaties with China; these rights have been emphasized and consistently asserted by the United States.

In this, as in all matters similarly affecting the general right of its citizens to engage in commercial and industrial enterprises in China, it has been the traditional policy of the American Government to insist upon the doctrine of equality for the nationals of all countries, and this policy, together with the other policies mentioned in the note of May 13, 1915, which I have quoted, are consistently maintained by this government. I may say that it is with especial pleasure that the Government of the United States finds itself now engaged in the act of reaffirming and defining, and I hope that I may add, revitalizing, by the proposed Nine-Power Treaty, these policies with respect to China.

After these statements it was proposed and decided in the committee that the statements thus made should be reported to the Conference to be spread upon its record. In the course of the vote Mr. Koo stated in the committee that his colleagues and he himself desire to indorse the Chairman's suggestion that all of the statements on this very important question would be spread upon the records of the Conference, it being understood of course that the Chinese Delegation reserved their right to seek a solution on all future appropriate occasions concerning those portions of the treaties and notes of 1915 which did not appear to have been expressly relinquished by the Japanese Government. The Chairman stated:

> Of course it is understood that the rights of all Powers are reserved with respect to the matters mentioned by Mr. Koo.

It was agreed that these statements should be spread upon the records of the Conference, and that the Chinese Delegation reserved their right to seek relief on all appropriate occasions, concerning those portions of the treaties and notes of 1915 which did not appear to have been expressly relinquished by the Japanese Government.

At the sixth plenary session of the Conference, held February 4, 1922, Baron Shidehara's and Dr. Wang's and Secretary Hughes' statements were read, *in extenso,* in order, as the Chairman said, that they might be formally placed upon the records of the Conference.

CHAPTER XXII

China's Commitments

Upon the Agenda of the Conference relating to China appeared the item "The Status of Existing Commitments." This topic was not reached in the Committee of the Whole until its twenty-first meeting, held January 19, when the Chairman introduced it with the statement that it would be of service if a clear understanding could be had, when the Conference ended, of the commitments which were claimed to exist with respect to China.

Chinese Proposals. The Chinese Delegation, as it had done with reference to the other subjects discussed by the Conference, took the lead. Dr. Koo, speaking in behalf of his Delegation, said that he had three suggestions to make: First, that all the Powers which had any claims on China should make them known, in other words that the principle of publicity should be applied to them; Second, that the validity of these commitments should be determined; and Third, that, after their validity had been determined, steps should be taken to harmonize them with one another and with the principles adopted by the Conference.

As to the first point, that of publicity, Dr. Koo referred to the fact that this principle had been provided for in Article XVIII of the Covenant of the League of Nations, and that there were special reasons why it should be observed with regard to China. These special reasons arose out of the fact that many of the commitments claimed to have been made by China were based on agreements entered into under very uncertain circumstances—in some cases in letters or verbal statements of a single Chinese official, not even of the Central Government. As long as the principle for which he contended was not applied, Dr. Koo continued, not only would speculations and suspicions be rife, but the Powers be led to adopt policies that would run counter to existing but unknown agreements. Moreover, China herself could not adopt sound economic or fiscal policies until she had a full knowledge of the claims which the Powers might advance against her. So far as China herself was concerned, she was ready, in accordance with the principle of full publicity for all international engagements, to place before the Conference the texts of all commitments to which she was a party and any other information regarding them which the other Delegations might desire. Dr. Koo added that, so far as the Chinese Delegation was aware, the only engagement which China had entered into the authentic text of which had not been published, and concerning which the other Powers had at times exhibited an interest, was the so-called Li-Lobanoff treaty of 1896 between China and Russia. This text he was ready to supply if there was a desire for it.[1]

[1] The summary of the text, obtained by cable from Peking, was supplied to the Committee at its twenty-fifth meeting.

Regarding the validity of such claims upon China as might be submitted, Dr. Koo said that it was especially desirable that those should be examined which had been obtained in doubtful circumstances.

As to the harmonizing of the commitments or claims with one another and with the principles adopted by the Conference, Dr. Koo said that while this would introduce the principle of retroactivity, the fact could not be overlooked that there were commitments which were in conflict with one another and that it was to the interest of all concerned that these possible causes of controversy should be removed: if an existing commitment were sound and just it would have nothing to fear since the course proposed would furnish an opportunity to confirm its validity.

Discussion. The Chairman, Secretary Hughes, spoke with emphatic approval of China's proposition that the Powers should make a full disclosure of all the claims which they had upon China, and that they should file with the Secretary-General of the Conference all treaties or other engagements upon which their Governments expected to rely.

Sir Auckland Geddes said that the British Empire was prepared to publish and file every such commitment upon which it relied. He suggested, however, that a certain time interval should be provided in which the lists should be submitted, and that, as most of the agreements were already published, a simple reference to some standard collection such as that of Mr. MacMurray, should be deemed sufficient.

Baron Shidehara said that Japan was prepared to supply such a list of agreements to which its Government was a party, but that Chinese obligations to individuals or companies to which the Government was not a party would be difficult to list since the Government was not, in all cases, in a position to ascertain their precise nature and terms. Also that there were some engagements, as, for example, those relating to the Chinese Eastern Railway, which were of serious concern to its nationals but to which the Government was not a party. He suggested, therefore, that the several Governments should list the engagements in which they had an interest, which were made by them, or in their behalf, or to which they were related, or of which they had knowledge.

Viscount d'Alte, of the Portuguese Delegation, asked if it was necessary, in the Chairman's opinion, to list local engagements entered into by colonial authorities and Chinese authorities, or whether only treaties were referred to. The Chairman replied that if there was an engagement of any character which was to be asserted against China, in favor of a Power or its nationals, it was desirable that the Conference should know what it was, and that this consideration applied to commitments of the local authorities as well as of the Central Government of China.

Draft Resolution. At the next (twenty-second) meeting of the Committee, Secretary Hughes submitted the following draft resolution:

The powers represented in this conference, considering it desirable that there should hereafter be full publicity with respect to all matters affecting the political and other international obligations of China and of the several powers in relation to China, are agreed as follows:

I. The several powers will at their earliest convenience file with the secretariat general of the conference for transmission to the participating powers a list of all treaties, conventions, exchanges of notes, or other international agreements which they may have with China, or with any other power or powers in relation to China, which they deem to be still in force and upon which they may desire to rely. In each case, citations will be given to any official or other publication in which an authoritative text of the documents may be found. In any case in which the document may not have been published, a copy of the text (in its original language or languages) will be filed with the secretariat general of the conference.

Every treaty or other international agreement of the character indicated shall hereafter be notified to the powers here represented within 60 days of its conclusion.

II. The several powers will file with the secretariat general of the conference at their earliest convenience for transmission to the participating powers a list, as nearly complete as may be possible, of all those contracts between their nationals, of the one part, and the Chinese Government or any of its administrative subdivisions, of the other part, on which their respective Governments propose to rely, which involve any concession, franchise, option or preference with respect to railway construction, mining, forestry, navigation, river conservancy, harbor works, reclamation, electrical communications, or other public works or public services, or for the sale of arms or ammunition, or which involve either a lien upon any of the public revenues or properties of the Chinese central Government or of the several provinces, or a financial obligation on the part of that Government or of the provinces exceeding $1,000,000 silver (peiyang $1,000,000). There shall be, in the case of each document so listed, either a citation to a published text, or a copy of the text itself.

Every contract of the character indicated shall hereafter be notified to the powers here represented within 60 days of its conclusion.

Discussion. Baron Shidehara, speaking upon this Resolution, said that when citations were made to MacMurray or to other compilations of agreements it should be with the understanding that the accuracy of the texts and of the translations was not to be considered as guaranteed by the Government making the citation. In the second place, he said, that, though the Japanese Delegation had a general knowledge of the important contracts concluded between Japanese nationals and the Chinese Government or local authorities, they had not at hand the full texts nor was there any legal means whereby the individuals firms or corporations could be compelled to supply them.

Secretary Hughes said that he saw no reason why texts or translations in compilations should not be subject to correction. As to the second point, he assumed that the lists were to include all contracts either between the Governments, or in which the Governments had an interest, and of which they had knowledge. He would assume that, in providing a list, a Government would give what would amount to an assurance that it was, in these respects, as complete as that Government could make it. The contracts referred to in Article II, he said

were concessions, franchises, options, or preferences with respect to railway construction, mining, forestry, navigation, river conservancy, harbor works, reclamations, electrical communications, or other public works or public services, for the sale of arms or munitions, or which involved either liens upon any of the public revenues or properties of the Chinese central government or of the several provinces, or financial obligations on the part of that government or of the provinces exceeding $1,000,000 silver. They were contracts or concessions of the character described, between the nationals of a Government on one part and the Chinese Government or any of its administrative subdivisions on the other. In other words, from the Chinese side it was a government contract; it was a government contract in relation to these classes of works of a very important character. Of course, with the information that this policy had been adopted, which could hardly fail to come to the attention of any concern seeking a concession or contract of this sort from the Chinese Government or its political subdivisions, he supposed that it might well be understood that the governments of the nationals concerned would be informed, if it were to be expected that they would later diplomatically support the undertaking. Also, as had just been pointed out to him, there was a further point that should be mentioned; the Government whose nationals were concerned, as well as the other Governments represented at this conference, would be at once informed by China of the making of the contract. So he felt that, so far as the future was concerned, their Japanese colleagues would not be in any danger of being taken by surprise.

Baron Shidehara said that perhaps he had not made his meaning entirely clear. There might be some contracts of the nature specified in Article II of which the Japanese Government had at present no knowledge, but with regard to which question might later arise. If these contracts were legitimate, the Japanese Government would have to support them. According to this article, each power would be required to supply a list of these contracts as nearly complete as possible. The Japanese Government would do everything in its power to supply such a list, but it could not guarantee that this would be complete. He also wished to call attention to the fact that the first paragraph of Article II specified that the several powers were to file with the secretary general of the conference, at their earliest convenience, for transmission to the participating powers, a list, as nearly complete as might be possible, of all those contracts between their nationals, etc., while the second paragraph of this same article did not contain such a limitation.

Mr. Balfour observed that China should herself be made a party to the proposed arrangement, that is, that she should supply a list of the commitments which she had made. He also suggested that provision be made for the adherence of other Powers not represented at the Conference.

At the twenty-third meeting of the Committee there was a further discussion of the subject during which Dr. Koo suggested that it appeared that one class of agreements, which were of great importance, was not included within the scope of the resolution. These were agreements which concerned China, but which were made between a set of nationals of one country with a set or sets of nationals of one or more other countries, Instances of these agreements were the Anglo-German bankers' arrangement concerning spheres of influence in railway construction of September 7, 1898, and the International Consortium agreement of October 15, 1920.

With reference to this point Mr. Root said that contracts of the kind referred to could be dealt with by the laws of China, and doubtless would be so dealt with when China had carried out her process of reorganization and stabilization. The real remedy, as he saw it, for such agreements as should in any way prejudice China, would be, not that the Governments should attempt to give notice of contracts of which they might have no knowledge, but that they should agree to a resolution of the following purport:

Resolved, That the signatory Powers will not support any agreement by their respective nationals with each other designed to create spheres of influence or to provide for the enjoyment of mutually exclusive opportunities in designated parts of Chinese territory.

Baron Shidehara asked if this resolution had not been covered by the Open Door resolution which had already been adopted. The Chairman, as to this, observed that the proposed resolution related not to agreements by Governments but to agreements between nationals and the support of such agreements by Governments: it might be within the spirit of the Open Door resolution but that it would be well to make a definite statement upon this particular point which would bind the consciences of the Governments. Mr. Root thought that the proposed resolution had not been covered by the Open Door resolution,—that it was aimed at proceedings which were illustrated by rules of law against agreements between bidders at public auctions. After quoting the terms of the Anglo-German bankers' agreement to which Dr. Koo had referred, Mr. Root said that he was of opinion that no two groups of bankers ought to be able to commit their Governments in that way, and that it ought to be understood that they could not.

Baron Shidehara repeated the statement of his opinion that the matter had been covered by the Open Door resolution previously adopted, whereupon Mr. Balfour pointed out that if the objection related only to a matter of repetition, it was surely not a serious one. The Chairman then put the resolution to vote and it was unanimously carried.

Baron de Cartier queried whether, by giving notification of a private contract upon the part of the nationals, a government might not be giving to that contract a status or dignity which it might not deserve.

Dr. Koo reserved the right of China during a public war to which she was a party, to refuse publications of texts of agreements for the purchase of arms and munitions. That to publish such contracts might be seriously detrimental to her was obvious. This reservation, however, he said, was not intended to apply to times of civil war.

Mr. Balfour suggested that the words " or a financial obligation on the part of that Government or of the provinces exceeding $1,000,000 silver," should be omitted from the resolution, as this provision appeared to have no reference to questions of monopoly or undue preference.

Senator Underwood expressed some doubt as to the desirability or possibility of publishing agreements by individuals or concerns which might result in making public trade secrets or private contracts. Mr. Root said that he agreed in general with Senator Underwood as to the requirement of publicity for trade agreements, but that, as he understood it, the resolution was aimed at a distinct class of contracts in which, upon the one side, there was a Government officer executing a trust for the public. In regard to these the only practical method yet discovered for securing honesty and fairness and just representation of the public was to make them known to the world. What was being attempted, he said, was to help, as far as possible, the development of government in China by means of self-denying ordinances on the part of the Powers, in order to restrain their own nationals from taking advantage of the disturbed conditions in China to secure preferences and advantages which would be injurious to China herself. He understood that the purpose of the resolution was, in an indirect way, to make certain that public contracts, made by public officers of whatever kind in China, would be made public, and that there would thus be a check upon the transaction of public business in China which, at some future time, China herself would provide for by her own laws.

Resolutions Adopted. As a result of these discussions the resolution as to the publishing and listing of commitments was given the following form and in that form unanimously approved by the Committee:

The Powers represented in this Conference, considering it desirable that there should hereafter be full publicity with respect to all matters affecting the political and other international obligations of China and of the several Powers in relation to China, are agreed as follows:

I. The several Powers other than China will at their earliest convenience file with the Secretariat General of the Conference for transmission to the participating Powers, a list of all treaties, conventions, exchange of notes, or other international agreements which they may have with China, or with any other Power or Powers in relation to China, which they deem to be still in force and upon which they may desire to rely. In each case, citations will be given to any official or other publication in which an authoritative text of the documents may be found. In any case in which the document may not have been published, a copy of the text (in its original language or languages) will be filed with the Secretariat General of the Conference.

Every treaty or other international agreement of the character described which may be concluded hereafter shall be notified by the

Governments concerned within sixty (60) days of its conclusion to the Powers who are signatories of or adherents to this agreement.

II. The several Powers other than China will file with the Secretariat General of the Conference at their earliest convenience for transmission to the participating Powers a list, as nearly complete as may be possible, of all those contracts between their nationals, of the one part, and the Chinese Government or any of its administrative subdivisions or local authorities, of the other part, which involve any concession, franchise, option or preference with respect to railway construction, mining, forestry, navigation, river conservancy, harbor works, reclamation, electrical communications, or other public works or public services, or for the sale of arms or ammunition, or which involve a lien upon any of the public revenues or properties of the Chinese Government or of any of its administrative subdivisions. There shall be, in the case of each document so listed, either a citation to a published text, or a copy of the text itself.

Every contract of the public character described which may be concluded hereafter shall be notified by the Governments concerned within sixty (60) days after the receipt of information of its conclusion to the Powers who are signatories of or adherents to this agreement.

III. The Chinese Government agrees to notify in the conditions laid down in this agreement every treaty agreement or contract of the character indicated herein which has been or may hereafter be concluded by that Government or by any local authority in China with any foreign Power or the nationals of any Foreign Power whether party to this agreement or not, so far as the information is in its possession.

IV. The Governments of Powers having treaty relations with China, which are not represented at the present Conference, shall be invited to adhere to this agreement.

The United States Government, as convener of the Conference, understakes to communicate this agreement to the Governments of the said Powers, with a view to obtaining their adherence thereto as soon as possible.

Additional Resolution moved by Mr. Root.

Resolved, That the Signatory Powers will not support any agreements by their respective nationals with each other designed to create Spheres of Influence or to provide for the enjoyment of exclusive opportunities in designated parts of Chinese territory.

At the fifth plenary session, held February 1, these resolutions were unanimously approved by the Conference.

Commitments without Time Limits. The Chinese Delegation, among the Ten Points which it submitted to the Conference, asked that reasonable definite terms of duration should be attached to China's existing commitments which were without time limits.

This request was brought before the Committee of the Whole by Dr. Koo at its twenty-fourth meeting, held January 23. The Chairman, Secretary Hughes, called attention to the fact that there were manifestly certain commitments which were intended to be without time limit,—examples of such commitments were the agreement of the Powers to recognize the territorial and administrative integrity of China, and their commitments regarding fair dealing with each other, the abstention from seeking special privileges at the expense of each other, and the like. He asked, therefore, that Dr. Koo should state more specifically the commitments to which he desired a time limit to be set.

Replying to this, Dr. Koo said that it had been the intention of the Chinese Delegation, not that time limits should be set to all commitments which, by their terms, were without time limit, but that, when it was essentially just or expedient to do so, in view of one or the other of the parties to the commitment, it should be done. The proposition which the Chinese Delegation had made was that this desideratum should be borne in mind by any committee and other body that might be created in order to bring existing commitments into harmony with one another or with the principles adopted by the Conference.

In the discussion that followed it appeared that it was the general opinion of the Committee that this matter was one which China should take up with the parties directly concerned in each case. The Chinese Delegation therefore did not deem it expedient to press further the point.

Construction of Commitments. Among the requests made by the Chinese Delegation in the Ten Points which it submitted to the Conference was that, in the interpretation of instruments granting special rights or privileges, the well-established principle of construction should be observed that such grants should be strictly construed in favor of the grantors.

This matter was brought before the Committee at the same time that the question of commitments without time limits was presented. It received, however, practically no discussion. The Chairman ruled that, in his opinion, it was not desirable to adopt an abstract principle, that is, one without regard to the specific agreements to which it was applied, and this opinion seemed to be shared by the other Delegations —at any rate no dissent to it was recorded.

China's Ninth and Tenth Points. The ninth and tenth of the points presented by the Chinese Delegation to the Conference on November 16 were as follows:

> 9. Provision is to be made for the peaceful settlement of international disputes in the Pacific and the Far East.
> 10. Provision is to be made for future Conferences to be held from time to time for the discussion of international questions relative to the Pacific and the Far East, as a basis for the determination of common policies of the Signatory Powers in relation thereto.

These two propositions, though presented by China, had, in fact, no exclusive relation to China, but exhibited a wish upon her part that, with reference to all the questions of the Pacific and Far East, the Conference should make provision for the peaceful settlement of all future controversies that might arise between the Powers concerned. The fact, therefore, that the Conference took no affirmative action regarding them was not a denial to China of rights to which she thought herself entitled, but only a general opinion that, with reference generally to the political situation in the Pacific and Far East it was not feasible, at that time, to create arbitral or other specific instrumentalities for the settlement of such international controversies as might arise. The Conference did, however, as has been earlier seen, make provision for a Board of Reference which should be empowered to consider and report upon questions that might be referred to it regarding the Open Door and discriminations upon the Chinese Railways as provided for in the Nine Power Treaty Relating to the Principles and Policies to be Followed in Matters Concerning China. Also is to be noted Article VII of the Nine Power Treaty according to which the Powers agree that, whenever a situation arises involving, in the opinion of any one of them, the application of the stipulations of that treaty, and which renders desirable a discussion of such application, there shall be a full and frank communication between the contracting Powers concerned.

At the twenty-fourth meeting of the Committee of the Whole, the Chairman, Secretary Hughes, referred to the fact that China was a member of the permanent court of arbitration at The Hague, and that, so far as concerned controversies between nations which were susceptible of settlement according to judicial standards, he doubted whether it was desirable to duplicate already existing machinery.

At the last (thirty-first) meeting of the Committee, Mr. Sze said that, in view of Article VII of the Nine Power Treaty, the Chinese Delegation desired to withdraw the ninth and tenth of its proposals. This Article, he said, amply covered what the Chinese Delegation had in mind when it proposed them.

CHAPTER XXIII

Shantung

As is well known, the long pending controversy between China and Japan with reference to the rights claimed by Japan in and over the leased area, of Kiaochow and in the Province of Shantung was not settled in the committee room of the Conference, but was adjusted in connection with that Conference by " Conversations " entered into between the Chinese and Japanese Delegations under the " good offices " of Secretary Hughes and Mr. Balfour. That these Conversations had been entered upon was reported to the Conference and several times referred to in the proceedings of that body, and, when an agreement was finally reached, the fact was reported to the Conference by its Chairman, and the text of the agreement spread upon its official records.

At the tenth meeting of the Committee of the Whole, held November 30, Baron Kato announced that, through the kind offices of Secretary Hughes and Mr. Balfour and at their suggestion and arrangement, conversations were to be entered upon with a view to the settlement, if possible, of the questions relating to Shantung. Secretary Hughes said that it had been a keen pleasure both to himself and to Mr. Balfour to make this suggestion, and Mr. Sze made the following statement:

The Chinese delegation has not solicited or asked for the meeting of the Chinese and Japanese delegations, as the Government and people of China have always hoped to be able to present this very important question to the consideration of the conference, not with any desire to add to the labors of the conference or to embarrass any delegation interested in this question, but merely in the hope of obtaining a fair and just settlement. The Chinese Government, however, deeply appreciates the friendly sympathy and interest which Mr. Hughes and Mr. Balfour, representing two great powers equally friendly to China and Japan, have manifested in offering their good offices, and the Chinese delegation, therefore, have the pleasure of accepting the kind offer, of course, in the hope that a fair and just settlement may be soon reached and reported to the Conference, and without qualifying its freedom to seek other methods of settlement in the unhappy event of inability to reach an agreement for a fair and just settlement.

When, at its fifth plenary session, held February 1, 1922, the Shantung Agreement was reported to the Conference, its Chairman, Secretary Hughes, said:

While the work of the Conference and of its Committees has been in progress, Conversations have been had between the representatives of China and Japan for the purpose of settling the controversy which has arisen in relation to Shantung. I am happy to be able to announce to the Conference that I have been informed by the representatives of the Governments of China and Japan that this controversy has been settled. I now propose to communicate to the Conference the terms of settlement as they have been agreed upon by the representatives of the two Governments.

Mr. Sze, in behalf of his Government and of the Chinese people, expressed the thanks of the Chinese Delegation for the extension of the good offices by Secretary Hughes and Mr. Balfour, which, he said, had made possible the Shantung conversations. He continued:

SHANTUNG

His Excellency, the President of the United States, in his invitation to the Powers to attend the Conference, expressed the hope that through the facilities of intercourse which it would provide, it might be possible to arrive at understandings with respect to matters which have been of international concern, and thus to promote enduring friendship among the nations whose interests have been involved. Animated by the same hope and desire, the Chinese Delegation, in the conversations which were held, with the valuable assistance of observers so kindly designated by Mr. Hughes and by Mr. Balfour, sought to accommodate its views, so far as it could consistently with China's rights and legitimate interests, to those of the Japanese Delegation, in order that a meeting of minds might be arrived at and a program provided whereby an end might be put to the controversy which not only has disturbed the friendly relations between the Chinese and Japanese people but has furnished a cause of concern to the other Powers.

This hope and this desire upon the part of the Chinese Government and of the Chinese people now appears certain to be realized. Such a program has found embodiment in the series of agreements and understandings which are to be incorporated into a treaty to be signed by the Governments of China and Japan.

The Chinese Delegation rejoices in the settlement of this question not only because a source of friction between its Government and that of Japan has been removed, but because the Chinese Government is thus able to aid in the realization of the beneficent aim for the attainment of which this Conference was convened.

It will be remembered that it was upon this occasion that Mr. Balfour declared the intention of the British Government to surrender to China the leased area of Weihaiwei.

At the sixth plenary session, Secretary Hughes announced to the Conference that the Shantung agreement which he had previously reported, had been put into final treaty form and was ready for signature by the representatives of the Governments of China and Japan. These signatures were attached on February 4.

Reasons for Resorting to the Conversations. Whether or not the Chinese Delegation should enter upon the Shantung Conversations was not an easy one for its members to decide. Upon the one hand, there had been an insistent demand upon the part of the articulate elements of the Chinese population that the Chinese Government should not enter upon any direct negotiations that would, in any way, imply that the Japanese had rights in Shantung such as would furnish a basis for negotiation, and that the whole question should be taken to the Conference with a view to obtaining its action thereupon. Upon the other hand, there was every reason to believe that, should this latter be taken, no remedial results would be obtained, with the result that the Japanese would be left in still firmer possession of the leased area of Kiaochow, the Shantung Railway and other interests in the Province, and with little likelihood that they would be dispossessed in the near future, if ever.

How futile would have been the hope of securing action on the Shantung Question by the Conference favorable to China was made plain—if indeed, it had not been abundantly plain before,—in a debate in the United States Senate upon a Resolution, introduced by Senator Walsh of Montana calling upon the President of the United States to state what steps had been taken by the American Government to give effect to various declarations which it had, from time to time, made with reference to Japan's actions in and towards China.

In that debate, held on January 20, 1922, two of the American Delegates to the Washington Conference, Senators Underwood and Lodge, stated in terms that could not be misunderstood that, should the Shantung Question be brought before the Conference, China could not expect any favorable action. If this was the feeling of the American Delegation, it could be predicted what the action of the other Delegations would be. Senator Underwood said:

> The attitude of the American Delegation at the Conference now being held in Washington has been exactly in accord with the representations made by the Government of President Wilson and the Government of President Harding, The question has not been directly before the Conference, and manifestly it cannot come before the Conference until it is settled between the Governments of China and Japan, because seven of the Powers sitting in the Conference are signatory to the Treaty of Versailles, and, of course, cannot deny the conclusions reached in that treaty with reference to this [Shantung] territory until an agreement is reached between China and Japan. Therefore, seven of the Powers are unable to discuss the question as between Japan and China because they have already committed themselves by treaty.

Senator Lodge was equally explicit upon this point. He said:

> I am in thorough accord with what the Senator [Underwood] has said . . . . The question is not directly before the Conference, for the reason that seven of the Powers are committed by the treaty [of Versailles], and the matter must be worked out between the Republic of China and the Empire of Japan before the Conference can do anything. If they can reach an agreement, then the other Powers can come in and ratify it and stand upon it. . . . . I can give my assurance to the Senator [Walsh] and the Senate that so far as the American Delegation is concerned, they are using every effort they legitimately and properly can to bring about a settlement along the lines suggested by the Senator from Montana.

If any further assurance were needed that the Chinese Delegation would have made a serious mistake had they insisted upon bringing the Shantung Question before the Conference, before seeking an agreement with Japan outside of but collateral to the Conference, the results obtained from the presentation to the Conference of the other portions of the Agreements of May 25, 1915, with Japan, resulting from Japan's Twenty-One Demands upon China, would furnish it. As has been already seen, the presentation of those Agreements to the Conference led to no other concrete results than the surrender by Japan of two of the less important of the preferential rights she had obtained in Manchuria, and to the declaration that Group V of her original demands were no longer to be deemed matters postponed for future negotiations. This explicit disclaimer by Japan was, of course, not without its importance, but the other engagements which Japan had entered into in union with the other Powers at the Conference had already made it impossible for Japan, without gross bad faith again, at any future time, to press the Group V demands.

As further evidence of the good judgment displayed by the Chinese Delegation when it consented to enter upon the Shantung Conversations with the Japanese Delegation are the following facts regarding the Conversations themselves.

In the first place, these Conversations were to be held at Washington and while the Conference was in session. This meant that the environment was to be an exceptionally favorable one for China—a consideration which, as every one who has participated in the conduct of internal relations knows, is of great importance. At this Conference Japan was definitely upon the defensive and striving in every way possible to create a conviction that she was disposed to be just and reasonable in her dealings with China. The Conference itself had for its purpose the removal, by mutual concession upon the part of the Powers concerned, of existing causes of international controversy in the Far East, and thus created, as it were, a general atmosphere that was favorable to a settlement of disputes upon which the Powers were not already so definitely committed that no change of policy upon their part could be expected.

In the second place, the holding of these Conversations was at the suggestion, and in pursuance of the " good offices," of Secretary Hughes, the head of the American Delegation, and Mr. Arthur Balfour, the head of the British Empire Delegation, and representatives of these gentlemen were to be present at all the Conversations and were to have the right, at any time, to interpose with friendly suggestions. Finally, the results of the Conversations were to be reported to the Conference, and thus the whole procedure, though technically not in the Conference, was to be connected with and ancillary to that body.[1]

[1] It is worthy of note that there arose at one time during the Conversations a difference of view between the Chinese and Japanese representatives as to the manner in which, or the extent to which, the "good offices" of Secretary Hughes and Mr. Balfour might be availed of.

At the nineteenth meeting, held January 5, when it seemed that an *impasse* had been reached, the Chinese representatives suggested that the friendly offices of Secretary Hughes and Mr. Balfour should be resorted to. At the next meeting, held January 6, Baron Shidehara said that the instruc-

Scope of the Conversations. One further fact regarding the Conversations requires to be mentioned. This is, that, in entering upon them, the Chinese Government was not required to make any admissions or concessions regarding the legal or treaty rights of the Japanese Government or of its nationals in Shantung. Before the Conversations were begun it was definitely understood between the two Delegations that the discussions should be upon what was termed a purely *de facto* basis, that is, no arguments should be based upon legal as distinguished from equitable or factual premises. In other

tions from Tokyo were so explicit regarding the matter at issue that the Japanese Delegation was not in a position to solicit these good offices. Dr. Koo then said that it had been the understanding of the Chinese Delegates that the Conversations had been entered upon because of the offer of these good offices, which offer they regarded as continuing in character and therefore available at any time. That this was so he argued from the fact that representatives of both Secretary Hughes and Mr. Balfour were present at all the meetings, and that, at the opening meeting, both of these gentlemen had said that they would be ready at any time, should occasion arise, to extend their good offices, and that, for this offer, they had been thanked by the Japanese representatives. At the opening meeting Mr. Balfour had said that "he joined Mr. Hughes in saying that if, in the course of the Conversations, any circumstances should come to pass which called for friendly intervention on their part, it would be his great pleasure to offer his services. He was in that case entirely at the disposal of Mr. Hughes and the representatives of Japan and China." Mr. Hughes said that "he was in full accord with Mr. Balfour in offering services whenever needed."

To the suggestion upon the part of the Chinese representatives that the good offices should be resorted to, Baron Shidehara replied that his Delegation was not in a position to request them. Dr. Koo then asked that Mr. Hughes and Mr. Balfour be invited to attend the next meeting. To this Baron Shidehara said that his Delegation would not object to their presence, but they would not invite them to come, and that he did not see how they would be disposed to participate unless invited by both Delegations—that without such invitation their participation would amount to intervention.

words, neither the Chinese nor the Japanese were to rely upon the terms of existing Sino-Japanese treaties or other agreements, nor were the Japanese to base any of their contentions upon the provisions of the Treaty of Versailles. For the purposes of the Conversations the situation was thus reduced to this: Japan was in possession and exercising certain powers or rights in Shantung, but was ready to surrender them, or most of them, to the Chinese upon certain conditions. Should these conditions be accepted by the Chinese the whole controversy was to be considered closed. The purpose and scope of the Conversations was therefore to determine whether or not the two parties could arrive at an agreement as to these conditions. It was further agreed that all of the matters involved in the Shantung controversy were to be deemed interdependent in the sense that unless agreements were reached as to them all there was to be no agreement whatever.

The foregoing explanations will show how far the Shantung Conversations were from being the same as, or equivalent to, the direct negotiations between the two Governments which Chinese Government had previously refused to enter upon, and in opposition to which Chinese public opinion had so loudly spoken.

The Status of the Shantung Question. The general features of the Shantung Question are so well known to the world that only the briefest statement of them will be here required. It will be necessary, however, to speak with somewhat more particularity regarding the status of the controversy after the Treaty of

Versailles and at the time the Conversations were initiated in Washington.

It will be remembered that, in 1914, Japan, in pursuance of what she affirmed to be her obligation under the Anglo-Japanese Alliance, sent a military expedition against the German leased area of Kiaochow at the Eastern end of Shantung Province; that, in the military operations thus carried on, Japan paid no attention to the rights of China as a neutral State, and not only occupied the leased area with the important city and port of Tsingtao, but took military possession of the entire length of the railway running from Tsingtao to the capital of the Province Tsinanfu, a distance of nearly three hundred miles, where it joined with the important railways running from the north, through Peking and Tientsin to Shanghai;[2] that Japan also took possession of, and operated, certain mines formerly German owned; that Japan took possession of other mines that had not been so owned; that she erected radio stations, and stationed troops at various points in the Province; that, in one way or another, her nationals came into possession and claimed ownership of considerable amounts of real estate in the Province; that the operation of such public enterprises as the electric lighting, telephone, water and laundry services was carried on under Japanese authority; and finally, that Japan had gone so far as to assume and exercise, at various places, civil governmental rights such as could properly be claimed only by a territorial sover-

[2] This Shantung Railway was owned and operated by a corporation chartered by the German Empire. A few of its shares were Chinese owned.

eign. In short, Japan had assumed and exercised powers within Shantung that were in considerable excess of those that had been claimed or exercised by Germany.[3]

In 1915 had come the Twenty-One demands by Japan upon China which resulted in the Agreements of May 25, 1915, among which was the treaty which provided:

ARTICLE 1. The Chinese Government agrees to give full assent to all matters upon which the Japanese Government may hereafter agree with the German Government relating to the disposition of all rights, interests and concessions which Germany, by virtue of treaties or otherwise, possesses in relation to the Province of Shantung.

ARTICLE 2. The Chinese Government agrees that as regards the railway to be built by China herself from Chefoo or Lungkow to connect with the Kiaochow-Tsinanfu railway, if Germany abandons the privilege of financing the Chefoo-Weihsien line, China will approach Japanese capitalists to negotiate for a loan.

ARTICLE 3. The Chinese Government agrees in the interest of trade and for the residence of foreigners, to open by China herself as soon as possible certain suitable places in the Province of Shantung as Commercial Ports.

In connection with this treaty the following further agreement was entered into by an Exchange of Notes:

When, after the termination of the present war, the leased territory of Kiaochow Bay is completely left to the free disposal of Japan, the Japanese Government will restore the said leased territory to China under the following conditions:

---

[3] This is irrespective of such other matters as the displacement of Chinese employees on the railway by Japanese nationals; the introduction of vast amounts of morphia into the country, the export, in violation of Chinese law, of many tons of copper " cash "; and the assertion of special rights with reference to the administration of the Chinese Maritime Customs service at Tsingtao.

1. The whole of Kiaochow Bay to be opened as a commercial port.

2. A Concession under the exclusive jurisdiction of Japan to be established at a place designated by the Japanese Government.

3. If the foreign Powers desire it, an International Concession may be established.

4. As regards the disposal to be made of the buildings and properties of Germany and the conditions and procedure relating thereto, the Japanese Government and the Chinese Government shall arrange the matter by mutual agreement before the restoration.

As is well known, because of the circumstances under which the Agreements of May 25, 1915, were entered into, and because of their substantive character, the people of China have ever asserted their right to escape from them at the first possible opportunity.

On September 24, 1918, the following letter from the Japanese Minister for Foreign Affairs was sent to the Chinese Minister at Tokyo:

> In view of the friendly relations existing between your country and Japan and in pursuance of the spirit of harmony and reconciliation, the Imperial Government considers it proper that the various questions in Shantung should be arranged in the following manner, and has decided to bring the matter to the notice of your Government.
>
> With regard to the Japanese troops stationed along the Kiaochow-Tsinan Railway, all the troops shall be concentrated at Tsingtao except for the stationing of a detachment at Tsinan.
>
> The guarding of the Kiaochow-Tsinan Railway is to be undertaken by your Government by the organization of a police force for the purpose.
>
> The expenditure required for the maintenance of the police force shall be defrayed by the Kiaochow-Tsinan Railway.
>
> Japanese shall be engaged for the headquarters of this police force, at the principal railway stations and at the police training school.

SHANTUNG 289

Chinese are to be engaged as employees on the Kiaochow-Tsinan Railway.

When the status of the Kiaochow-Tsinan Railway shall have been established it shall be conjointly worked by Japanese and Chinese.

The Civil Administration now in force shall be abolished.

I shall deem it a great favor if you will let me know your opinion concerning the above matter.

MacMurray in his compilation of the *Treaties and Agreements with and Concerning China* (p. 1445) in a footnote to the text of the foregoing letter, says that, according to an Associated Press dispatch from Paris, February 25, 1919, the Chinese Minister replied to the letter, saying: " I beg to acquaint you in reply that the Chinese Government gladly agree to the proposals of the Japanese Government above alluded to."

By an agreement of September 28, 1918, between the Chinese Minister to Japan and the Industrial Bank of Japan representing a syndicate of Japanese banks, the Chinese Government was represented as agreeing that all money necessary for the construction of railways between Tsinan in Shantung and Shunte in Chihli Province, and between Kaomi in Shantung and Hsuchow in Kiangsu Province, would be obtained from the Japanese banks in the form of gold bonds, with the proviso that, should, after survey, the railways be deemed unprofitable undertakings, the Chinese Government should confer with the banks regarding a change of their routes.

As is also well known, the Treaty of Versailles signed by the Allied Powers with Germany, was not signed by China because it contained the following provisions regarding the disposition of the former German rights in Shantung:[4]

ARTICLE 156. Germany renounces, in favour of Japan, all her rights, title and privileges—particularly those concerning the territory of Kiaochow, railways, mines and submarine cables—which she acquired in virtue of the Treaty concluded by her with China on March 6, 1898, and of all other arrangements relative to the Province of Shantung.

All German rights in the Tsingtao-Tsinanfu Railway, including its branch lines, together with its subsidiary property of all kinds, stations, shops, fixed and rolling stock, mines, plant and material for the exploitation of the mines, are and remain acquired by Japan, together with all rights and privileges attaching thereto.

The German State submarine cables from Tsingtao to Shanghai and from Tsingtao to Chefoo, with all the rights, privileges and properties attaching thereto, are similarly acquired by Japan, free and clear of all charges and encumbrances.

ART. 157. The movable and immovable property owned by the German State in the territory of Kiaochow, as well as all the rights which Germany might claim in consequence of the works or improvements made or of the expenses incurred by her, directly or indirectly, in connection with this territory, are and remain acquired by Japan, free and clear of all charges and encumbrances.

ART. 158. Germany shall hand over to Japan within three months from the coming into force of the present Treaty the archives, registers, plans, title-deeds and documents of every kind, wherever they may be, relating to the administration, whether civil, military, financial, judicial or other, of the territory of Kiaochow.

Within the same period Germany shall give particulars to Japan of all treaties, arrangements or agreements relating to the rights, title or privileges referred to in the two preceding Articles.

For the purposes of this chapter it is not necessary to review the grounds upon which the Chinese Government refused to recognize the operative force of

[4] These provisions also played a considerable part in the refusal of the United States to sign the treaty.

the foregoing provisions of the Versailles Treaty. Of course China, not being a signatory party to that treaty, could not be bound by its provisions taken by themselves. This none of the Powers, including Japan, could claim. It was, however, asserted that, independently of that treaty, and prior to it, namely by the Shantung Treaty of May 25, 1925, China had agreed to abide by any disposition that Germany might make of her Shantung rights. As to this it is sufficient to say that the Chinese Government held that, even if it should be granted *arguendo* that the Agreements of May 25, 1915, were binding upon itself, the Shantung treaty had ceased to have any force in 1919, and, furthermore, that, at the time the Paris Treaty was signed Germany had, in fact, no valid rights in Shantung—that these had disappeared when China declared war against Germany and announced that thereby all treaties between herself and that country were abrogated.

Correspondence Between China and Japan. The statement of the foregoing facts has been necessary in order to explain the *impasse* that had been reached between China and Japan with reference to the presence of the Japanese in Shantung. Japan wished to negotiate with China with regard to a definitive settlement of the whole controversy, but China could not consistently do this so long as Japan insisted that these negotiations should be predicated upon treaties and other agreements the validity or pertinency of which she, China, did not admit.

In a statement issued at Tokyo on June 15, 1920, the Japanese ministry of Foreign Affairs expressed the regret that, though it had sought to open negotiations with China for the restoration of Kiaochow to China and the settlement of other matters relating thereto, it had received no reply to its communication of January 24, 1920, until May 22, when the Chinese Government had said (in part):

> The Chinese Government have noted that it is the intention of the Japanese Government now that the Treaty of Peace [with Germany] has come into force to restore Kiaochow to China and to prepare for the withdrawal of the troops from along the Kiaochow-Tsinanfu Railway. China, however, has not signed the Treaty of Peace with Germany, and is not therefore in a position to negotiate directly with Japan on the question of Tsingtao on the basis of that Treaty. Furthermore, as the Japanese Minister at Peking is very well aware, the whole people of China have assumed a strongly antagonistic attitude in regard to the question in hand. For these two reasons, and because of the importance they have attached to amity between Japan and China, the Chinese Government naturally felt it inconvenient to make a reply at the time. On the other hand, the Japanese military establishments within and without the leased territory of Kiaochow have been rendered unnecessary and, as it is the hearty desire of the people and Government of China to have the conditions along the Shantung Railway restored to the pre-war footing, the Chinese Government proposes to form at an early date a proper organization to take the place of the Japanese troops in guarding the whole line. However, this proposition has nothing to do with the settlement of the question of Kiaochow and the Chinese Government trust that the Japanese Government will not delay the withdrawal of the troops on account of that question.

To this communication the Japanese Government replied by asserting that the Chinese Government had given its formal agreement to the disposition that might be made, and which was made in the Treaty of Versailles, of the German rights in Shantung. As to the withdrawal of its troops stationed in

Shantung, it declared that this was but one of the several questions to be determined when a settlement of the Shantung Question as a whole should be reached.[5]

Japanese Note of September 7, 1921. On September 7, 1921, the Japanese Government again addressed the Chinese Government with reference to Shantung, this time stating specifically the conditions upon which it was prepared to settle the entire controversy. As these conditions and the Chinese answer to them constituted, in considerable measure, the basis upon which the " Conversations " were carried on, it is desirable to state them in full. They were as follows:

1. To return to China the Lease of the Kiaochow Bay Territory and the right relating to the Neutral Zone.

2. In case the Chinese Government on its own initiative throws open the entire Leased Territory as a commercial port, recognizes the liberty of residence, commerce, industry, agriculture, and other lawful undertakings of foreigners, and respects and recognizes the vested rights of foreigners, the Japanese Government agrees to the withdrawal of the proposal for the establishment of a special and international settlements. With a view to foreign residence and commerce the Chinese Government will as soon as possible throw open suitable cities and marts in the Province of Shantung. The regulations governing the opening as marts of the above-mentioned places will be formulated by the Chinese Government in consultation with the interested countries.

3. The Shantung Railway and the mines thereto appertaining are to be considered as an organization under joint Chinese and Japanese operation.

[5] For the foregoing correspondence, see *China Year Book*, 1921-1922, pp. 716-719.

4. All preferences and options relating to the employment of persons and the supply of capital and materials that are based on the Kiaochow Convention are to be renounced.

5. The Right to the extension of the Shantung Railway and any option with regard to the Chefoo-Weihsien and other railways are to be assigned to the common undertakings of the new Consortium.

6. The Customs Administration at Tsingtao is to be made even more truly and clearly than the system under the German régime an integral part of the Chinese Customs Administration.

7. The Administrative government properties within the Leased Territory is in principle to be ceded to China, but further agreements will be made relating to the administration and maintenance of public constructions.

8. For the conclusion of further agreements relative to the details involved in the execution of the above-mentioned arrangements and to other matters the Chinese and Japanese Governments shall as soon as possible appoint delegates.

9. Although further agreements are to be concluded between China and Japan relative to the organization of the Special Police Force for the Shantung Railway, upon the receipt of the notification from the Chinese Government of the organization of the Police Force the Japanese Government shall, according to its repeated declarations, immediately announce the withdrawal of its troops and shall withdraw them upon the handing over of the functions of policing the railway to the Police Force.

China's Answer. The answer of the Chinese Government, dated October 5, declared:

The reason why China has not until now been able to commence negotiations with Japan is because of the fact that the basis upon which Japan claims to negotiate are all of a nature either highly objectionable to the Chinese Government and the Chinese people, or such to which they have never given their recognition. . . . After careful consideration the Chinese Government feels that much in Japan's new proposals is still incompatible with the repeated declarations of the Chinese Government, with the hopes and expectations of the entire Chinese people, and with the principles laid down in treaties between China and the foreign Powers. If these proposals are to be considered the final concession on the part of Japan, they surely fall short to prove the sincerity of Japan's desire to settle the question.

The Chinese communication then went on to examine, *seriatim,* the Japanese proposals, indicating the respects in which they were deemed unsatisfactory. The lease of Kiaochow, it was declared, had expired immediately upon China's declaration of war against Germany and, therefore, Japan had over that area nothing more than bare military posession—no leasehold right whatever. Agricultural pursuits, it was said, concern a fundamental means of existence of the people of a country and, according to the usual practice of all countries, foreigners are not permitted, without express authority, to engage in them. The opening of additional Treaty Ports in Shantung was one to be determined wholly by China's judgment. The joint operation of the Shantung Railway, the Chinese Government declared " is objected to by the entire Chinese people." The Custom House at Tsingtao should be under the complete control and management of the Chinese Government and should have a status no different from that of any other Custom House in the Chinese Maritime Customs Administration. All public properties in the former leased area should be handed over to China without conditions necessitating special arrangements. The Japanese troops in Shantung should be immediately withdrawn and without regard to the restoration of the Kiaochow territory. The communication closed with the statement that " in view of the marked difference of opinion between the two countries, and apprehending that the case may long remain unsettled, China reserves to herself the freedom of seeking a solution of the question whenever a suitable occasion presents itself.''

On October 18, 1921, the Japanese Government again submitted a long communication to the Chinese Government in which it traversed the Chinese statement that the Kiaochow lease had been annulled by the Chinese declaration of war against Germany, and, in support of this contention, referred to the declaration of the German representative in May, 1921, to the Chinese Government that, by reason of the Versailles Treaty, Germany was unable to restore Kiaochow to China,—a declaration of fact, which, the Japanese note asserted, China had accepted. The note also called attention to the fact that the value of the railway and mines in Shantung held by Japan had been appraised by the Reparations Commission under the Versailles Treaty, and the amounts deducted from the sums due to Japan from Germany by way of reparations,—that, in this way, Japan had paid for these properties.

To this Japanese note the Chinese Government replied by repeating its regret that the Japanese Government should propose a basis of settlement so far from the hopes and expectations of the Chinese people that it could not be even considered, and by denying that it had given to the Japanese Government an assurance that it would open negotiations if that Government would present concrete proposals for consideration.

As for the declaration of the German representative to China in the preceding May, the Chinese Government pointed out that that statement was nothing more than one of regret upon the part of the German Government that, by *force majeure,* it was unable to restore Kiaochow to China, and that China had merely acknowledged this explanation as such and nothing more, and thus had given no recognition whatever of the validity of the Versailles Treaty.[6]

As to the Shantung Railway, somewhat misunderstanding the proposition that Japan had made with regard to its ownership and operation, and conceiving that Japan had expressed its willingness to vest half of its ownership in China, the Chinese Government declared its willingness to pay Japan for its half and thus to become the sole owner of the road.

Reasons why the Other Powers were Unwilling to have the Shantung Question Brought before the Conference. The correspondence which has been quoted or summarized serves to show the status of the Shantung Question at the time of the convening of the Washington Conference. The reasons why it would

[6] On May 5, 1921, an "Accord" was signed between China and Germany, as a basis for a definitive treaty, according to which amity and commerce between the two countries were restored, and the appointment of diplomatic and consular officials provided for. In connection with this agreement the German representative declared that Germany formally consented to the abrogation, so far as its nationals were concerned, of extraterritorial jurisdiction in China. With regard to Shantung the following statement was made:

"Constate que l'Allemagne par les événements de la guerre et par le traité de Versailles a été obligée de renouncer à tout ses droits, titres et privileges qu'elle a acquis, en vertu du traité passé par clle avec la Chine le 6 Mars 1898 et de tous autres actes concernant la province du Chantoung, et se trouve ainsi privée de la possibilité de les restitutuer à la China."

not be advantageous to China to insist that the entire matter should be brought before that Conference to the exclusion of any other mode of adjustment have been given. To these reasons it may be added that the other Powers participating in the Conference were, for reasons of their own, anxious that the controversy should not be brought before them in such a manner as to compel their action upon it. That Japan should not look forward with approval to a general discussion of her acts in and concerning Shantung was but natural, and it is known that she would have asserted that the matter was one which the Conference could not properly consider—that it was one to be decided wholly between herself and China. Thus it will be remembered that when the Treaties and Agreements of May 25, 1915, including of course the Shantung Treaty, were first brought before the Conference on January 5, 1922, Mr. Hanihara, speaking for the Japanese Delegation, said that " the question was one to be taken up between Japan and China, if it were to be taken up at all, and not at this Conference. He wished to make this point clear." It is also practically certain that the other Powers which signed the Treaty of Versailles, and especially Great Britain, had unwillingly agreed to the Shantung provisions, but had been compelled to do so because of agreements which they had entered into with Japan during the progress of the war. However, should the matter be again brought before them they would feel themselves obliged to honor their signatures to the Versailles Treaty. The United States was exceedingly anxious that justice should be done China in the matter, and that, in the interests of peace in the Far East, this disturbing controversy between China and Japan should be removed. Its hands were free, so far as the Versailles Treaty was concerned, but it clearly perceived, as has been earlier pointed out, that no repudiation of the Shantung clauses of that treaty by the Powers signatory to it could be expected. Therefore, it also was anxious that the matter should not be brought before the Conference. In addition to the futility of such a course which it perceived, it feared lest the success of the entire work of the Conference should be endangered by the discussions which would probably ensue. The United States would feel compelled to side with China, but this would result in no benefit to China since the other Powers would be obliged to support the *status quo* or, at any rate, the provisions of the Versailles Treaty. Thus the Conference would find itself openly and irreconcilably divided upon this important matter.

Conversations Agreed Upon. The foregoing were the considerations which led Secretary Hughes and Sir Arthur Balfour to extend to the Chinese and Japanese Delegations their " good offices " with a view to persuading them to enter into friendly Conversations outside the Conference, in order that they might, if possible, come to some agreement regarding Shantung, or, at any rate, to determine the specific points upon which they could reach an agreement, and thus reduce the entire controversy to the simplest and most definite form possible in case it should be finally found necessary to bring it before the Conference.

This suggestion, emanating from the chiefs of the American and British Delegations, the Chinese and Japanese Delegations accepted, and Conversations entered upon on December 1, which, extending to thirty-six in number, were terminated on January 31, and resulted in a full agreement upon all points, which agreement was embodied in a Treaty signed February 4, 1922.

Persons Participating in the Conversations. The Chinese Delegation was represented by its three Chief Delegates, Dr. Sze, Dr. Koo, and Dr. Wang and their secretaries.

The Japanese Delegation was represented at the first meeting by Baron Kato, Mr. Hanihara and Mr. Debuchi, and their secretaries. Beginning with the second meeting Baron Kato was replaced by Prince Tokogowa who was succeeded by Baron Shidehara.

His Excellency Mr. Hughes, representing America, and Mr. Balfour, representing Great Britain, were present at the first meeting. Thereafter, America was represented by Mr. J. V. A. MacMurray and Mr. Edward Bell; and Great Britain by Sir John Jordan (later replaced by Mr. A. Gwatkin) and Mr. M. W. Lampson.

Procedure. At the first meeting it was decided that the meetings should be informal; without a president or presiding officer; that as much publicity as possible should be given to the proceedings; that Dr. Koo and Mr. Hanihara should supervise the drafting of the press communiques; that minutes should be kept by the secretaries of the Chinese and Japanese Delegations with the assistance, when necessary, of the American and British representatives; that substitutes might be sent in place of plenipotentiaries; that the whole communications between Japan and China in relation to the Shantung Question might be used as a basis for discussions; and that at the close of each meeting the date should be agreed upon for the next meeting.

In the account of the discussions which follows the topical method of presentation will be adopted—a method which will most clearly exhibit the complexity of the controversy, and the significance of the specific agreements reached.

Restoration of Kiaochow. It was agreed without discussion that Japan should restore to China the former German leased area of Kiaochow. The details of the transfer, it was agreed, should be arranged for and carried out by a Joint Commission composed of six members, three of whom were to be appointed by the Chinese Government and three by the Japanese Government. This Commission, it was declared, should meet immediately upon the coming into force of the treaty, and the transfer of the administration of the leased area and of public properties to be completed as soon as possible, and, in any case, not later than six months from the coming into force of the Shantung Treaty.

It was specifically agreed by the Japanese Delegation that, at the time of the transfer of the leased area, Japan would hand over to China such archives, registers, plans, title deeds, and other documents, as she, Japan, might possess, or certified copies thereof, and which might be necessary for such transfer or be later useful to China in the administration of the area and the fifty kilometre zone around Kiaochow Bay.

It was also agreed that Japan would not seek the establishment in the former leased area of an exclusive Japanese "settlement" or an international settlement.

The Chinese Delegation, upon its part, agreed that the Government of China, pending the enactment and general application of laws regulating the system of local self-government in China, would ascertain the views of the foreign residents in Kiaochow in municipal matters directly affecting their welfare and interests. Also that the entire former leased area should be opened to foreign trade, and that, within it, foreign nationals should be permitted freely to reside and carry on commerce, industry and other lawful pursuits.

Customs. In its note of September 7, 1921, to the Chinese Government, the Japanese Government had declared that it desired that the Customs Administration at Tsingtao should be "even more truly and clearly than the system under the German régime an integral part of the Chinese Customs Administration." However, Mr. Hanihara, in behalf of his Delegation, asked that the Japanese language should be made one of the official languages of Customs Administration, and that there should be appointed upon the customs staff at Tsingtao a sufficient number of persons versed in that language. To these proposals Dr. Sze replied:

> We like our customs service to be the same everywhere; it is not convenient to have different languages in different ports. The Inspector General [of Maritime Customs] would be glad to give facilities to the traders of Japan, but we hardly think it possible to use a foreign language.

It was finally agreed that the Chinese Delegation should recommend to its Government that Japanese traders should be permitted to communicate in the Japanese language with the customs administration at Tsingtao, and that the Inspector-General in the selection of a suitable staff at Tsingtao should give consideration, within the limits of its established service regulations, to the diverse needs of the trade at Tsingtao. It was agreed that, with this understanding, the provisional Sino-Japanese agreement of August 6, 1915, with reference to the customs administration was to be deemed abrogated.

Public Properties. The return to China of the various public properties and public works or services in Tsingtao, their valuation, and the operation of them after their return, was one of the most difficult matters which the Delegations had to discuss.

The Japanese Delegation agreed, without discussion, that all public properties which Japan had acquired without cost to herself should be returned to China without compensation except for such improvements as she might have made upon them; and that this principle should apply not only to properties originally belonging to China and transferred to Germany at the time of the treaty of lease, but also to properties acquired and buildings or works constructed by Germany during the German régime. However, as to property acquired, or buildings or works constructed by Japan during Japanese occupation, compensation from China would be asked for. The Japanese Delegation further said that a few buildings and premises for the use of the Japanese consulate and for Japanese public schools, a cemetery, shrines, and other properties of a similar nature should be handed over to the Japanese community in Tsingtao for maintenance and preservation.

As to such public works as roads, water-works, parks, drainage and sanitary equipment, etc., the Japanese Delegation asked that, after being handed over to China, arrangement should be made for their satisfactory maintenance and management in the interest and welfare of the general public; and that such enterprises as the electric light, telephone, stock yard, etc., hitherto under Government management, should be handed over to Chinese corporations, to be organized for the purpose and with foreign stockholders.

The Chinese Delegation refused to accept the principle of compensation to be made by China for any properties properly belonging to the category of public properties, but said that they were willing that suitable properties, as above mentioned, might be reserved for use by the Japanese consulate and by the Japanese community at Tsingtao. As to properties acquired or buildings or works constructed by Japanese during the Japanese occupation, China would make a reasonable payment, due consideration being given to depreciation and to the fact that China had contributed 20 per cent of the Tsingtao customs revenues towards the expense of the leased area, and that the Japanese had made considerable profit from the operation of certain of the public works.

As to the maintenance and operation of public service after their return to China, the Chinese Delegation said that foreign interests in Tsingtao would be given a fair representation, but that no undertaking could be given as to the form of government that Tsingtao was to have.

After extended discussion it was agreed by the two Delegations that the Government of Japan should transfer to the Chinese Republic all public properties, including lands, buildings, works or establishments, public enterprises such as the telephone system, electric light, stock yard and laundry in the former leased area whether formerly possessed by the German authorities or purchased or constructed by the Japanese authorities during the period of Japanese administration; that, for this transfer, no compensation should be asked of the Chinese Government, but that for properties purchased or constructed by the Japanese authorities, and for improvements or additions to those formerly possessed by the German authorities, a fair and equitable proportion of the expense actually incurred by Japan (due regard being had to the principle of depreciation and continuing value) should be refunded by China. Also that such public properties as might be needed for the Japanese consulate to be established at Tsingtao should be retained by Japan; and those properties especially required for the benefit of the Japanese community, including public schools, shrines and cemeteries, should be left in the hands of that community.

Specifically it was agreed that, in the management and maintenance of the public works transferred, the foreign community in the former leased area should have fair representation; that, in the management of the telephone system due consideration would be given by the Chinese Government to requests of the foreign community for such extensions and improvements as might be reasonably required in the interests of the public; and that the Government of China, upon receiving the electric light, stock yard and laundry enterprises would re-transfer them to the Chinese municipal authorities of Tsingtao, which, in turn, should cause commercial companies to be formed for their operation and management subject to municipal regulation and supervision.

Vested Rights. As to these, after considerable discussion, it was agreed that " vested rights lawfully and equitably acquired by foreign nationals " in the former leased area, whether under the German régime or during the period of the Japanese administration, would be respected by the Chinese Government; and that all questions relating to the status or validity of such rights claimed by Japanese subjects or Japanese companies should be adjusted by the Joint Commission later to be referred to.

Salt. During the Japanese occupation, Japanese nationals became largely interested in the production of salt in Shantung; with the result that the annual output of salt, which, under the German régime, had been 84,000 tons had increased to 270,000 tons; and that very considerable amounts had been exported to Japan, which country was in great need of that commodity. The contention of the Japanese Delegation was that the interests of their nationals in this industry should be recognized and protected. This, the Chinese Delegation said, would be effected if the present Japanese interests were protected, but the industry prevented from so developing as to compete with the Chinese Government monopoly of the production and sale of salt, and at the same time, an arrangement made for the export to Japan of a fixed amount of salt. Reference was made by the Chinese Delegation to the fact that, during Japanese occupation, considerable amounts of salt had been smuggled to other parts of China by the Japanese. Mr. Hanihara said that he did not know that this was the case, but that the Japanese would be willing to cooperate with the Chinese Government to prevent smuggling in the future.

It was finally agreed that the interests of Japanese subjects or companies actually engaged in the salt industry along the coast of Kiaochow Bay should be purchased by the Chinese Government at a fair valuation and that the exportation to Japan of a quantity of salt produced by such industry along this coast should be permitted on reasonable terms.

Mines. It was agreed that the mines of Tsechwan, Fangtze and Chinlingchen, rights for which had been formerly granted to Germany, should be handed over to a company to be formed under a special charter to be granted by the Chinese Government, and according to which the amount of Japanese capital invested therein should not exceed that of the Chinese capital.

Withdrawal of Japanese Troops. As has been earlier seen, Japan had several times declared her readiness to withdraw her troops along the Shantung Railways as soon as a Chinese police or other military force should be sent to replace them. This undertaking was reaffirmed in the Conversations, with the specific understanding that this replacement should be effected in sections, and the entire withdrawal to be completed within three months, if possible, and, in any case, not more than six months from the date of the signing of the Shantung Treaty. The Japanese garrison at Tsingtao, it was agreed, should be withdrawn simultaneously, if possible, with the transfer to China of the administration of Kiaochow, and, in any case, within thirty days thereafter.

Wireless Stations. It was agreed that the Government of Japan should transfer to the Chinese Government for a fair compensation the Japanese wireless stations at Tsingtao and Tsinanfu upon the withdrawal of the Japanese troops at those places.

Submarine Cables. It was agreed that all the rights, titles and privileges concerning the former German submarine cables between Tsingtao and Chefoo and between Tsingtao and Shanghai, should become vested in China with the exception of those portions of these cables which had been utilized by the Government of Japan for laying a cable between Tsingtao and Sesabo, Japan. All questions relating to the landing and operation at Tsingtao of this last named cable, it was agreed, should be determined by the Joint Commission, later to be described, subject to the terms of existing contracts to which China is a party.

Renunciation by Japan of Preferential Rights in Shantung. It was agreed that the Government of Japan would renounce all preferential rights with respect to foreign assistance in persons, capital and material, which had been granted by China to Germany in the Treaty of lease of March 6, 1898. Also that, provided it were constructed with Chinese capital, Japan would not claim that the option for financing the proposed Chefoo-Weihsien Railway should be open to the common activity of the International Financial Consortium.

The Shantung Railway. Overshadowing in importance perhaps even the return to China of the administration of the Kiaochow area, was the question as to the conditions under which the Shantung Railway running from Tsingtao to Tsinanfu was to be restored to China. More than one-half of the Conversations were devoted to the consideration of this one subject, and it was upon this matter that the two Delegations found themselves deadlocked for a period of approximately a month.

The controversy centered mainly around the two points as to the form in which China should make payment to Japan for the road, and the amount of interest or control Japan should retain in the management and operation of the road after its surrender to the Chinese Government. However, there was also considerable difficulty in arriving at an agreement as to the manner in which valuation of the road and its appurtenant properties should be determined.

The Valuation of the Railway and Appurtenant Properties. There seemed to be some confusion at first as to the manner in which the Japanese Government had eliminated the German financial interests in the Railroad. This road, it will be remembered, had been owned and operated by a German chartered corporation in which the Chinese had a few (360) shares of 1000 marks each. The earlier offer of the Chinese Government to pay Japan one-half of the value of the railway properties upon their control and ownership being vested in the Chinese Government, had been based upon the assumption that those properties had been public property of Germany, and therefore subject to military seizure and condemnation, although it was of course not conceded that the Japanese had ever had a right to take possession or to assert ownership of any part of the line or properties outside of the leased area. However, as soon as it appeared that the railway properties had been regarded by the Japanese as private German property, and that the Japanese Government had agreed that their value—assessed by the Reparations Commission as 53,406,141 Gold Marks—should be deducted from the total of the pecuniary reparations due from Germany to Japan, the Chinese Delegation expressed its willingness to pay to Japan the entire value of the railway properties, less the surplus profit received by the Japanese from their operation of the road, and less also the amount represented by the Chinese-held shares in the German railway corporation.

Improvements and Additions. The question of improvements of and additions to the properties by the Japanese was then raised. The Chinese Delegation said that these would be compensated for in so far as they were permanent in character, were improvements or additions as distinguished from mere upkeep or replacement, and in so far as they had not been paid for by the Japanese out of the revenues of the railway itself.

Baron Shidehara asserted that since her occupation of the railway Japan had not been operating it as an agent of China and that, therefore, Japan should not be held accountable to China for the profits accruing from such operation. He admitted, however, that, since occupation, the Japanese had not accounted for any of the profits to the shareholders of the corporation in which the legal title to the railway had been vested.

Mr. Sze asked whether it was correct to assume that China would not be asked to pay for the go-downs, warehouses, as well as dock No. 3 which were connected with the Railway but were public properties. Baron Shidehara said that this was correct except as to any improvements that the Japanese might have made upon them. Mr. Sze asked further as to barracks for Japanese troops as well as wireless stations along the railway. Baron Shidehara said that these could be handed over at their actual value. Mr. Sze observed that they would have only a "residuary" value to the Chinese Government and should only be paid for upon such a basis. It was therefore agreed that the principles of depreciation and continuing value should receive their proper application.

As to the mode of determining the actual value of the road, the Chinese Delegation proposed the following formula:

China to pay the actual value of the Shantung Railway properties as represented by the Reparations Commission figure plus the actual amount, minus the depreciation, that was expended for such permanent improvements on or additions to the Railway properties as were effected by Japan during the period of her administration of the railway.

After considerable discussion regarding phraseology and other matters, and especially as to whether the term "Reparation Commission figure" should be replaced by a statement of the exact amount, the following formula was agreed to by both Delegations.

(1) Japan to transfer to China the Tsingtao-Tsinanfu Railway and its branches together with all the properties appurtenant thereto, including wharves and warehouses and other similar properties, it being understood that the question of the mines appurtenant to the Railway shall be set apart for separate consideration. The said transfer to be completed as soon as practicable and not later than nine months after the coming into force of the agreement of the whole Shantung question.

(2) China to pay to Japan the actual value of the Tsingtao-Tsinanfu Railway properties, consisting of the sum of 53,406,141 Gold Marks, or its equivalent, which is the assessed value of such railway properties, as were left behind by the Germans, plus the amount which Japan, during the period of her administration of the

Railway, has actually expended for permanent improvements on and additions to the railway properties, less a suitable allowance for depreciation. It is understood that no charge will be made for the transfer to China of wharves and warehouses and other similar properties mentioned in the preceding clause, except for such permanent improvements on and additions to them as may have been effected by Japan, less a suitable amount for depreciation.

Joint Railway Commission. It was also agreed that the Governments of China and Japan should each appoint three Commissioners to form a Joint Railway Commission, with power to appraise the actual value of the railway properties in accordance with the principles agreed upon. Furthermore, the understanding, to be embodied in an Exchange of Notes, was arrived at that should this Railway Commission fail to reach an agreement on any of the matters submitted to it, the points at issue would be taken up by the two Governments for discussion and adjustment by means of diplomacy.

In the Conversations the Chinese Delegation urged that these differences should be referred for discussion to a board of neutral experts to be chosen by mutual agreement upon the part of the two Governments, but this was declared unacceptable by the Japanese Delegation, the reason alleged being that this might produce the misgiving in the minds of the Japanese people that neutrals would be asked to settle differences between the two countries. In this connection it is interesting to note that, throughout the Conversations, the Japanese showed an unwillingness to accept any sort of procedure that savored of international arbitration. With regard, however, to the Joint Railway Commission they did agree that, in reaching its decisions it might, if necessary, obtain recommendations of an expert or experts of a third Power who should be designated by the mutual agreement of the Chinese and Japanese Governments.

Mode of Payment and Conditions to be Attached Thereto. An agreement between the two Delegations upon the foregoing matters having been reached, the question of the manner in which China should pay for the Railway and its properties was taken up.

The Chinese Delegation asked whether it was the desire of the Japanese Government that China should discharge her obligations as quickly as possible. The reply was that that was not the desire of Japan; but that she wished to retain a certain amount of interest in the Railway as was the case with regard to other Chinese Railways operated with the help of foreign loans. Asked if Japan would object to a cash payment, the Japanese Delegation said that she would.

Mr. Sze stated that the Chinese bankers had offered the Chinese Government a loan with a view to the purchase of the Railway, and, if that offer were accepted there would be no need for a foreign loan. Baron Shidehara, however, said that the Japanese Government would consider it discriminatory against itself should the Chinese Government decline the offer of Japan to make a loan. Mr. Sze pointed out that it was difficult to see how the Japanese Government could consider itself discriminated against in the matter of railway loans when its financial interests already held so many Chinese Railway loans,— loans aggregating 21,600,000 Yen in amount—an amount exceeded by the railway loans of only one other country. Mr. Sze further observed that it would be exceedingly difficult to explain to the Chinese people why the offer of a loan from their own banks was not accepted. Baron Shidehara said that the purpose in retaining a Japanese interest in the railway was not only to safeguard the commercial interests of the Japanese people, but mostly for the purpose of escaping criticism that might otherwise be created in Japan: that Japan had made concession as to joint operation, but wished to retain at least an interest in the railway.

The Chinese Delegation then proposed that the payment for the railway should be made in six installments at intervals of six months each, so that by the end of three years total payment would be made. The first installment would be made in cash, and the remaining five in Treasury Notes secured by revenues of the railway. Interest at a reasonable rate would be paid upon the deferred payments. Furthermore, the Chinese Government would give an assurance that in the operation of the railway there would be no discrimination against traders of any foreign nationality.

Japanese Propose Loan by Japanese Capitalists and Employment of Japanese as Chief Engineer, Chief Accountant, and Traffic Manager. Commenting upon this proposal, the Japanese Delegation found it unsatisfactory since it made no provision for continuing Japanese interest in the railway. Now for the first time the proposition was advanced by the Japanese Delegation that, not only should the railway be paid for by China by a loan from Japan, but that, during the currency of the loan, a Japanese Chief Engineer, a Japanese Traffic Manager and a Japanese Chief Accountant, nominated by the Japanese capitalists should be employed by the railway—these officials to be subject to supervision and control of the higher railway authorities. This arrangement, it was declared, would not interfere in any way with the complete ownership and operation or with the plan of unification of the Chinese Railways, which, it was understood, China was aiming at.

Some attempt was made by the Japanese to support this proposal upon the ground that the efficiency of the operation of the railway would thereby be advanced. This argument was, however, only mentioned, and no serious attempt made to sustain its validity. Indeed, as was later brought out, the statistics of the railways administered by the Chinese Government showed better results, viewed from the standpoint of efficiency, than those operated by the Japanese Government. The point more strongly pressed by the Japanese Delegation was that their proposal for the employment upon the Shantung Railway of a Japanese Chief Engineer, Traffic Manager and Chief Accountant was in conformity with conditions existing upon other Chinese railways and provided for in recent railway foreign loans.

As to this argument the Chinese Delegation had no difficulty in showing that the practice of employing foreign railway experts had grown up in China not because the nations had found any dissatisfaction with the management and administration of the Chinese railways, but because, at the time of the constructing of the railways and in the course of construction, the Bankers had simply seized the opportunity thus given them to obtain for their nationals these appointments. The Shantung Railway stood upon a wholly different footing. It was not a projected railway which was to be built, but was already constructed and in operation. Furthermore, it was quite possible that the Shantung Railway after its return to China's control would be operated in conjunction with the Tientsin-Pukow line, in which case the Chief Engineer, Traffic Manager and Accountant of that line could take care of the Shantung line. In other words, that there would be an unnecessary and expensive duplication of these officials should separate ones be appointed for the Shantung line.

It thus developed that the Japanese Delegation was anxious that the loan which the Chinese Government should obtain from Japanese capitalists should be a long term one and without an option of redemption upon the part of China until a considerable number of years should elapse. Upon reference being made to other long term railway loans, the Chinese Delegation was able to point out that they had been made for the purpose of constructing the railways concerned and not for financing or for the purchase of roads already built.

The Japanese Delegation then stated that it was desirable that the right of option upon the part of China to redeem the entire loan should not arise until after ten years, and that the term of the loan should be twenty years, and that China should engage to employ as Chief Engineer, Traffic Manager and Chief Accountant of the road three Japanese to be recommended by the Japanese capitalists making the loan, but who should be subject to the supervision of the Chinese Managing Director. Any intention upon the part of the Japanese Government to control the operation of the road was disclaimed but nevertheless it was declared that Japan placed great importance upon these appointments.

Mr. Sze pointed out that the main aim of the Chinese Government in operating the road would be economy and efficiency: that foreign experts already employed by the Government could be utilized: that the Shantung line was only 280 miles in length and would in all probability be operated in connection with the Tientsin-Pukow line, and, therefore, could utilize, without extra expense, the services of the Chief Engineer, Traffic Manager and Accountant of that line. Mr. Sze said that it might be possible to have a Japanese District Engineer to look after the maintenance of the Shantung line who might be selected from Japanese Engineers already in the Chinese Railway service, but that there was no necessity for a separate Traffic Manager or Chief Accountant. He pointed out that upon the Peking-Hankow Railway, which was as long as the Tientsin-Pukow and Tsingtao-Tsinan lines put together, there was but one Traffic Manager. In fact, said Mr. Sze, there would be no real need for a separate District Engineer for the Shantung line after its union with the Tientsin-Pukow line, and he had made the suggestion that such a post might be created and filled by a

Japanese only to show the willingness of the Chinese to meet, as far as possible, the wishes of the Japanese Delegation.

Baron Shidehara insisted that what the Japanese Delegation wanted was a Japanese Traffic Manager and a Chief Accountant, that a Japanese Chief Engineer would not be insisted upon, and that unless this arrangement was arrived at, it would be difficult for Japan to accept payment in Treasury Notes.

The Japanese Delegation asked whether, if cash payment were agreed upon, the Chinese would pay the entire sum into the bank of a neutral Power prior to or at the time that the process of transferring the railroad should begin, which bank should pay the amount to Japan as soon as the transfer was completed.

To this question the Chinese Delegation replied that such a procedure would not only lead to a disturbance of the money market but necessarily entail upon China a very considerable loss in interest, since, while the money would be in the bank, only a very low rate of interest upon it would be paid as compared with that which the Chinese bankers could obtain from its use. Also there was the difficulty that at present the Chinese Delegation did not know how large the total sum would be, the value of the improvements and additions made by Japan not having been determined. It was therefore suggested by the Chinese Delegation that the Joint Commission for determining values, when it had finished its work, should decide how much money should be deposited at the outset in the bank of the third Power, and that the remaining amounts be paid in, *pari-passu* as the transfer of the Railway and its appurtenant properties was proceeded with. Concretely, Mr. Sze suggested that two-fifths of the total amount should be paid in at the end of the first three months after the conclusion of the Shantung agreement; that at the end of another three months another fifth be paid in; and that the last two-fifths be paid in at the end of nine months after the signing of the agreement.

The Japanese Delegation said that it objected to this plan upon the ground that it did not furnish a sufficient guarantee that, after the transfer of the railway properties had begun, the remaining three-fifths would surely be paid into the bank. To this the Chinese Delegation pointed out that no business transactions were possible without some degree of confidence in one another's good faith and ability,— that merchants sold and delivered goods upon the understanding that they would be paid for when received. The Japanese Delegation, however, stood firmly upon the condition that, if cash payment were made the entire amount would have to be paid into a bank of a third Power before the transfer of the road should begin.

A deadlock having been reached upon the foregoing points, the Conversations were discontinued on December 20 until the Japanese Delegation could receive further instructions from its Government, and it was thus not until January 6 that the next meeting was had. After discussions running through two more meetings, the two Delegations found themselves still in disagreement and it was at this time, as

SHANTUNG 321

has been earlier referred to, that the Chinese Delegates suggested that the " good offices " of Secretary Hughes and Mr. Balfour be resorted to—a suggestion which the Japanese representatives expressed themselves as unwilling, or unable under their instructions, to accept. The meetings were thereupon adjourned *sine die,* pending further developments.

The Issue Drawn. In the Communique issued to the press the situation that had been reached was stated in the following terms:

The Japanese Delegates proposed a railway loan agreement plan for the settlement of this question on the basis of the terms of ordinary railway loan agreements entered into by China with various foreign capitalists during recent years, namely, on the following general lines:

1. The term of the loan shall be fixed at fifteen years while China shall retain an option of redeeming the whole outstanding liabilities upon six months' notice after five years from the date of the agreement.

2. A Japanese Traffic Manager and a Chief Accountant shall be engaged in the service of the Shantung Railway.

3. The details of the financial arrangement shall be worked out at Peking between the representatives of the two parties to the loan.

This plan was not found acceptable to the Chinese Delegation.

The Chinese Delegates, on their part, proposed the following two alternative plans:

1. China to make a cash payment for the railway and its appurtenant properties with a single deposit in a bank of a third Power at a specified date either before the transfer of the properties or when such transfer is effected.

2. China to make a deferred payment either in Treasury Notes or Notes of the Chinese Bankers' Union secured upon the revenues of the railway properties, extending over a period of twelve years with an option on the part of China at any time after three years

upon giving six months' notice to pay all the outstanding liabilities. The first installment to be paid on the day on which the transfer of the railway and properties is completed.

China to select and employ in the service of the Tsingtao-Tsinanfu Railway a district Engineer of Japanese nationality.

Neither of these plans was found acceptable to the Japanese Delegation in their present form.

Informal Conversations and Interviews. Meetings of the two Delegations were resumed on January 11 for the consideration of other questions involved in the Shantung controversy, but it was not until January 30 that the two Delegations found themselves in a position again to take up the matter of the railway.

During this interval of more than three weeks a number of plans emanating from American and British sources were brought to the attention of the Chinese and Japanese representatives with a view to bringing them, if possible, into agreement. Also personal and, of course, wholly informal interviews were held with Secretary Hughes, Mr. Balfour and other representatives of the American and British Governments. Mr. Sze, of the Chinese Delegation, also had an interview with Mr. Harding, President of the United States. As a result of these efforts, it finally appeared that an agreement might be reached upon certain terms that had been brought to the attention of both Delegations, and, therefore, with this expectation in view, the matter of the Shantung Railway was again taken up in the Conversations at the meeting held January 30.

Agreement Reached. At this and the next meeting, held the following day, the following agreements in addition to those previously reached, were arrived at:

(1) The transfer of the railway and its appurtenant properties to the Chinese Government to be completed as soon as possible and in any case not later than nine months from the date of the coming into force of the Shantung Treaty;

(2) China to make payment for the railway in Chinese Government Treasury Notes, secured on the properties and revenues of the railway, and running for a period of fifteen years, but redeemable, whether in whole or in part, at the option of China, at the end of five years from the date of the delivery of the Notes, or at any time thereafter upon six months' previous notice;

(3) Pending the redemption of these Notes the Government of China to select and appoint a Japanese subject as Traffic Manager of the road and another Japanese subject as Chief Accountant jointly with a Chinese Chief Accountant with coordinate functions; these officials to be under the "direction, control and supervision" of the Chinese Managing Director of the road and to be removable for cause.

Understandings Recorded in the Minutes. The following additional understandings were reached in the Conversations and recorded upon their Minutes:

1. That the redemption by China of the Treasury Notes will not be effected with funds raised from other than Chinese sources.

2. That financial details of a technical character relating to the Notes will be determined in mutual accord between the Chinese and Japanese authorities as soon as possible, but in any case not later than six months from the coming into force of the Shantung Agreement.

3. That the transfer of the road shall be completed as soon as possible, and in any case, not later than six months from the date of the coming into force of the Shantung agreement.

4. That all light railways, including the lands appurtenant thereto, built by Japan in Shantung during her military occupation

shall be transferred to China at the time the Shantung Railway is transferred.

5. That, after two and a half years from the date of the transfer of the Railway, the Chinese Government may appoint an Assistant Traffic Manager of Chinese Nationality, for a period of two and a half years, and that such Assistant Chinese Traffic Manager may also be appointed at any time after six months' notice for the redemption of the Treasury Notes is given by the Chinese Government.

6. That Japan has no intention to claim that China is under any obligation to appoint Japanese nationals as members of the subordinate staff of the Japanese Traffic Manager or of the Japanese Chief Accountant. The discussion showed, as to this understanding, that Japan would make no such claim as a matter either of legal right or of fact.

7. That the Chinese Managing Director of the Railway will appoint the entire subordinate staff of the Japanese Traffic Manager and the Japanese Chief Accountant.

8. That, in the selection of Japanese experts for the positions of Traffic Manager and Chief Accountant, the Chinese Government will ask the Japanese Government for such information as may be useful in making suitable selections.

9. That, on the taking over of the Shantung Railway, the Chinese authorities are to have full power and discretion to continue or to remove the present employees of Japanese nationality in the service of the Railway, and that reasonable notice of dismissal may be given before the date of the transfer of the Railway. Detailed arrangements regarding the replacements, which are to take effect immediately upon the transfer of the Railway, are to be made by the Chinese and Japanese authorities.

10. That, pending the transfer to China of the Shantung Railway, no new agreements or contracts will be made on that railway by the present administration; and that as to existing contracts or other commitments, which may conflict with Chinese railway policy or interests, the present administration will see to it that their operation ceases with the transfer of the Railway to China, but that this understanding is not to prevent the Japanese authorities from buying material for making repairs that are absolutely necessary to the Railway.

11. That the construction of the Chefoo-Weihsien Railway is to be financed by Chinese capitalists.

12. That the telegraph administration is part of the Shantung Railway and will be handed back to China at the time the Railway is transferred.

13. That all the Japanese post-offices in Shantung outside of the leased area of Kiaochow will be withdrawn before January 1, 1923, if the Shantung Agreement has come into force before that date; and that, otherwise, they will be withdrawn not later than that date. That all Japanese post-offices within the leased area will be withdrawn at the time of the transfer to China of the administration of that area.

14. That the forestry in the leased area connected with the conservation of water supply will be transferred to China in the same category as the other public properties formerly belonging to Germany.

15. That all claims for restitution of land in Shantung belonging to Chinese citizens but occupied by Japanese authorities without satisfactory arrangements, and all claims for compensation arising from injuries caused in Shantung to the public property of China or to persons and property of Chinese citizens by Japanese authorities, during the period of Japanese occupation, shall be jointly investigated by a Sino-Japanese Commission and if they are found just, the Japanese Government will cause fair reparation to be made.

16. That all claims for lands in Shantung belonging to Chinese citizens but occupied by Japanese subjects, without satisfactory arrangements, and all claims for compensation arising from injuries caused in Shantung to the public property of China or to the persons or property of Chinese citizens by Japanese subjects, during the period of Japanese occupation, shall be similarly investigated for final adjustment.

17. That the omission of reference in the Shantung Treaty to questions of claims shall not be deemed to prejudice any claims which China or Chinese citizens may have against the Japanese Government or against Japanese subjects arising during the period of Japanese occupation.

Joint Commission. For the settlement of various matters and details upon which it was not possible to come to a precise and definite agreement in the Conversations, or to provide for in the Shantung Treaty itself, it was agreed that there should be created a Joint Commission of six members, three to be appointed by each of the two Governments, which was to have the following functions and powers:

To make and carry out detailed arrangements relating to the transfer of the administration of the former German Leased Territory of Kiaochow and to the transfer of public properties in the said Territory and to settle other matters likewise requiring adjustment. (Article II of Shantung Treaty.)

By other provisions of the Shantung Treaty this Commission is specifically authorized:

1. To arrange details regarding the transfer of public properties;
2. To arrange the mode and terms upon which the mines of Tsechwan, Fangtze and Chinlingchen are to be vested in a Chinese chartered corporation.
3. To adjust all questions relating to the status or validity of vested rights acquired in Kiaochow by Japanese subjects or companies.
4. To make arrangements for the transfer to China of Japanese interests in the salt industries and the exportation to Japan of a quantity of salt produced by such industries.
5. To arrange details of the transfer of and compensation for, the Japanese wireless stations at Tsingtao and Tsinanfu.

Results of the Conversations Communicated to Secretary Hughes and Mr. Balfour. It was agreed that the results of the Conversations should be reported to Secretary Hughes and Mr. Balfour. This was done by both the Delegations on February 1, and, as has been earlier mentioned, Mr. Hughes in turn reported these results to the Conference.

An Estimate of the Merits of the Shantung Agreement. Inasmuch as, in the opinion of the writer, Japan never had equitable rights in Shantung save, possibly, such as might have accrued to her during the period when her occupation of Kiaochow was justified by strict military necessity, it can scarcely be said that there was an equitable basis for such concessions as were made to her by the Chinese in the final Shantung settlement. It is clear, however, that, from the juristic point of view, Japan had in Shantung legal rights *vis a vis* China which could only be denied by denying the validity of the Sino-Japanese Agreements of 1915 and 1918. But, leaving aside questions both of equitable and legal rights, and regarding the situation that existed at the time the Conversations were entered upon, namely, that Japan was in actual possession and China was without the power to dispossess her, it is easily demonstrable that China won an almost complete victory. The Kiaochow lease and the other rights that had been granted to Germany are wholly abrogated. China is to get back all the public properties in Tsingtao and the Province generally under conditions as regards compensation, etc., that are essentially reasonable and such as she would presumably have been fully willing to grant to Germany had Germany, before the war, offered to surrender them to China. Every vestige of special German or Japanese treaty or contractual rights in the Province disappears, with only the following exceptions so far as Japan is concerned:

1. Such public properties in the former leased area as may be needed for the Japanese Consulate, are to be retained by Japan and properties for the special benefit of the Japanese community in Kiaochow, such as public schools, shrines and cemeteries, are to be left in the hands of that community.

2. The mines of Tsechwan, Fangtze and Chinlingchen are to be operated by a company chartered by the Chinese Government in which Japanese capital may equal the Chinese capital.

3. The exportation to Japan of a quantity of salt produced by salt industries along the coast of Kiaochow Bay is to be permitted by the Chinese Government, on reasonable terms.

4. In the management and maintenance of the public works in the former leased area, the foreign community (most of whom are now Japanese) are to have fair representation; and, in the operation of the telephone system due consideration is to be given to requests from the foreign community for such extensions and improvements as may be reasonably demanded by the general interests of the public.

5. In the administration of the Maritime Customs Japanese traders are to be permitted to communicate with the Customs House of Tsingtao in their own language, and the Inspector-General is to be instructed to give consideration, within the limits of the established service regulations, to the diverse needs of the trade of Tsingtao, in the selection of a suitable staff for such Customs House.

6. For a limited period of time, the Chinese Government is to employ upon the Shantung Railway a Japanese as Traffic Manager, and, in coordination with a Chinese Chief Accountant, a Japanese as Chief Accountant.

Only as to this last-named concession to Japan can there be any question as to reasonableness, or as to a possible jeopardizing of Chinese interests. And, even as to this concession, an examination of its extent shows that if the Chinese authorities make proper use of the rights of administration control reserved to them, the Japanese Traffic Manager and Chief Accountant, during the limited period of time they are to be employed, will not have the power to discriminate against or otherwise injure legitimate Chinese interests, even should they be disposed to do so. As to this the writer can do no better than quote the following statement of Mr. John E. Baker, Adviser since 1917 to the Chinese Ministry of Communications:

> The Chinese people are to be congratulated upon the settlement of the Shantung question. By agreeing to the railway settlement the whole Shantung question is settled. China gets rid of 2,000 Japanese employees at the price of retaining only two. The price to be paid for the railway is to be no greater than that which Japan paid for it, and will probably be less than it would cost to reproduce the railway today. China has five years or fifteen years at her option, within which to raise the purchase price. The railway can be made to pay for itself within the fifteen year limit. While it would have been desirable to get rid of all Japanese participation in this railway immediately, there will be certain benefits accruing to a campaign extending for five years during which the purpose of eliminating Japanese influence from Shantung is placed before the Chinese people.
>
> There has been a very real fear that if employees of Japanese nationality remained upon the railway, some means will be found by Japan to retain possession of the line. If that were the ultimate intention of Japan there was no need whatever for her to have entered into these negotiations. Supporting her position in Shantung, she had the signed agreement of the three most powerful European nations. This support Japan has now signed away. In the case of Siberia, Japan had no support of this kind, yet she openly defied the United States and the expressed opinion of other Delegations, and got away with it. If she had intended to remain in Shantung, she could have done so.
>
> Furthermore, the Japanese Traffic Manager and the Japanese Chief Accountant (the latter of whom acts jointly with the Chinese Chief Accountant) are so hedged about with limitations to their powers that under a vigorous Chinese administration they should

be harmless. They are "under the direction, control and supervision of the Chinese Managing Director." Take the case of the Traffic Manager. By no means will he have unrestricted liberty of action in the performance of his duties. Upon the Chinese Government railways there are at present two organizations of the Traffic Managers; (1) the Through-traffic Conference and (2) the General Traffic Conference. Both of these conferences meet at least once a year, but generally an extra conference or two is called by the Ministry of Communications for specific purposes. The first is composed of representatives of the through-traffic lines and of the Through-traffic Administration in the Ministry of Communications, while the second is composed of Traffic Managers of all Government lines together with representatives of the General Traffic section of the Ministry of Communications.

The Traffic Manager of the Shantung Railway will go into one or the other or both of these conferences. These conferences act as a legislative body which passes the laws governing the traffic department upon all the lines participating in such conferences. The law comes into effect when approved by the Minister of Communications, and is administered by the Traffic Manager as the representative, under the Managing Director, of the Ministry of Communications. Thus this Traffic Manager will be subject to the control which comes from association with technical representatives of other lines as well as the control of his own Managing Director. To escape from such control either he must defy his colleagues in the conference or deliberately disobey the Ministry of Communications, in which case he is subject to removal by the Director, power to do which is expressly reserved in the agreement.

Such conferences have already prescribed a uniform classification of goods; uniform rules for the carriage of goods and passengers, baggage and parcels; uniform rules for car distribution and reporting of car performance. The formulation of uniform operating rules, signalling rules, and civil service rules is already under way. Other subjects will follow.

A similar condition will be found governing the Chief Accountant, who will be subject to the scrutiny of a Chinese Chief Accountant, as well as of the Managing Director. The uniform classifications of accounts on Chinese railways have been in force for several years.

The conferences of the Accountants have had nearly eight years of successful history. Practically the whole field of accounts has been covered, and these classifications and accounting rules are a part of the railway law of China which the Japanese Chief Accountant will be compelled to follow.

The accounts and statistics required of Chinese railways are considered by experts to be among the best in the world. If used intelligently they hold to rigid accountability both the integrity and efficiency of operating officers. If care is taken to appoint a vigorous and intelligent Managing Director, China has little to fear from the presence of a Japanese Traffic Manager or Accountant.

As a matter of fact this settlement secures better terms for China than are to be found in any other railway contracts negotiated under the Republic. All such other contracts place a mortgage on the line and yield commissions on foreign supplies purchased by the railway or limit the freedom of the government as to banks with which it will deal. All of this is avoided in the Shantung Agreement. All of them provide for a foreign Chief Accountant who acts alone, while this agreement gives China an associate Chief Accountant. All of them provide for foreign Chiefs of Maintenance of Way, of Locomotives and of Traffic, or else for a foreign General Manager, compared with a mere Traffic Manager on the Shantung Railway. Besides, all of these agreements were made in days before China possessed any of the machinery described above for circumscribing the powers of any of these officers. Today, China can safely be far more liberal in appointments of foreigners than she could be five or six years ago, yet this agreement is much more conservative than those negotiated by Sun Yat Sen and others in 1913, 1914 and 1915.

In fact, on lines where the Government is under little or no compulsion to use foreigners, China has voluntarily placed foreign accountants, engineers and mechanical experts in much larger numbers than are required in their contract.

There is nothing to fear from the present arrangement if China will merely use ordinary vigor, intelligence and integrity in her handling of the situation.

In case there should be any disposition to defy such established conditions—a disposition which is not expected at present by any one conversant with these negotiations—the machinery has been provided by conference for the establishment of a Board of Reference which will make an attempt on the part of Japan to take advantage of China's weakness publicly apparent. There can be no greater protection at the present time.[7]

If further evidence were needed of the satisfaction with which the Chinese people should receive the Shantung settlement reached at Washington, attention may be called to the fact that the terms of that settlement are decidedly more favorable to China than were those which the Chinese Government instructed its representative, Dr. Koo, to present in 1921 to the League of Nations at Genoa. These provided that the Tsinanfu-Shunteh and Kaomihsu railways should be given over to the new International Banking Consortium for operation, and that the Tsingtao-Tsinanfu road should be operated by China herself; or, a future date for the return of this road having been agreed upon, pending that return, it should be operated on a joint capital and business basis. As to the operation of the mines, they might be made a joint Sino-Japanese undertaking.

---

[7] Mr. Baker was in Washington during most of the time the Conference was in session, and his expert advice was of great value to the Chinese Delegation.

CHAPTER XXIV

Results

We are now in a position to summarize the results of the Conference so far as China is concerned as well as to draw some conclusions as to the bearing of these results upon the general political situation in the Far East.

It is doubtless true that China did not obtain all that she wished to obtain, or all that her friends hoped she would secure. None of the Powers represented at the Conference did that,—not even the most powerful of them. But it is certain that China obtained all, and possibly more than, it was reasonable to expect that, under the existing circumstances, she would be able to obtain. The Conference was one of Sovereign States. It was called to promote peace and not to bring controversies to an acute issue. It was therefore impossible for any of the Powers to obtain action except with regard to matters upon which a unanimous agreement could be reached. It was hoped that, at the Conference, the Powers would exhibit an intelligent cooperation and, by making mutual concessions, create a situation in the Pacific and Far East that would be of mutual advantage to them all. But it was too much to expect that the nations would suddenly free themselves from all selfish and purely nationalistic aims, and no one, therefore, looked forward to results that would be wholly dictated by altruism and enlightened humanitarianism.

It is furthermore to be observed that though, upon its political side, the Conference devoted itself almost exclusively to a consideration of problems of China, it had not been called primarily for that purpose. Its primary purpose was to clear up the general political situation in the Pacific and Far East so as to render less likely, in the future, international controversies or possible wars. It was only as incidental to this end, that China's problems were involved. In other words, it was only in so far as the rehabilitation of China as an autonomous Power with a stable and efficient government was conceived to be a condition precedent to a correction of the general political situation in the Far East, that the Conference was under obligation or necessity to give any attention whatever to China's case. This fact is to be steadily borne in mind in considering what China had a right to expect from the Conference.

In a communication to the November, 1921, issue of the *Chinese Students' Monthly,* the writer called attention to the fact that it was China's great good fortune that she was able to approach the Conference table with no acts of aggression of her own toward other friendly Powers which needed to be explained or defended, and that she would appear as a petitioner for the recognition of principles which would be not only just in themselves but of benefit to all the Powers. In another respect, however, China was, as has been earlier dwelt upon, very unfortunately circumstanced at Washington. This was due to the fact that, for several years, there had been disorder in her own household; that some of her administrative services had been notoriously ineffective; that her armies had not been under adequate control by the civil authorities; and that there were a number of her provinces which had openly refused to recognize the legitimacy of the Government at Peking whose Delegates were at the Conference, and had given their nominal allegiance to an organization with headquarters at Canton which claimed to be the only government of China with a constitutional status; and that, finally, to make matters still worse for the Chinese Delegation at Washington, just before the opening of the Conference, the Peking Government had been obliged to make default upon certain of its foreign loans.

The foregoing facts lay in the minds of the Delegates of all of the Powers represented at the Conference, and necessarily influenced their policies. They were facts from the influence of which the Chinese Delegation could not hope to escape. Indeed, it is well known that, because of them, China came to the Conference with anxious fears as well as with eager hopes. There was ever present in the minds of her public men the apprehension lest the Powers, when assembled in the conference, should deem it desirable, and seize the opportunity by common agreement, to improve conditions in China by the imposition upon her of additional forms of administrative control instead of waiting for the perhaps slower processes of autonomous political development.

336   CHINA AT THE CONFERENCE

No New Bonds Upon China. It was, therefore, a great victory for China when the Powers at the beginning of the Conference declared their firm intention to respect the sovereignty, the independence, and the territorial and administrative integrity of China; to provide for her the fullest opportunity to develop and maintain for herself an effective and stable Government; and to refrain from taking advantage of existing conditions in China in order to seek special rights or privileges which would abridge the rights of subjects or citizens of friendly States and from countenancing action inimical to the security of such States.

Under the guidance of these principles, the Powers abstained throughout the Conference from attempting to create Boards or Commissions or other bodies which should function in China without China's consent, or which, in any case, would have legislative, executive or administrative powers. Thus the Tariff Revision Commission, which is to meet at Shanghai, has only the function of revising tariff valuations so as to increase China's revenues; the Special Conference which is to be convened, is to have for its function the preparation of the way for the speedy abolition of Likin—a result desired by China—and for the fulfillment of other conditions whereby China may be enabled to obtain a greatly increased return from her maritime customs;[1] the Extraterritorial Commission is organized to inquire into the present

---

[1] This Special Conference has also been authorized to suggest a detailed plan for the Board of Reference to which may be referred questions arising out of the application of the Open Door principle.

practice of extraterritorial rights in China, and into the laws and judicial administration of China in order that it may make recommendations—but recommendations only—as to the means whereby existing conditions of the administration of justice in China may be so improved as to warrant the Powers in progressively or otherwise relinquishing their extraterritorial rights. It is declared that the Chinese Government shall have the right to appoint a representative to sit as a member of this Commission, and that China is to be deemed free to accept or reject any or all of the recommendations of the Commission. The Board of Reference, which is provided for by one of the Resolutions adopted by the Conference for dealing with questions arising in connection with Open Door provisions of the " Nine Power Treaty Relating to Principles and Policies to be Followed in Matters Concerning China " has only powers of investigation and report, and these powers it may exercise, not upon its own initiative, but only as to matters that may be referred to it.

It was at one time suggested in the Conference that the Powers should establish some sort of Board or Commission authorized to make a general inquiry into conditions of law and order in China in order to determine whether or not certain of the Powers were justified in maintaining their troops in China; but, at the suggestion of the Chinese Delegation, this proposal was changed so as to provide merely that, if and when China should so request, the representatives of the Powers at Peking might, in association with three representatives of the Chinese Government, make such an inquiry as regards not of all of China but as to troops maintained in particular localities.

As regards the railways of China the Powers placed themselves upon record, as expressed in a formal resolution, that it is their hope that the future development of Chinese railways will be so conducted as to enable the Chinese Government to effect their unification into a single system under Chinese control with such foreign financial and technical assistance as may be necessary in the interests of the system, it of course being understood that the Chinese Government shall determine when this financial or technical assistance is to be asked for, and what its character shall be. Even with regard to the Chinese Eastern Railway, the Conference forebore to disregard the wishes of the Chinese representative upon the technical committee that was asked to report upon the road's future status, and contented itself with merely declaring that it was desirable that better protection should be given to the railway and to those using it; that it should be more efficiently operated, and that China would be held responsible for the obligations to foreign creditors of the road resulting from the contracts under which the road had been built and the action of China thereunder.

Despite, then, the undeniable breakdown of the authority of the Central Government of China; despite the fact that it had been obliged to make default upon certain of its foreign debts; despite the fact that there was in the south of China a political party and political organization which denied, *in toto,* the legitimacy of the Peking Government itself, China came from the Conference not only without any new administrative or other limitations upon its autonomous powers, but with the formal and unqualified assurance that the Powers would not take any advantage of existing conditions to impose any new restraints upon her freedom of action.

In this connection the writer cannot refrain from expressing his admiration of the manner in which the Chinese Delegates took jealous and successful care to place upon the records of the Conference, in clear and unmistakable terms, the principles which the Government of China asserts with regard to those matters concerning which full and immediate relief could not be obtained. An examination of these records shows that no concessions or admissions were made upon China's part which, in the future, can be brought forward to plague her, or to operate as an estoppel to her efforts to obtain, upon appropriate occasion, further and complete release from the treaty bonds which still restrain the autonomous exercise of her powers, or relief from those violations of her territorial sovereign rights which, to a certain extent, still oppress her.

Specific Results Gained by China. Turning now to the affirmative work of the Conference it is seen that China obtained the following substantial benefits:

China is to have an immediate revision of tariff valuations so as to be able to collect an effective five per cent upon her imports, thereby being able, it is estimated, to increase her revenue by $17,000,000 silver. By means of steps to be arranged for by a

Special Conference, she is to be allowed to levy a surtax which should yield $27,000,000 silver, and a further surtax on luxuries which will yield something over $2,000,000 silver. Also, when the work of the Special Conference is completed and the abolition of Likin effected, the additional revenue to be secured by China from her maritime customs, it is calculated, will amount to $156,000,000 silver.

A Commission is to be appointed which is to report within a year as to the steps to be taken in the future whereby China may be aided to effect such legislative and judicial reforms, in addition to those already achieved, as will warrant the Powers in relinquishing, progressively or otherwise, their respective rights of extraterritoriality in China.

All foreign post offices in China are to be removed by the end of the current year, and, pending this removal, the Powers concerned are pledged to afford full facilities to the Chinese customs authorities to examine all postal matter, except ordinary letters, with a view to determining whether or not they contain dutiable or contraband goods. Thus China will be able not only to prevent frauds upon her customs revenues, but to check what, in the past, has been a great evil, namely, the introduction into China, through the Japanese parcels posts, of great amounts of morphine.

It is provided that China can, at any time that she wishes to do so, obtain from the representatives of the Powers at Peking an inquiry as to whether there is justification for the retaining upon her soil of foreign troops or police, either generally or in particular localities.

Radio stations, installed in China without the express consent of her Government, are to be removed or sold at a fair valuation to China, with, however, the proviso that questions as to the removal of stations in leased areas, in the South Manchuria Railway zones or the French Settlement at Shanghai are to be discussed with the Powers concerned.

A further resolution of the Conference, which will undoubtedly rebound to the great advantage of China, is that the Powers are to supply and make public lists of all treaties, conventions, exchange of notes and other agreements which they claim to have with China or with any other Power or Powers in relation to China which they deem to be in force and upon which they desire to rely. They are also similarly pledged to supply lists as nearly complete as may be possible of all contracts between their nationals on the one part, and the Chinese Government or any of its administrative subdivisions or local authorities on the other part, which involve any concession, franchise, option or preference with respect to railway construction, mining, forestry, navigation, river conservancy, harbor works, reclamation, electrical communications, or other public works or public services, or for the sale of arms or munitions, or which involve a lien upon any of the public revenues or properties of the Chinese Government or of any of its administrative subdivisions.

As regards Leased Areas, China is to receive back Weihaiwei from Great Britain, and France has agreed to enter into negotiations with China for the return of Kwanchow-wan.

Finally, in connection with, if not technically in, the Conference, China won, as has been seen, an almost complete victory in the Shantung controversy.

Principles and Policies Relating to China. In addition to the foregoing specific items of relief which China obtained either in, or in connection with, the Conference, are to be added the emphatic statements of Principles and Policies which, in the Nine to recognize and pursue in the future in all their relations with China. Much will naturally depend upon the good faith with which these promises are carried out, but there is no good reason for supposing that they will not be observed. If this proves true, the general political situation in the Pacific and Far East, and especially as regards China, will be a much better one than it has been in the past.

One thing is certain, upon the surface the situation has been much improved. Not only have certain matters been clarified, but specific remedial action has been taken. The claims of particular Powers to Spheres of Interest in China which, because undefined and vague as to their implications, are provocative of controversy, have been definitely abandoned. The Open Door doctrine has, for the first time, received as clear a definition as, from the nature of the case, it is possible to give it, and has been embodied in treaty form. The Lansing-Ishii Agreemen and the Anglo-Japanese Alliance with their recognition by the United States and Great Britain that Japan has certain undetermined " special interests " in China have no longer any force. Henceforth the principle of publicity is to be applied to all commitments of political significance between the Powers or their nationals on the one side and the public authorities of China upon the other side. All past agreements upon which the Powers continue to rely are to be made known, and all future engagements are to be similarly published. China's rights as a neutral are to be respected in all future wars to which she is not a party. Furthermore, the eight Powers, other than China, represented at the Conference have, in a formal treaty to which all other Powers with Far Eastern interests are asked to adhere, pledged themselves generally to respect the sovereignty, the independence, and the territorial and administrative integrity of China; to provide for her the fullest and most unembarrassed opportunity to develop and maintain an effective and stable government; to use their influence for the purpose of effectually establishing and maintaining the principle of equal opportunity for the commerce and industry of all nations throughout the territory of China; and to refrain from taking advantage of conditions in China in order to seek special rights of subjects or citizens of friendly States, and from countenancing action inimical to the security of such States. And these Powers further engage " not to enter into any treaty, agreement, or understanding, either with one another, or, individually or collectively, with any Power or Powers which would infringe or impair " these principles. By the Four Power Pact the United States, Great Britain, France and Japan agree that should any controversy develop between themselves arising out of any Pacific question and involving their rights in relation to their several insular possessions or insular dominions in the region of the Pacific Ocean, which is likely to affect their friendly relations, they will jointly confer for their consideration and adjustment; and that if these rights should be threatened by the aggressive action of any other Power, they will communicate with one another fully and frankly in order to arrive at an understanding as to the most efficient measures to be taken jointly or separately to meet the exigencies of the particular situation. So far as this pact is calculated to preserve the peace in the Pacific and Far East, China will of course obtain benefit from it.

Anglo-Japanese Alliance. As a result of the Four Power Pact between the United States, Great Britain, France and Japan, China is relieved from what she has justly deemed the threatening possibilities of the Anglo-Japanese Alliance. Though not a party to this Alliance, China objected to it as in derogation of her dignity as a sovereign State insofar as the two Parties to it recognized or claimed special interests within her own territory, and as dangerous to her safety in that these Powers agreed to consider in common the measures to be taken to safeguard those rights or interests.

That China was justified in not being reassured by the declaration of the Alliance that her own independence and integrity were to be preserved is evident when one considers that although Korea's sovereignty and independence had been similarly guaranteed by the Alliance in its first form, that unfortunate country three years later passed under the administrative control of Japan and, five years later, was annexed by that country and incorporated into its empire. That China had formally protested to the British Government the renewal of the Alliance is well known.[2]

That Japan used her Alliance with Great Britain as an occasion for herself coming into the war and thus bringing its military operations into the Far East and upon the soil of China is, of course, well known. In her Imperial Rescript of August 23, 1914, declaring war against Germany, the Japanese Emperor declared: " the action of Germany has at length compelled Great Britain, Our Ally, to open hostilities against that country, and Germany is at Kiaochow, its leased territory in China, busy with warlike preparations, while her armed vessels, cruising the seas of East Asia, are threatening Our commerce and that of Our Ally. The peace of the Far East is thus in jeopardy. Accordingly, Our Government, and that of His Britannic Majesty, after a full and frank communication with each other, agreed to take such measures as may be necessary for the pro-

[2] In the Memorandum which it submitted to the British Government the Chinese Government said: " Chinese opinion is not unnaturally distrustful of any renewal of this Agreement, all men holding that China has suffered enough from its operation during the World War in the matter of Shantung. Furthermore, as China became a member of the League of Nations she is advised that a contract regarding her affairs between the other members of the League of Nations cannot be entered into without her prior consent. Article X of the Covenant is sufficient guarantee that her territorial integrity will be respected."

tection of the general interests contemplated in the Agreement of Alliance."³

It is scarcely open to doubt that the existence of her alliance with Great Britain gave to Japan a reasonable assurance that she would not be effectively interfered with in the pursuance of the aggressive policies embodied in her Twenty-One Demands upon China, just as it had been that same alliance which had given her the courage in 1904 to bring her controversies with Russia to the issue of war.

It is not to be doubted that Great Britain was not in sympathy with Japan's acts in 1915. It is indeed reasonably certain that she was not given notification by Japan that her Demands were to be made. By acting as she did in 1915 Japan clearly violated two articles of the Alliance,—that of the Preamble which declared that one of its purposes was to preserve " the common interests of all the Powers in China by insuring the independence and integrity of

³ The well-known British publicist, Robert Young, editor of the *Japan Chronicle*, in an article contributed to the *Contemporary Review* under the title, " The Anglo-Japanese Alliance," argues that the Alliance gave to Japan an excuse rather than an occasion for entering the war. He calls attention to the fact that it was not until August 15, eleven days after Great Britain's declaration of war against Germany, that Japan presented to Germany demands that were in the nature of an ultimatum. In other words, that Japan did not conceive that her Alliance operated automatically and necessarily to bring her into the war. And, furthermore, that, had Germany acceded to the terms of Japan's ultimatum, Japan would not have felt herself obligated to come into the war at all. The rejection by Germany of this ultimatum brought Japan into the war three weeks late, " a delay which," says Mr. Young, " had consequences as widely dispersed as the bombardment of Madras, the sinking of a new Blue Funnel liner with a million pounds' worth of rubber in the Arabian Sea, the annihilation of Sir Reginald Cradock's squadron, with its gallant crews, and the battle of the Falkland Islands."

the Chinese Empire and the principle of equal opportunities for the commerce and industry of all nations in China," and Article III which provided that neither of the Contracting Parties would, without consulting the other, enter into separate arrangements with another Power to the prejudice of the objects described in the Preamble in the Agreement. The fact that Great Britain did not at the time protest against these acts of bad faith upon the part of her Ally gives point to the observation which students of international relations have often made that the existence of an alliance between two Powers, so far from giving to the one a means or opportunity to bring pressure to bear upon the other, operates more often to deter the one from expressing that disapproval or exerting that influence for deterrence that it otherwise might have expressed or exerted. The fact, also, that the American Government and the American people were anxious that the Anglo-Japanese Alliance should be brought to end gives additional proof as to the effect that it might have upon political conditions in the Far East. In the debate in the United States Senate, at the time of the approval by that body of the Four Power Pact, Senator Lodge said: " The chief and most important point in the treaty is the termination of the Anglo-Japanese Alliance. That was the main object of the treaty." Again, he declared: " It is sufficient to say that in my judgment the Anglo-Japanese Alliance was the most dangerous element in our relations with the Far East and with the Pacific. Wars come from suspicions which develop into hatreds and hatreds which develop into wars. The Anglo-Japanese Alliance caused a growing feeling of suspicion not only in the United States but in Canada. On the other hand it tended to give a background to Japan which encouraged the war spirit and large preparations both by land and sea for future conflict. It immobilized England and prevented the exercise of her influence in the East for the cause of peace."

That this peace was chiefly threatened by the known imperialistic ambitions of Japan no one, outside of Japan, has attempted seriously to deny. That Japan attached great importance to the Alliance is equally well known. Count Hayashi, who negotiated the Alliance in its first form, declared in his *Secret Memoirs:*[4] "The Anglo-Japanese Alliance is the established policy of Japan. It is the basis of the country's foreign policy." And Baron Kato, who signed the Alliance in its final form, in 1911, is reported to have said:

> The Anglo-Japanese Alliance is revered and respected in Japan as long as it can be used as a stepping stone in China. It will remain in the future, as in the past, the shaft on which the wheels of Japanese diplomacy revolve.

It is true that, in 1916, the Japanese press, which is known to take its cue in such matters from the Japanese Government, raised a concerted and vehement outcry against the Alliance, but this was at a time when the military situation in the world War was not an encouraging one so far as Great Britain was concerned, and when, moreover, by the treaty

[4] Edited by A. M. Pooley, and published in 1915. See p. 207.

secretly entered into in July, 1916, Japan had formed a strong military alliance with Russia.[5]

Siberia. China cannot but view with interest and concern the future policies of Japan in Eastern Siberia, for that there will be a close connection between these policies and the ones which she may be expected to pursue in Manchuria and Mongolia there is every reason to believe. It will therefore be proper to give a summary of the statements that were made in the Conference with reference to this matter.

In the statement which the American Delegation made in the Conference with reference to the Siberian situation, attention was drawn to the circumstances and conditions under which the allied military intervention in Siberia had been undertaken. At the time this intervention was decided upon it was stated that this would be solely for the purpose of helping the Czecho-Slovaks to consolidate their forces and get into successful cooperation with their Slavic kinsmen; to steady any efforts at self-government or self-defense in which the Russians might themselves be willing to accept assistance; and to guard the military

[5] Mr. Robert Young, in the article to which reference has earlier been made, says: "There can be little doubt that the instrument was intended as a substitute for the Anglo-Japanese Alliance, and it is significant that its conclusion was coincident with the press campaign against the existing agreement with Britain, which it widely declared shackled the hands of Japan in dealing with China."

In view of what Japan had already done to China in 1915 while the Alliance was in force, one cannot but be curious to know what further action with regard to China Japanese jingoists desired their Government to take.

stores at Vladivostok. " It was stated," said Secretary Hughes in his statement to the Conference, " that the American Government proposed to ask all associated in this course of action to unite in assuring the people of Russia in the most public and solemn manner that none of the Governments uniting in action either in Siberia or in Northern Russia contemplated any interference of any kind with the political sovereignty of Russia, any intervention in her internal affairs, or any impairment of her territorial integrity either now or thereafter, but that each of the associated Powers had the single object of affording such aid as should be acceptable, and only such aid as should be acceptable, to the Russian people in their endeavor to regain control of their own affairs, their own territory, and their own destiny."

At this time, also, the Japanese Government declared that it was anxious to act in harmony with this understanding, and that " the Japanese Government remains unshaken in their constant desire to promote relations of enduring friendship with Russia and the Russian people, and reaffirms their avowed policy of respecting the territorial integrity of Russia and of abstaining from all interference in her internal policies. They further declare that, upon the realization of the projects above indicated, they will immediately withdraw all Japanese troops from Russian territory, and will leave wholly unimpaired the sovereignty of Russia in all its phases whether political or military."

As is well known the Powers other than Japan withdrew their troops from Siberia in 1920 because they considered that the purposes of the military intervention had been achieved so far as it was possible to achieve them by such intervention, but that Japan has continued to retain her troops in considerable numbers in that country. Also it has been known that although the original understanding of the United States and the other intervening Powers with Japan had been that she would send no more than a number of troops approximately equal to those sent by the United States, she, in fact, soon sent some eight or ten times that number. Still further it is known that Japan has taken military occupation of the northern half of the Island of Sakhalin, in alleged reprisal of what she has termed a massacre of her nationals by the Russians at Nikolaievsk.

It has also been charged that the Japanese troops, acting under direction of the Japanese authorities, have interfered actively in the factional domestic affairs of Siberia; that Japanese nationals have secured from organizations claiming to be the *de facto* or *de jure* governments of the Siberian peoples, various and valuable economic concessions, and that it is insisted by the Japanese Government that the validity of these concessions shall be recognized and guaranteed by the Russian or Siberian authorities as a condition precedent to the withdrawal of Japanese troops from Eastern Siberia.

That the American Government was not at all satisfied with the actions of Japan was shown in its correspondence with the Japanese Government. Thus, in the statement which he read to the Conference, the American Government Secretary Hughes said:

It must be frankly avowed that this correspondence has not always disclosed an identity of views between the two Governments. The United States has not been unmindful of the direct exposure of Japan to Bolshevism in Siberia, and the special problems which the conditions existing there have created for the Japanese Government; but it has been strongly disposed to the belief that the public assurances, given by the two Governments at the inception of the joint expedition, nevertheless required the complete withdrawal of Japanese troops from all Russian territory—if not immediately after the departure of the Czecho-Slovak troops, then within a reasonable time.

As to the occupation of Sakhalin, in reprisal for the massacre of the Japanese at Nikolaievsk, the United States was not unimpressed by the serious character of that catastrophe; but, having in mind the conditions accepted by both Governments at the outset of the joint expedition, of which the Nikolaievesk must be considered an incident, it has regretted that Japan should deem necessary the occupation of Russian territory as a means of assuring a suitable adjustment with a future Russian Government.

Secretary Hughes then read to the Conference extracts from a communication of his Government on May 31, 1921, to the Japanese Government in which it had protested against the longer continuance of Japanese troops in Siberia, and which had contained the following statement:

In view of the conviction that the course followed by the Government of Japan brings into question the very definite understanding concluded at the time troops were sent to Siberia, the Government of the United States must in candor explain its position and say to the Japanese Government that the Government of the United States can neither now nor hereafter recognize as valid any claims or titles arising out of the present occupation and control, and that it cannot acquiesce in any action taken by the Government of Japan which might impair existing treaty rights or the political or territorial integrity of Russia.

Secretary Hughes concluded his statement to the Conference with a reiteration of the hope of his Government that Japan would find it possible to carry out within the near future her expressed intention of terminating finally the Siberian expedition and of restoring Sakhalin to the Russian people.

In the formal statement which he made in explanation of Japan's retention of troops in Siberia, and of the conditions under which they would be withdrawn, Baron Shidehara adverted to the fact that there were many Japanese nationals in Siberia who had lawfully established themselves there prior to the Bolshevik uprising, and who looked to Japanese troops for protection of their lives and property. Also that, due to geographical propinquity, the general situation in the districts around Vladivostok and Nikolsk was bound to affect the security of the Korean frontier. In particular, he said, it was known that these districts had long been the base of Korean conspiracies against Japan, and that, should the Japanese troops be withdrawn, there was every likelihood that, at the first favorable opportunity, these conspirators would penetrate Korea itself.

" It should be made clear," he said, " that no part of the maritime province is under Japan's military occupation. Japanese troops are still stationed in the southern portion of that province, but they have not set up any civil or military administration to displace local authorities. Their activity is confined to measures of self-protection against the menace to their own safety and to the safety of their country and nationals. . . . . The Japanese Government is anxious to see an orderly and stable authority speedily reestablished in the Far Eastern possessions of Russia.[6] . . . . The Japanese Government are now seriously considering plans which would justify them in carrying out their decision of the complete withdrawal of Japanese troops from the maritime province with reasonable precaution for the security of Japanese residents and of the Korean frontiers regions. It is for this purpose that negotiations were opened some time ago at Dairen between the Japanese representatives and the agents of the Chita Government. Those regulations at Dairen are in no way intended to secure for Japan any right or advantage of exclusive nature.[7] They have been solely actuated by a desire to adjust some of the more pressing questions with which Japan is confronted in relation to Siberia. They have essentially in view the conclusion of provisional commercial arrangements, the removal of the existing menace to the security of Japan and to the lives and property of Japanese residents in Eastern Siberia, the provision of guarantees for the freedom of lawful undertakings in that region, and the prohibition of Bolshevik propaganda over the Siberian border. Should adequate provisions be arranged on the line indicated, the Japanese Government will at once proceed to the complete withdrawal of Japanese troops from the maritime province.

These conditions, even if one takes them at their full face value, show how far Japan has departed from the original conditions upon which she had

[6] In the communication of May 31, 1921 from the American to the Japanese Government, extracts from which Secretary Hughes read to the Conference, the American Government said that, in its view, the continued occupation by the Japanese troops of the strategic centers in Eastern Siberia, and the seizure of the Russian portion of Sakhalin and the establishment there of a civil administration " inevitably lends itself to misconception and antagonism—tends rather to increase than to allay the unrest and disorder in that region."

[7] It has, however, been understood that Japan has insisted that the Chita or Far Eastern Republic Government should recognize as valid the numerous economic concessions in Siberia which the Japanese nationals have obtained from one or the other political organizations that have from time to time been in existence in Siberia.

agreed with the American and other Governments she would withdraw her troops.

As to the occupation of the Russian Province of Sakhalin—that is, the northern part of the Island and certain points on the mainland opposite to the island—Baron Shidehara said that the situation was a different one both as to its nature and origin. These points had been occupied by Japan by way of reprisal for the killing of her nationals at Nikolaievsk, and would continue to be occupied until there was established in Russia a responsible authority with which Japan could communicate in order to obtain due satisfaction.

Secretary Hughes, in his statement to the Conference, said that he understood Japan's assurances to mean that she did not seek "through her military operation in Siberia, to impair the rights of the Russian people in any respect, or to absorb for her own use the Siberian fisheries, or to set up an exclusive exploitation either of the resources of Sakhalin or of the maritime province." To this statement the Japanese Delegation made no reply by way of either affirmation or denial or qualification.

Has a Fundamental Change of Policy on the Part of the Powers Been Effected? The results of such a Conference as the Washington cannot, however, be summed up in a series of specific achievements. They are not to be found explicitly stated in the agreements or formal resolutions which are signed by the participating Powers, for, in addition to these agreements and resolutions, there is the still more important question whether, as a result of the discussions that have been had, a new and changed spirit has found its way into the foreign policies that are henceforth to be pursued. Monsieur Briand, in the address which he made in the third plenary session of the Conference, struck a note to which all those who heard him responded when he said: "It is not enough to reduce armies and to decrease the munitions of war. That is the material side of things. There is another consideration which one has no right to overlook when facing such a problem—a consideration which goes to the heart of questions vital to the welfare of a nation. A nation must be surrounded by what I may call an atmosphere of peace; disarmament must be moral as well as material."

Monsieur Briand was speaking in defense of the continued maintenance by his country of her considerable land forces, but whether or not one is convinced of the necessity, under existing circumstances, of the large armies still maintained by France, the truthfulness and pertinency of the statement which had been quoted cannot be denied. If, then, we paraphrase this statement and apply it to political conditions in the Far East we have the equally true proposition that the answer to the question whether the Conference achieved the primary purpose for which it was convened depends largely upon the other question whether, as a result of its deliberations, the Nations with Pacific and Far Eastern interests have come to a firm intention to substitute cooperation for nationalistic competition, to do stricter justice to the weaker peoples than they have done in the past, and to guide themselves by the avowed spirit as well as by the strict letter of the agreements which they have signed and by the various declarations which their delegates have made in the Conference and which are incorporated in its official records. Whether or not they have come to this firm intention and will continue to hold it, only future events can reveal.

The Future. What the future is to bring forth will depend in large measure upon the answer it gives to the question stated in the preceding paragraph. If we analyze this question into its chief parts they will be found to be the following: (1) the extent to which Japan, in reversal of its former policies, will be guided and controlled by a strict regard for the spirit as well as for the letter of its international engagements, and will sincerely seek, or, at least avoid the placing of obstacles in the way of, the welfare of its great neighbors, China and Russia; (2) the extent to which Great Britain and the United States will cooperate in the Far East; and (3) the extent to which China herself will exhibit a power to make use of the opportunity that the Powers have agreed to give her to establish and maintain for herself a strong central government and to create efficiently operated public administrative services.

That Japan's economic and political future is bound up in her ability to import increasing amounts of foodstuffs and raw materials for her manufacturing establishments there can be no doubt. It appears to be now evident to the Japanese themselves that immigration does not furnish them with a solution to the problem presented by their increasing population:—their emigrants will not be received by those countries which supply the conditions under which they can economically flourish, and experience has shown that they cannot successfully compete with the natives of Asia or Polynesia. Even in Korea, where they have had the aid of their own government and of colonization societies, the Japanese have shown themselves unable to supplant the Koreans.

Unless, then, the population of Japan proper ceases to increase, the islands will have to continue that process of industrialization and commercialization which has already made such considerable progress. This, in turn, will mean that increasing amounts of foodstuffs and raw materials for manufacturing will have to be imported. For these, as the Japanese Delegation several times frankly said in the Conference, Japan will look especially to China, and, they might have added, to Eastern Siberia. Respect for the rights of these countries as well as for those of the other Powers and for her own covenants will require that Japan should take her chances in the open competitive market in order to obtain these necessities for her national economic existence. It may be safely assumed, however, that she will at least seek by every legitimate means possible to increase her investments in China and especially in Manchuria and Mongolia, and also in Eastern Siberia, in order that she may have increased assurance of obtaining the supplies her peoples and industries will demand. It is also to be expected that she will be especially insistent that law and order are maintained in those regions in order that no serious impediments may be placed in the way of the production, sale and shipment of these supplies.

This is as far as Japan, in this respect, can legitimately go, for she cannot validly appeal to her own economic necessities in order to justify her in taking from another friendly country what she conceives herself to need—that would be to take a leaf out of the book of Prussian political philosophy—and, furthermore, it is clear that, so far as Manchuria and Mongolia are concerned, China already needs them as outlets for her own rapidly expanding populations, and soon will need their mineral resources for her own developing industries.

As regards the second factor that is likely to determine the future in the Far East—the extent to which Great Britain and the United States will cooperate—it need only be said that harmonious action upon the part of these the two most powerful States of the world, must necessarily be efficient to secure the results aimed at, and that the present indications are that this entente exists. This, of course, does not mean that any secret or formulated understanding has been arrived at between these two Powers, but that their governments see clearly that it is to their mutual advantage as well as to the advantage of the other Powers, including China and even Japan, that peace shall be preserved in the Far East; that the Open Door doctrine shall be observed; and that the sovereignty and administrative integrity of China shall be respected. Those who watched carefully the proceedings of the Washington Conference and were in a position to judge intelligently the forces operating to bring about the results that were reached, know how close was the cooperation between Great

Britain and the United States, and how nearly eye to eye these two Powers now stand in their Far Eastern policies. The abrogation of the Anglo-Japanese Alliance is, of course, of especial significance in this respect, since it leaves Great Britain free to pursue without embarrassment, this Anglo-American community of opinion and interest.

The last factor in the Far Eastern political future is China herself. After all, upon her will rest the greatest responsibility for what the next few years are to bring forth in her part of the world. She is now to have the opportunity to give substance to her claim to sovereignty and reality to her administrative integrity. A State that claims that its sovereignty and independence shall be scrupulously respected by other States gives the implied assurance that it is able to exercise a reasonable amount of effective political control over the territories and peoples which it claims as its own. China cannot, therefore, ask of these States that they exercise a forbearance towards herself for a longer period than is reasonably necessary for her to place her own household in order, and thus to be in a position not only to fulfill her own international obligations but to promote the welfare of her own peoples. At any rate it is necessary that she should make steady even if only slow political progress. Thus there now rests upon China the immediate duty of reducing her military forces to a reasonable number and of bringing them into due subordination to the civil authorities; of creating and operating efficient administrative services; of purging her politics of corruption; and, in general, of establishing a stable Central Government which will command the respect and obedience of all of her millions of people. Especially must her patriotic leaders maintain unremitting vigilance that no commitments are made that will impose new restraints upon her freedom of action or which will sacrifice economic rights which should be retained for the exclusive benefit of her own citizens. Against the possibility of such improvident or disloyal action upon the part of her own Government or officials, no Conference of Powers could protect her except by denying to her the exercise of treaty and other rights which belong to her as a sovereign State and which, of course she would not be willing to surrender.

It is the writer's opinion that, by their actions in the Washington Conference, the Western Powers have shown a real disposition to release China from the limitations upon her administrative autonomy as rapidly as existing conditions in China fairly warrant them in doing so. They are now in a frame of mind, he believes, that will lead them to grant further relief to China if China can exhibit to them the picture of a united people with a stable and efficient national Government.

Aside, however, from what she is able to do for herself, China needs to be especially anxious as to the course of Japanese influence in Manchuria and Mongolia. Japan, it is clear from the unambiguous statements made in the Conference, will be loath to surrender her lease of the Liaotung Peninsula and her railways and other rights in Manchuria. But, even as to these, the query may be raised whether, through the " good offices " of the other Powers some satisfactory situation between China and Japan may not be brought about. So conspicuously successful were the Shantung Conversations in clearing up that most disturbing controversy between the two countries, one is encouraged to ask whether similar good results might not be secured with reference to the remaining provisions of the Treaties to Agreements of 1915, if Great Britain and the United States would again extend their " good offices " for the purpose, and the Governments of China and Japan be persuaded to accept and employ them. It is scarcely conceivable that China would refuse such an offer, and it is likely that Japan would do the same if she can secure in her own country a due control of the militaristic forces which, unhappily for her and for her neighbors, have, during recent years, exercised such predominant control. And this suggests what probably should have been included as a fourth factor in the Far Eastern situation,—the course of constitutional and political development in Japan. Is she to obtain a type of government and to apply principles of political right which will bring her into true fellowship with the other enlightened nations of the world, or is she to remain under the domination of her bureaucrats and militarists?

APPENDICES

APPENDIX I: TREATIES

A Treaty Between the United States of America, the British Empire, France, and Japan, Signed December 13, 1921, Relating to Their Insular Possessions and Insular Dominions in the Pacific Ocean

The United States of America, the British Empire, France and Japan,

With a view to the preservation of the general peace and the maintenance of their rights in relation to their insular possessions and insular dominions in the region of the Pacific Ocean,

Have determined to conclude a Treaty to this effect and have appointed as their Plenipotentiaries:

The President of the United States of America:
 Charles Evans Hughes,
 Henry Cabot Lodge,
 Oscar W. Underwood and
 Elihu Root,
  citizens of the United States;
His Majesty the King of the United Kingdom of Great Britain and Ireland and of the British Dominions beyond the Seas, Emperor of India:
 The Right Honourable Arthur James Balfour, O. M., M. P., Lord President of His Privy Council;
 The Right Honourable Baron Lee of Fareham, G. B. E., K. C. B., First Lord of His Admiralty;
 The Right Honourable Sir Auckland Campbell Geddes, K. C. B., His Ambassador Extraordinary and Plenipotentiary to the United States of America;
And
 for the Dominion of Canada:
  The Right Honourable Robert Laird Borden, G. C. M. G., K. C.;

for the Commonwealth of Australia:
  The Honourable George Foster Pearce, Minister of Defence;
for the Dominion of New Zealand:
  Sir John William Salmond, K. C., Judge of the Supreme Court of New Zealand;
for the Union of South Africa:
  The Right Honourable Arthur James Balfour, O. M., M. P.;
for India:
  The Right Honourable Valingman Sankaranarayana Srinivasa Sastri, Member of the Indian Council of State;
The President of the French Republic:
  Mr. René Viviani, Deputy, Former President of the Council of Ministers;
  Mr. Albert Sarraut, Deputy, Minister of the Colonies;
  Mr. Jules J. Jusserand, Ambassador Extraordinary and Plenipotentiary to the United States of America, Grand Cross of the National Order of the Legion of Honour;
His Majesty the Emperor of Japan:
  Baron Tomosaburo Kato, Minister for the Navy, Junii, a member of the First Class of the Imperial Order of the Grand Cordon of the Rising Sun with the Paulownia Flower;
  Baron Kijuro Shidehara, His Ambassador Extraordinary and Plenipotentiary at Washington, Joshii, a member of the First Class of the Imperial Order of the Rising Sun;
  Prince Iyesato Tokugawa, Junii. a member of the First Class of the Imperial Order of the Rising Sun;
  Mr. Masanao Hanihara, Vice-Minister for Foreign Affairs, Jushii, a member of the Second Class of the Imperial Order of the Rising Sun;
Who, having communicated their Full Powers, found in good and due form, have agreed as follows:

I

The High Contracting Parties agree as between themselves to respect their rights in relation to their insular possessions and insular dominions in the region of the Pacific Ocean.

If there should develop between any of the High Contracting Parties a controversy arising out of any Pacific question and involving their said rights which is not satisfactorily settled by diplomacy and is likely to affect the harmonious accord now happily subsisting between them, they shall invite the other High Contracting Parties to a joint conference to which the whole subject will be referred for consideration and adjustment.

II

If the said rights are threatened by the aggressive action of any other Power, the High Contracting Parties shall communicate with one another fully and frankly in order to arrive at an understanding as to the most efficient measures to be taken, jointly or separately, to meet the exigencies of the particular situation.

III

This Treaty shall remain in force for ten years from the time it shall take effect, and after the expiration of said period it shall continue to be in force subject to the right of any of the High Contracting Parties to terminate it upon twelve months' notice.

IV

This Treaty shall be ratified as soon as possible in accordance with the constitutional methods of the High Contracting Parties and shall take effect on the deposit of ratifications, which shall take place at Washington, and thereupon the agreement between Great Britain and Japan, which was concluded at London on July 13, 1911, shall terminate. The Government of the United States will transmit to all the Signatory Powers a certified copy of the *procès-verbal* of the deposit of ratifications.

The present Treaty, in French and in English, shall remain deposited in the Archives of the Government of the United States, and duly certified copies thereof will be transmitted by that Government to each of the Signatory Powers.

In faith whereof the above named Plenipotentiaries have signed the present Treaty.

Done at the City of Washington, the thirteenth day of December, One Thousand Nine Hundred and Twenty-One.

      Charles Evans Hughes [l. s.]
      Henry Cabot Lodge [l. s.]
      Oscar W. Underwood [l. s.]
      Elihu Root [l. s.]
      Arthur James Balfour [l. s.]
      Lee of Fareham [l. s.]
      A. C. Geddes [l. s.]
[l. s.] R. L. Borden
[l. s.] G. F. Pearce
[l. s.] John W. Salmond
[l. s.] Arthur James Balfour
[l. s.] V. S. Srinivasa Sastri
[l. s.] René Viviani
[l. s.] A. Sarraut
[l. s.] Jusserand
[l. s.] T. Kato
[l. s.] K. Shidehara.
[l. s.] Tokugawa Iyesato
[l. s.] M. Hanihara

Declaration Accompanying the Above Four-Power Treaty

In signing the Treaty this day between The United States of America, The British Empire, France and Japan, it is declared to be the understanding and intent of the Signatory Powers:

1. That the Treaty shall apply to the Mandated Islands in the Pacific Ocean; provided, however, that the making of the Treaty shall not be deemed to be an assent on the part of The United States of America to the mandates and shall not preclude agreements between The United States of America and the Mandatory Powers respectively in relation to the mandated islands.

2. That the controversies to which the second paragraph of Article I refers shall not be taken to embrace questions which according to

principles of international law lie exclusively within the domestic jurisdiction of the respective Powers.

Washington, D. C., December 13, 1921.

> CHARLES EVANS HUGHES
> HENRY CABOT LODGE
> OSCAR W. UNDERWOOD
> ELIHU ROOT
> A. M. JAMES BALFOUR
> LEE OF FAREHAM
> A. C. GEDDES
> R. L. BORDEN
> G. F. PEARCE
> JOHN W. SALMOND
> ARTHUR JAMES BALFOUR
> V. S. SRINIVASA SASTRI
> RENÉ VIVIANI
> A SARRAUT
> JUSSERAND
> T. KATO
> K. SHIDEHARA
> TOKUGAWA IYESATO
> M. HANIHARA

A Treaty Between the Same Four Powers, Supplementary to the Above, Signed February 6, 1922

The United States of America, the British Empire, France and Japan have, through their respective Plenipotentiaries, agreed upon the following stipulations supplementary to the Quadruple Treaty signed at Washington on December 13, 1921:

The term "insular possessions and insular dominions" used in the aforesaid Treaty shall, in its application to Japan, include only Karafuto (or the Southern portion of the island of Sakhalin), Formosa and the Pescadores, and the islands under the mandate of Japan.

The present agreement shall have the same force and effect as the said Treaty to which it is supplementary.

The provisions of Article IV of the aforesaid Treaty of December 13, 1921, relating to ratification shall be applicable to the present Agreement, which in French and English shall remain deposited in the Archives of the Government of the United States, and duly certified copies thereof shall be transmitted by that Government to each of the other Contracting Powers.

In faith whereof the respective Plenipotentiaries have signed the present Agreement.

Done at the City of Washington, the sixth day of February, One Thousand Nine Hundred and Twenty-two.

	CHARLES EVANS HUGHES	[L. S.]
	HENRY CABOT LODGE	[L. S.]
	OSCAR W. UNDERWOOD	[L. S.]
[L. S.]	ELIHU ROOT	
[L. S.]	ARTHUR JAMES BALFOUR	
[L. S.]	LEE OF FAREHAM	
[L. S.]	A. C. GEDDES	
[L. S.]	R. L. BORDEN	
[L. S.]	G. F. PEARCE	
[L. S.]	JOHN W. SALMOND	
[L. S.]	ARTHUR JAMES BALFOUR	
[L. S.]	V. S. SRINIVASA SASTRI	
	A. SARRAUT	[L. S.]
	JUSSERAND	[L. S.]
	T. KATO	[L. S.]
	K. SHIDEHARA	[L. S.]
	M. HANIHARA	[L. S.]

A Treaty Between All Nine Powers Relating to Principles and Policies to be Followed in Matters Concerning China

The United States of America, Belgium, the British Empire, China, France, Italy, Japan, the Netherlands and Portugal:

Desiring to adopt a policy designed to stabilize conditions in the Far East, to safeguard the rights and interests of China, and to promote intercourse between China and the other Powers upon the basis of equality of opportunity;

Have resolved to conclude a treaty for that purpose and to that end have appointed as their respective Plenipotentiaries:

The President of the United States of America:
  Charles Evans Hughes,
  Henry Cabot Lodge,
  Oscar W. Underwood,
  Elihu Root,
    citizens of the United States;
His Majesty the King of the Belgians:
  Baron de Cartier de Marchienne, Commander of the Order of Leopold and of the Order of the Crown, His Ambassador Extraordinary and Plenipotentiary at Washington;
His Majesty the King of the United Kingdom of Great Britain and Ireland and of the British Dominions beyond the Seas, Emperor of India:
  The Right Honourable Arthur James Balfour, O. M., M. P., Lord President of His Privy Council;
  The Right Honourable Baron Lee of Fareham, G. B. E., K. C. B., First Lord of His Admiralty;
  The Right Honourable Sir Auckland Campbell Geddes, K. C. B., His Ambassador Extraordinary and Plenipotentiary to the United States of America;
And
  for the Dominion of Canada:
    The Right Honourable Sir Robert Laird Borden, G. C. M. G., K. C.;
  for the Commonwealth of Australia:
    Senator the Right Honourable George Foster Pearce, Minister for Home and Territories;
  for the Dominion of New Zealand:
    The Honourable Sir John William Salmond, K. C., Judge of the Supreme Court of New Zealand;
  for the Union of South Africa:
    The Right Honourable Arthur James Balfour, O. M., M. P.;
  for India:
    The Right Honourable Valingman Sankaranarayana Srinivasa Sastri, Member of the Indian Council of State;

The President of the Republic of China:
  Mr. Sao-Ke Alfred Sze, Envoy Extraordinary and Minister Plenipotentiary at Washington;
  Mr. V. K. Wellington Koo, Envoy Extraordinary and Minister Plenipotentiary at London;
  Mr. Chung-Hui Wang, former Minister of Justice;
The President of the French Republic:
  Mr. Albert Sarraut, Deputy, Minister of the Colonies;
  Mr. Jules J. Jusserand, Ambassador Extraordinary and Plenipotentiary to the United States of America, Grand Cross of the National Order of the Legion of Honour;
His Majesty the King of Italy:
  The Honourable Carlo Schanzer, Senator of the Kingdom;
  The Honourable Vittorio Rolandi Ricci, Senator of the Kingdom, His Ambassador Extraordinary and Plenipotentiary at Washington;
  The Honourable Luigi Albertini, Senator of the Kingdom;
His Majesty the Emperor of Japan:
  Baron Tomosaburo Kato, Minister for the Navy, Junii, a member of the First Class of the Imperial Order of the Grand Cordon of the Rising Sun with the Paulownia Flower;
  Baron Kijuro Shidehara, His Ambassador Extraordinary and Plenipotentiary at Washington, Joshii, a member of the First Class of the Imperial Order of the Rising Sun;
  Mr. Masanao Hanihara, Vice-Minister for Foreign Affairs, Jushii, a member of the Second Class of the Imperial Order of the Rising Sun;
Her Majesty the Queen of The Netherlands:
  Jonkheer Frans Beelaerts van Blokland, Her Envoy Extraordinary and Minister Plenipotentiary;
  Jonkheer Willem Hendrik de Beaufort, Minister Plenipotentiary, Chargé d' Affaires at Washington;
The President of the Portuguese Republic:
  Mr. José Francisco de Horta Machado da Franca, Viscount d' Alte, Envoy Extraordinary and Minister Plenipotentiary at Washington;

Mr. Ernesto Julio de Carvalho e Vasconcellos, Captain of the Portuguese Navy, Technical Director of the Colonial Office.

Who, having communicated to each other their full powers, found to be in good and due form, have agreed as follows:

Article I

The Contracting Powers, other than China, agree:

(1) To respect the sovereignty, the independence, and the territorial and administrative integrity of China;

(2) To provide the fullest and most unembarrassed opportunity to China to develop and maintain for herself an effective and stable government;

(3) To use their influence for the purpose of effectually establishing and maintaining the principle of equal opportunity for the commerce and industry of all nations throughout the territory of China;

(4) To refrain from taking advantage of conditions in China in order to seek special rights or privileges which would abridge the rights of subjects or citizens of friendly States and from countenancing action inimical to the security of such States.

Article II

The Contracting Powers agree not to enter into any treaty, agreement, arrangement, or understanding, either with one another, or, individually or collectively, with any Power or Powers, which would infringe or impair the principles stated in Article I.

Article III

With a view to applying more effectually the principles of the Open Door or equality of opportunity in China for the trade and industry of all nations, the Contracting Powers, other than China, agree that they will not seek, nor support their respective nationals in seeking

(a) any arrangement which might purport to establish in favour of their interests any general superiority of rights with respect to commercial or economic development in any designated region of China;

(b) any such monoply or preference as would deprive the nationals of any other Power of the right of undertaking any legitimate trade or industry in China, or of participating with the Chinese Government, or with any local authority, in any category of public enterprise, or which by reason of its scope, duration or geographical extent is calculated to frustrate the practical application of the principle of equal opportunity.

It is understood that the foregoing stipulations of this Article are not to be so construed as to prohibit the acquisition of such properties or rights as may be necessary to the conduct of a particular commercial, industrial, or financial undertaking or to the encouragement of invention and research.

China undertakes to be guided by the principles stated in the foregoing stipulations of this Article in dealing with applications for economic rights and privileges from Governments and nationals of all foreign countries, whether parties to the present Treaty or not.

ARTICLE IV

The Contracting Powers agree not to support any agreements by their respective nationals with each other designed to create Spheres of Influence or to provide for the enjoyment of mutually exclusive opportunities in designated parts of Chinese territory.

ARTICLE V

China agrees that, throughout the whole of the railways in China, she will not exercise or permit unfair discrimination of any kind. In particular there shall be no discrimination whatever, direct or indirect, in respect of charges or of facilities on the ground of the nationality of passengers or the countries from which or to which they are proceeding, or the origin or ownership of goods or the country from which or to which they are consigned, or the nationality or ownership of the ship or other means of conveying such passengers or goods before or after their transport on the Chinese Railways.

The Contracting Powers, other than China, assume a corresponding obligation in respect of any of the aforesaid railways over which they or their nationals are in a position to exercise any control in virtue of any concession, special agreement or otherwise.

ARTICLE VI

The Contracting Powers, other than China, agree fully to respect China's rights as a neutral in time of war to which China is not a party; and China declares that when she is a neutral she will observe the obligations of neutrality.

ARTICLE VII

The Contracting Powers agree that, whenever a situation arises which in the opinion of any one of them involves the application of the stipulations of the present Treaty, and renders desirable discussion of such application, there shall be full and frank communication between the Contracting Powers concerned.

ARTICLE VIII

Powers not signatory to the present Treaty, which have Governments recognized by the Signatory Powers and which have treaty relations with China, shall be invited to adhere to the present Treaty. To this end the Government of the United States will make the necessary communications to nonsignatory Powers and will inform the Contracting Powers of the replies received. Adherence by any Power shall become effective on receipt of notice thereof by the Government of the United States.

ARTICLE IX

The present Treaty shall be ratified by the Contracting Powers in accordance with their respective constitutional methods and shall take effect on the date of the deposit of all the ratifications, which shall take place at Washington as soon as possible. The Government of the United States will transmit to the other Contracting Powers a certified copy of the procès-verbal of the deposit of ratifications.

The present Treaty, of which the French and English texts are both authentic, shall remain deposited in the archives of the Government of the United States, and duly certified copies thereof shall be transmitted by that Government to the other Contracting Powers.

In faith whereof the above-named Plenipotentiaries have signed the present Treaty.

Done at the City of Washington, the Sixth day of February, One Thousand Nine Hundred and Twenty-Two.

	Charles Evans Hughes	[L. S.]
	Henry Cabot Lodge	[L. S.]
	Oscar W. Underwood	[L. S.]
	Elihu Root	[L. S.]
	Baron de Cartier de Marchienne	[L. S.]
	Arthur James Balfour	[L. S.]
	Lee of Fareham	[L. S.]
	A. C. Geddes	[L. S.]
	R. L. Borden	[L. S.]
	G. F. Pearce	[L. S.]
	John W. Salmond	[L. S.]
	Arthur James Balfour	[L. S.]
	V. S. Srinivasa Sastri	[L. S.]
[L. S.]	Sao-Ke Alfred Sze	
[L. S.]	V. K. Wellington Koo	
[L. S.]	Chung-Hui Wang	
[L. S.]	A. Sarraut	
[L. S.]	Jusserand	
[L. S.]	Carlo Schanzer	
[L. S.]	V. Rolandi Ricci	
[L. S.]	Luigi Albertini	
	T. Kato	[L. S.]
	K. Shidehara	[L. S.]
	M. Hanihara	[L. S.]
	Beelaerts van Blokland	[L. S.]
	W. de Beaufort	[L. S.]
	Alte	[L. S.]
	Ernesto de Vasconcellos	[L. S.]

A Treaty Between the Nine Powers Relating to Chinese Customs Tariff

The United States of America, Belgium, the British Empire, China, France, Italy, Japan, The Netherlands and Portugal:

With a view to increasing the revenues of the Chinese Government, have resolved to conclude a Treaty relating to the revision of

the Chinese customs tariff and cognate matters, and to that end
have appointed as their Plenipotentiaries:

The President of the United States of America:
    Charles Evans Hughes,
    Henry Cabot Lodge,
    Oscar W. Underwood,
    Elihu Root,
        citizens of the United States;

His Majesty the King of the Belgians:
    Baron de Cartier de Marchienne, Commander of the Order of
        Leopold and of the Order of the Crown, His Ambassador
        Extraordinary and Plenipotentiary at Washington;

His Majesty the King of the United Kingdom of Great Britain
and Ireland and of the British Dominions beyond the Seas, Emperor of India:
    The Right Honourable Arthur James Balfour, O. M., M. P.,
        Lord President of His Privy Council;
    The Right Honourable Baron Lee of Fareham, G. B. E.,
        K. C. B., First Lord of His Admiralty;
    The Right Honourable Sir Auckland Campbell Geddes,
        K. C. B., His Ambassador Extraordinary and Plenipotentiary to the United States of America;

And
    for the Dominion of Canada:
        The Right Honourable Sir Robert Laird Borden, G. C. M. G.,
            K. C.;
    for the Commonwealth of Australia:
        Senator the Right Honourable George Foster Pearce, Minister
            for Home and Territories;
    for the Dominion of New Zealand:
        The Honourable Sir John William Salmond, K. C., Judge of
            the Supreme Court of New Zealand;
    for the Union of South Africa:
        The Right Honourable Arthur James Balfour, O. M., M. P.;
    for India:
        The Right Honourable Valingman Sankaranarayana Srinivasa
            Sastri, Member of the Indian Council of State;

The President of the Republic of China:
  Mr. Sao-Ke Alfred Sze, Envoy Extraordinary and Minister Plenipotentiary at Washington;
  Mr. V. K. Wellington Koo, Envoy Extraordinary and Minister Plenipotentiary at London;
  Mr. Chung-Hui Wang, former Minister of Justice;
The President of the French Republic:
  Mr. Albert Sarraut, Deputy, Minister of the Colonies;
  Mr. Jules J. Jusserand, Ambassador Extraordinary and Plenipotentiary to the United States of America, Grand Cross of the National Order of the Legion of Honour;
His Majesty the King of Italy:
  The Honourable Carlo Schanzer, Senator of the Kingdom;
  The Honourable Vittorio Rolandi Ricci, Senator of the Kingdom. His Ambassador Extraordinary and Plenipotentiary at Washington;
  The Honourable Luigi Albertini, Senator of the Kingdom;
His Majesty the Emperor of Japan:
  Baron Tomosaburo Kato, Minister for the Navy, Junii, a member of the First Class of the Imperial Order of the Grand Cordon of the Rising Sun with the Paulownia Flower;
  Baron Kijuro Shidehara, His Ambassador Extraordinary and Plenipotentiary at Washington, Joshii, a member of the First Class of the Imperial Order of the Rising Sun;
  Mr. Masanao Hanihara, Vice-Minister for Foreign Affairs, Jushii, a member of the Second Class of the Imperial Order of the Rising Sun;
Her Majesty the Queen of The Netherlands:
  Jonkheer Frans Beelaerts van Blokland, Her Envoy Extraordinary and Minister Plenipotentiary;
  Jonkheer Willem Hendrik de Beaufort, Minister Plenipotentiary, Chargé d' Affaires at Washington;
The President of the Portuguese Republic:
  Mr. José Francisco de Horta Machado da Franca, Viscount d'Alte, Envoy Extraordinary and Minister Plenipotentiary at Washington;
  Mr. Ernesto Julio de Carvalho e Vasconcellos, Captain of the Portuguese Navy, Technical Director of the Colonial Office;

Who, having communicated to each other their full powers, found to be in good and due form, have agreed as follows:

ARTICLE I

The representatives of the Contracting Powers having adopted, on the fourth day of February, 1922, in the City of Washington, a Resolution, which is appended as an Annex to this Article, with respect to the revision of Chinese Customs duties, for the purpose of making such duties equivalent to an effective 5 per centum *ad valorem*, in accordance with existing treaties concluded by China with other nations, the Contracting Powers hereby confirm the said Resolution and undertake to accept the tariff rates fixed as a result of such revision. The said tariff rates shall become effective as soon as possible but not earlier than two months after publication thereof.

ANNEX

With a view to providing additional revenue to meet the needs of the Chinese Government, the Powers represented at this Conference, namely the United States of America, Belgium, the British Empire, China, France, Italy, Japan, The Netherlands, and Portugal, agree:

That the customs schedule of duties on imports into China adopted by the Tariff Revision Commission at Shanghai on December 19, 1918, shall forthwith be revised so that the rates of duty shall be equivalent to 5 per cent effective, as provided for in the several commercial treaties to which China is a party.

A Revision Commission shall meet at Shanghai, at the earliest practicable date, to effect this revision forthwith and on the general lines of the last revision.

This Commission shall be composed of representatives of the Powers above named and of representatives of any additional Powers having Governments at present recognized by the Powers represented at this Conference and who have treaties with China providing for a tariff on imports and exports not to exceed 5 per cent ad valorem and who desire to participate therein.

The revision shall proceed as rapidly as possible with a view to its completion within four months from the date of the adoption of this Resolution by the Conference on the Limitation of Armament and Pacific and Far Eastern Questions.

The revised tariff shall become effective as soon as possible but not earlier than two months after its publication by the Revision Commission.

The Government of the United States, as convener of the present Conference, is requested forthwith to communicate the terms of this Resolution to the Governments of Powers not represented at this Conference but who participated in the Revision of 1918, aforesaid.

ARTICLE II

Immediate steps shall be taken, through a Special Conference, to prepare the way for the speedy abolition of likin and for the fulfillment of the other conditions laid down in Article VIII of the Treaty of September 5th, 1902, between Great Britain and China, in Articles IV and V of the Treaty of October 8th, 1903, between the United States and China, and in Article I of the Supplementary Treaty of October 8th, 1903, between Japan and China, with a view to levying the surtaxes provided for in those articles.

The Special Conference shall be composed of representatives of the Signatory Powers, and of such other Powers as may desire to participate and may adhere to the present Treaty, in accordance with the provisions of Article VIII, in sufficient time to allow their representatives to take part. It shall meet in China within three months after the coming into force of the present Treaty, on a day and at a place to be designated by the Chinese Government.

ARTICLE III

The Special Conference provided for in Article II shall consider the interim provisions to be applied prior to the abolition of likin and the fulfillment of the other conditions laid down in the articles of the treaties mentioned in Article II; and it shall authorize the levying of a surtax on dutiable imports as from such date, for such purposes, and subject to such conditions as it may determine.

The surtax shall be at a uniform rate of $2\frac{1}{2}$ per centum *ad valorem*, provided, that in case of certain articles of luxury which, in the opinion of the Special Conference, can bear a greater increase without unduly impeding trade, the total surtax may be increased but may not exceed 5 per centum *ad valorem*.

ARTICLE IV

Following the immediate revision of the customs schedule of duties on imports into China, mentioned in Article I, there shall be a further revision thereof to take effect at the expiration of four years following the completion of the aforesaid immediate revision, in order to ensure that the customs duties shall correspond to the *ad valorem* rates fixed by the Special Conference provided for in Article II.

Following this further revision there shall be, for the same purpose, periodical revisions of the customs schedule of duties on imports into China every seven years, in lieu of the decennial revision authorized by existing treaties with China.

In order to prevent delay, any revision made in pursuance of this Article shall be effected in accordance with rules to be prescribed by the Special Conference provided for in Article II.

ARTICLE V

In all matters relating to customs duties there shall be effective equality of treatment and opportunity for all the Contracting Powers.

ARTICLE VI

The principle of uniformity in the rates of customs duties levied at all the land and maritime frontiers of China is hereby recognized. The Special Conference provided for in Article II shall make arrangements to give practical effect to this principle; and it is authorized to make equitable adjustments in those cases in which a customs privilege to be abolished was granted in return for some local economic advantage.

In the meantime, any increase in the rates of customs duties resulting from tariff revision, or any surtax hereafter imposed in pursuance of the present Treaty, shall be levied at a uniform rate *ad valorem* at all land and maritime frontiers of China.

ARTICLE VII

The charge for transit passes shall be at the rate of $2\frac{1}{2}$ per centum *ad valorem* until the arrangements provided for by Article II come into force.

ARTICLE VIII

Powers not signatory to the present Treaty whose Governments are at present recognized by the Signatory Powers, and whose present treaties with China provide for a tariff on imports and exports not to exceed 5 per centum *ad valorem,* shall be invited to adhere to the present Treaty.

The Government of the United States undertakes to make the necessary communications for this purpose and to inform the Governments of the Contracting Powers of the replies received. Adherence by any Power shall become effective on receipt of notice thereof by the Government of the United States.

ARTICLE IX

The provisions of the present Treaty shall override all stipulations of treaties between China and the respective Contracting Powers which are inconsistent therewith, other than stipulations according most favored nation treatment.

ARTICLE X

The present Treaty shall be ratified by the Contracting Powers in accordance with their respective constitutional methods and shall take effect on the date of the deposit of all the ratifications, which shall take place at Washington as soon as possible. The Government of the United States will transmit to the other Contracting Powers a certified copy of the procès-verbal of the deposit of ratifications.

The present Treaty, of which the English and French texts are both authentic, shall remain deposited in the archives of the Government of the United States, and duly certified copies thereof shall be transmitted by that Government to the other Contracting Powers.

In faith whereof the above-named Plenipotentiaries have signed the present Treaty.

Done at the City of Washington the sixth day of February, One Thousand Nine Hundred and Twenty-two.

APPENDIX II: RESOLUTIONS
Resolution Regarding a Board of Reference for Far Eastern Question

The representatives of the Powers assembled at the present Conference at Washington, to wit:

The United States of America, Belgium, the British Empire, China, France, Italy, Japan, The Netherlands, and Portugal:

Desiring to provide a procedure for dealing with questions that may arise in connection with the execution of the provisions of Articles III and V of the Treaty to be signed at Washington on February 6th, 1922, with reference to their general policy designed to stabilize conditions in the Far East, to safeguard the rights and interests of China, and to promote intercourse between China and the other Powers upon the basis of equality of opportunity;

Resolve that there shall be established in China a Board of Reference to which any questions arising in connection with the execution of the aforesaid Articles may be referred for investigation and report.

The Special Conference provided for in Article II of the Treaty to be signed at Washington on February 6th, 1922, with reference to the Chinese Customs Tariff, shall formulate for the approval of the Powers concerned a detailed plan for the constitution of the Board.

Adopted by the Conference on the Limitation of Armament at the Sixth Plenary Session, February 4th, 1922.

Resolution Regarding Extraterritoriality in China

The representatives of the Powers hereinafter named, participating in the discussion of Pacific and Far Eastern questions in the Conference on the Limitation of Armament, to wit, the United States of America, Belgium, the British Empire, France, Italy, Japan, the Netherlands, and Portugal,—

Having taken note of the fact that in the Treaty between Great Britain and China dated September 5, 1902, in the Treaty between the United States of America and China dated October 8, 1903, and in the Treaty between Japan and China dated October 8, 1903, these several Powers have agreed to give every assistance towards the attainment by the Chinese Government of its expressed desire to reform its judicial system and to bring it into accord with that of Western nations, and have declared that they are also " prepared to relinquish extraterritorial rights when satisfied that the state of the Chinese laws, the arrangements for their administration, and other considerations warrant " them in so doing;

Being sympathetically disposed towards furthering in this regard the aspiration to which the Chinese delegation gave expression on November 16, 1921, to the effect that " immediately, or as soon as circumstances will permit, existing limitations upon China's political, jurisdictional and administrative freedom of action are to be removed ";

Considering that any determination in regard to such action as might be appropriate to this end must depend upon the ascertainment and appreciation of complicated states of fact in regard to the laws and the judicial system and the methods of judicial administration of China, which this Conference is not in a position to determine;

Have resolved

That the Governments of the Powers above named shall establish a Commission (to which each of such Governments shall appoint one member) to inquire into the present practice of extraterritorial jurisdiction in China, and into the laws and the judicial system and the methods of judicial administration of China, with a view to reporting to the Governments of the several Powers above named their findings of fact in regard to these matters, and their recommendations as to such means as they may find suitable to improve the existing conditions of the administration of justice in China, and to assist and further the efforts of the Chinese Government to effect such legislation and judicial reforms as would warrant the several Powers in relinquishing, either progressively or otherwise, their respective rights of extraterritoriality;

That the Commission herein contemplated shall be constituted within three months after the adjournment of the Conference in accordance with detailed arrangements to be hereafter agreed upon by the Governments of the Powers above named, and shall be instructed to submit its report and recommendations within one year after the first meeting of the Commission;

That each of the Powers above named shall be deemed free to accept or to reject all or any portion of the recommendations of the Commission herein contemplated, but that in no case shall any of the said Powers make its acceptance of all or any portion of such recommendations either directly or indirectly dependent on the granting by China of any special concession, favor, benefit or immunity, whether political or economic.

ADDITIONAL RESOLUTION

That the non-signatory Powers, having by treaty extraterritorial rights in China, may accede to the resolution affecting extraterritoriality and the administration of justice in China by depositing within three months after the adjournment of the Conference a written notice of accession with the Government of the United States for communication by it to each of the signatory Powers.

ADDITIONAL RESOLUTION

That China, having taken note of the resolutions affecting the establishment of a Commission to investigate and report upon extraterritoriality and the administration of justice in China, expresses its satisfaction with the sympathetic disposition of the Powers hereinbefore named in regard to the aspiration of the Chinese Government to secure the abolition of extraterritoriality in China, and declares its intention to appoint a representative who shall have the right to sit as a member of the said Commission, it being understood that China shall be deemed free to accept or to reject any or all of the recommendations of the Commission. Furthermore, China is prepared to cooperate in the work of this Commission and to afford to it every possible facility for the successful accomplishment of its tasks.

Adopted by the Conference on the Limitation of Armament at the Fourth Plenary Session, December 10, 1921.

Resolution Regarding Foreign Postal Agencies in China

A. Recognizing the justice of the desire expressed by the Chinese Government to secure the abolition of foreign postal agencies in China, save or except in leased territories or as otherwise specifically provided by treaty, it is resolved:

(1) The four Powers having such postal agencies agree to their abandonment subject to the following conditions:
  (a) That an efficient Chinese postal service is maintained;
  (b) That an assurance is given by the Chinese Government that they contemplate no change in the present postal administration so far as the status of the foreign Co-Director General is concerned.
(2) To enable China and the Powers to make the necessary dispositions, this arrangement shall come into force and effect not later than January 1, 1923.

B. Pending the complete withdrawal of foreign postal agencies, the four Powers concerned severally undertake to afford full facilities to the Chinese customs authorities to examine in those agencies all postal matter (excepting ordinary letters, whether registered or not, which upon external examination appear plainly to contain only written matter) passing through them, with a view to ascertaining whether they contain articles which are dutiable or contraband or which otherwise contravene the customs regulations or laws of China.

Adopted by the Conference of the Limitation of Armament at the Fifth Plenary Session, February 1st, 1922.

Resolution Regarding Armed Forces in China

WHEREAS, The Powers have from time to time stationed armed forces, including police and railway guards, in China to protect the lives and property of foreigners lawfully in China;

AND WHEREAS, It appears that certain of these armed forces are maintained in China without the authority of any treaty or agreement;

AND WHEREAS, The Powers have declared their intention to withdraw their armed forces now on duty in China without the authority of any treaty or agreement, whenever China shall assure the protection of the lives and property of foreigners in China;

AND WHEREAS, China has declared her intention and capacity to assure the protection of the lives and property of foreigners in China;

Now, To the end that there may be clear understanding of the conditions upon which in each case the practical execution of those intentions must depend;

It is resolved, That the Diplomatic Representatives in Pekin of the Powers now in Conference at Washington, to wit, the United States of America, Belgium, the British Empire, France, Italy, Japan, The Netherlands and Portugal, will be instructed by their respective Governments, whenever China shall so request, to associate themselves with three representatives of the Chinese Government to conduct collectively a full and impartial inquiry into the issues raised by the foregoing declarations of intention made by the Powers and by China and shall thereafter prepare a full and comprehensive report setting out without reservation their findings of fact and their opinion with regard to the matter hereby referred for inquiry, and shall furnish a copy of their report to each of the nine Governments concerned which shall severally make public the report with such comment as each may deem appropriate. The representatives of any of the Powers may make or join in minority reports stating their differences, if any, from the majority report.

That each of the Powers above named shall be deemed free to accept or reject all or any of the findings of fact or opinions expressed in the report but that in no case shall any of the said Powers make its acceptance of all or any of the findings of fact or opinions either directly or indirectly dependent on the granting by China of any special concession, favor, benefit or immunity, whether political or economic.

Adopted by the Conference on the Limitation of Armament at the Fifth Plenary Session, February 1st, 1922.

Resolution Regarding Radio Stations in China and Accompanying Declarations

The representatives of the Powers hereinafter named participating in the discussion of Pacific and Far Eastern questions in the Conference on the Limitation of Armament—to wit: The United States of America, Belgium, The British Empire, China, France, Italy, Japan, The Netherlands and Portugal,

Have resolved

1. That all radio stations in China whether maintained under the provisions of the international protocol of September 7, 1901, or in fact maintained in the grounds of any of the foreign legations in China, shall be limited in their use to sending and receiving government messages and shall not receive or send commercial or personal or unofficial messages, including press matter: Provided, however, that in case all other telegraphic communication is interrupted, then, upon official notification accompanied by proof of such interruption to the Chinese Ministry of Communications, such stations may afford temporary facilities for commercial, personal or unofficial messages, including press matter, until the Chinese Government has given notice of the termination of the interruption;

2. All radio stations operated within the territory of China by a foreign government or the citizens or subjects thereof under treaties or concessions of the Government of China, shall limit the messages sent and received by the terms of the treaties or concessions under which the respective stations are maintained;

3. In case there be any radio station maintained in the territory of China by a foreign government or citizens or subjects thereof without the authority of the Chinese Government, such station and all the plant, apparatus and material thereof shall be transferred to and taken over by the Government of China, to be operated under the direction of the Chinese Ministry of Communications upon fair and full compensation to the owners for the value of the installation, as soon as the Chinese Ministry of Communications is prepared to operate the same effectively for the general public benefit;

4. If any questions shall arise as to the radio stations in leased territories, in the South Manchurian Railway Zone or in the French Concession at Shanghai, they shall be regarded as matters for discussion between the Chinese Government and the Governments concerned.

5. The owners or managers of all radio stations maintained in the territory of China by foreign powers or citizens or subjects thereof shall confer with the Chinese Ministry of Communications for the purpose of seeking a common arrangement to avoid interference in the use of wave lengths by wireless stations in China, subject to such general arrangements as may be made by an interna-

tional conference convened for the revision of the rules established by the International Radio Telegraph Convention signed at London, July 5, 1912.

Adopted by the Conference on the Limitation of Armament at the Fifth Plenary Session, February 1st, 1922.

DECLARATION CONCERNING THE RESOLUTION ON RADIO STATIONS IN CHINA OF DECEMBER 7, 1921

The Powers other than China declare that nothing in paragraphs 3 or 4 of the Resolutions of 7th December, 1921, is to be deemed to be an expression of opinion by the Conference as to whether the stations referred to therein are or are not authorized by China.

They further give notice that the result of any discussion arising under paragraph 4 must, if it is not to be subject to objection by them, conform with the principles of the Open Door or equality of opportunity approved by the Conference.

CHINESE DECLARATION CONCERNING RESOLUTION OF DECEMBER 7TH REGARDING RADIO STATIONS IN CHINA

The Chinese Delegation takes this occasion formally to declare that the Chinese Government does not recognize or concede the right of any foreign Power or of the nationals thereof to install or operate, without its express consent, radio stations in legation grounds, settlements, concessions, leased territories, railway areas or other similar areas.

Resolution Regarding Unification of Railways in China and Accompanying Declaration by China

The Powers represented in this Conference record their hope that to the utmost degree consistent with legitimate existing rights, the future development of railways in China shall be so conducted as to enable the Chinese Government to effect the unification of railways into a railway system under Chinese control, with such foreign financial and technical assitance as may prove necessary in the interests of that system.

Adopted by the Conference on the Limitation of Armament at the Fifth Plenary Session, Feburary 1st, 1922.

STATEMENT REGARDING CHINESE RAILWAYS MADE ON JANUARY 19, 1922, BY THE CHINESE DELEGATION

The Chinese Delegation notes with sympathetic appreciation the expression of the hope of the Powers that the existing and future railways of China may be unified under the control and operation of the Chinese Government with such foreign financial and technical assistance as may be needed. It is our intention as speedily as possible to bring about this result. It is our purpose to develop existing and future railways in accordance with a general programme that will meet the economic, industrial and commercial requirements of China. It will be our policy to obtain such foreign financial and technical assistance as may be needed from the Powers in accordance with the principles of the Open Door or equal opportunity; and the friendly support of these Powers will be asked for the effort of the Chinese Government to bring all the railways of China, now existing or to be built, under its effective and unified control and operation.

Resolution Regarding the Reduction of Chinese Military Forces

Whereas the Powers attending this Conference have been deeply impressed with the severe drain on the public revenue of China through the maintenance in various parts of the country, of military forces, excessive in number and controlled by the military chiefs of the provinces without coordination,

And whereas the continued maintenance of these forces appears to be mainly responsible for China's present unsettled political conditions,

And whereas it is felt that large and prompt reductions of these forces will not only advance the cause of China's political unity and economic development but will hasten her financial rehabilitation;

Therefore, without any intention to interfere in the internal problems of China, but animated by the sincere desire to see China develop and maintain for herself an effective and stable government alike in her own interest and in the general interest of trade;

And being inspired by the spirit of this Conference whose aim is to reduce, through the limitation of armament, the enormous disbursements which manifestly constitute the greater part of the encumbrance upon enterprise and national prosperity;

APPENDICES 389

It is resolved: That this Conference express to China the earnest hope that immediate and effective steps may be taken by the Chinese Government to reduce the aforesaid military forces and expenditures.

Adopted by the Conference on the Limitation of Armament at the Fifth Plenary Session, February 1st, 1922.

Resolution Regarding Existing Commitments of China or With Respect to China

The Powers represented in this Conference, considering it desirable that there should hereafter be full publicity with respect to all matters affecting the political and other international obligations of China and of the several Powers in relation to China, are agreed as follows:

I. The several Powers other than China will at their earliest convenience file with the Secretariat General of the Conference for transmission to the participating Powers, a list of all treaties, conventions, exchange of notes, or other international agreements which they may have with China, or with any other Power or Powers in relation to China, which they deem to be still in force and upon which they may desire to rely. In each case, citations will be given to any official or other publication in which an authoritative text of the documents may be found. In any case in which the document may not have been published, a copy of the text (in its original language or languages) will be filed with the Secretariat General of the Conference.

Every Treaty or other international agreement of the character described which may be concluded hereafter shall be notified by the Governments concerned within sixty (60) days of its conclusion to the Powers who are signatories of or adherents to this agreement.

II. The several Powers other than China will file with the Secretariat General of the Conference at their earliest convenience for transmission to the participating Powers a list, as nearly complete as may be possible, of all those contracts between their nationals, of the one part, and the Chinese Government or any of its administrative subdivisions or local authorities, of the other part, which involve any concession, franchise, option or preference with respect to railway construction, mining, forestry, navigation, river conservancy, harbor works, reclamation, electrical communications, or other public works or public services, or for the sale of arms or ammunition, or which involve a lien upon any of the public revenues or properties of the Chinese Government or of any of its administrative subdivisions. There shall be, in the case of each document so listed, either a citation to a published text, or a copy of the text itself.

Every contract of the public character described which may be concluded hereafter shall be notified by the Governments concerned within sixty (60) days after the receipt of information of its conclusion to the Powers who are signatories of or adherents to this agreement.

III. The Chinese Government agrees to notify in the conditions laid down in this agreement every treaty agreement or contract of the character indicated herein which has been or may hereafter be concluded by that Government or by any local authority in China with any foreign Power or the nationals of any foreign Power whether party to this agreement or not, so far as the information is in its possession.

IV. The Governments of Powers having treaty relations with China, which are not represented at the present Conference, shall be invited to adhere to this agreement.

The United States Government, as convener of the Conference, undertakes to communicate this agrement to the Governments of the said Powers, with a view to obtaining their adherence thereto as soon as possible.

Adopted by the Conference on the Limitation of Armament at the Fifth Plenary Session, February 1st, 1922.

Resolution Regarding the Chinese Eastern Railway, Approved by All the Powers Including China

Resolved, That the preservation of the Chinese Eastern Railway for those in interest requires that better protection be given to the railway and the persons engaged in its operation and use, a more careful selection of personnel to secure efficiency of service, and a more economcial use of funds to prevent waste of the property.

That the subject should immediately be dealt with through the proper Diplomatic channels.

Adopted by the Conference on the Limitation of Armament at the Sixth Plenary Session, February 4th, 1922.

Resolution Regarding the Chinese Eastern Railway, Approved by All the Powers Other Than China

The Powers other than China in agreeing to the resolution regarding the Chinese Eastern Railway, reserve the right to insist hereafter upon the responsibility of China for performance or non-performance of the obligations towards the foreign stockholders, bondholders and creditors of the Chinese Eastern Railway Company which the Powers deem to result from the contracts under which the railroad was built and the action of China thereunder and the obligations which they deem to be in the nature of a trust resulting from the exercise of power by the Chinese Government over the possession and administration of the railroad.

APPENDIX III: TREATY FOR THE SETTLEMENT OF OUTSTANDING QUESTIONS RELATIVE TO SHANTUNG

China and Japan, being equally animated by a sincere desire to settle amicably and in accordance with their common interest outstanding questions relative to Shantung, have resolved to conclude a treaty for the settlement of such questions, and have to that end named as their Plenipotentiaries, that is to say:

His Excellency the President of the Chinese Republic:
    Sao-Ke Alfred Sze, Envoy Extraordinary and Minister Plenipotentiary;
    Vikyuin Wellington Koo, Envoy Extraordinary and Minister Plenipotentiary; and
    Chung-Hui Wang, Former Minister of Justice;

His Majesty the Emperor of Japan:
    Baron Tomosaburo Kato, Minister of the Navy;
    Baron Kijuro Shidehara, Ambassador Extraordinary and Plenipotentiary; and
    Masanao Hanihara, Vice-Minister for Foreign Affairs;

Who, having communicated to each other their respective full powers, found to be in good and due form, have agreed upon the following Articles:

SECTION I
RESTORATION OF THE FORMER GERMAN LEASED TERRITORY OF KIAOCHOW

ARTICLE I

Japan shall restore to China the former German Leased Territory of Kiaochow.

ARTICLE II

The Government of the Chinese Republic and the Government of Japan shall each appoint three Commissioners to form a Joint Commission, with powers to make and carry out detailed arrangements relating to the transfer of the administration of the former German Leased Territory of Kiaochow and to the transfer of public properties in the said Territory and to settle other matters likewise requiring adjustment.

For such purposes, the Joint Commission shall meet immediately upon the coming into force of the present Treaty.

ARTICLE III

The transfer of the administration of the former German Leased Territory of Kiaochow and the transfer of public properties in the said Territory, as well as the adjustment of other matters under the preceding Article, shall be completed as soon as possible, and, in any case, not later than six months from the date of the coming into force of the present Treaty.

ARTICLE IV

The Government of Japan undertakes to hand over to the Government of the Chinese Republic upon the transfer to China of the administration of the former German Leased Territory of Kiaochow, such archives, registers, plans, title-deeds and other documents in the possession of Japan, or certified copies thereof, as may be necessary for the transfer of the administration, as well as those that may be useful for the subsequent administration by China of the said Territory and of the Fifty Kilometre Zone around Kiaochow Bay.

SECTION II
Transfer of Public Properties
ARTICLE V

The Government of Japan undertakes to transfer to the Government of the Chinese Republic all public properties including land, buildings, works or establishments in the former German Leased Territory of Kiaochow, whether formerly possessed by the German authorities, or purchased or constructed by the Japanese authorities during the period of the Japanese administration of the said Territory, except those indicated in Article VII of the present Treaty.

ARTICLE VI

In the transfer of public properties under the preceding Article, no compensation will be claimed from the Government of the Chinese Republic: Provided, however, that for those purchased or constructed by the Japanese authorities, and also for the improvements on or additions to those formerly possessed by the German authorities, the Government of the Chinese Republic shall refund a fair and equitable proportion of the expenses actually incurred by the Government of Japan, having regard to the principle of depreciation and continuing value.

ARTICLE VII

Such public properties in the former German Leased Territory of Kiaochow as are required for the Japanese Consulate to be established in Tsingtao shall be retained by the Government of Japan, and those required more especialy for the benefit of the Japanese community, including public schools, shrines and cemeteries, shall be left in the hands of the said community.

ARTICLE VIII

Details of the matters referred to in the preceding three Articles shall be arranged by the Joint Commission provided for in Article II of the present Treaty.

SECTION III
Withdrawal of Japanese Troops
ARTICLE IX

The Japanese troops, including gendarmes, now stationed along the Tsingtao-Tsinanfu Railway and its branches, shall be withdrawn as soon as the Chinese police or military force shall have been sent to take over the protection of the Railway.

ARTICLE X

The disposition of the Chinese police or military force and the withdrawal of the Japanese troops under the preceding Article may be effected in sections.

The date of the completion of such process for each section shall be arranged in advance between the competent authorities of China and Japan.

The entire withdrawal of such Japanese troops shall be effected within three months, if possible, and, in any case, not later than six months, from the date of the signature of the present Treaty.

ARTICLE XI

The Japanese garrison at Tsingtao shall be completely withdrawn simultaneously, if possible, with the transfer to China of the administration of the former German Leased Territory of Kiaochow, and, in any case, not later than thirty days from the date of such transfer.

SECTION IV
Maritime Customs at Tsingtao
ARTICLE XII

The Custom House of Tsingtao shall be made an integral part of the Chinese Maritime Customs upon the coming into force of the present Treaty.

ARTICLE XIII

The Provisional Agreement of August 6, 1915, between China and Japan, relating to the reopening of the Office of the Chinese Maritime Customs at Tsingtao shall cease to be effective upon the coming into force of the present Treaty.

SECTION V
TSINGTAO-TSINANFU RAILWAY
ARTICLE XIV

Japan shall transfer to China the Tsingtao-Tsinanfu Railway and its branches, together with all other properties appurtenant thereto, including wharves, warehouses and other similar properties.

ARTICLE XV

China undertakes to reimburse to Japan the actual value of all the Railway properties mentioned in the preceding Article.

The actual value to be so reimbursed shall consist of the sum of fifty-three million four hundred and six thousand, one hundred and forty-one (53,406,141) gold Marks (which is the assessed value of such portion of the said properties as was left behind by the Germans), or its equivalent, plus the amount which Japan, during her administration of the Railway, has actually expended for permanent improvements on or additions to the said properties, less a suitable allowance for depreciation.

It is understood that no charge will be made with respect to the wharves, warehouses and other similar properties mentioned in the preceding Article, except for such permanent improvements on or additions to them as may have been made by Japan, during her administration of the Railway, less a suitable allowance for depreciation.

ARTICLE XVI

The Government of the Chinese Republic and the Government of Japan shall each appoint three Commissioners to form a Joint Railway Commission, with powers to appraise the actual value of the Railway properties on the basis defined in the preceding Article, and to arrange the transfer of the said properties.

ARTICLE XVII

The transfer of all the Railway properties under Article XIV of the present Treaty shall be completed as soon as possible, and, in any case, not later than nine months from the date of the coming into force of the present Treaty.

ARTICLE XVIII

To effect the reimbursement under Article XV of the present Treaty, China shall deliver to Japan simultaneously with the completion of the transfer of the Railway properties, Chinese Government Treasury Notes, secured on the properties and revenues of the Railway, and running for a period of fifteen years, but redeemable, whether in whole or in part, at the option of China, at the end of five years from the date of the delivery of the said Treasury Notes, or at any time thereafter upon six months' previous notice.

ARTICLE XIX

Pending the redemption of the said Treasury Notes under the preceding Article, the Government of the Chinese Republic will select and appoint, for so long a period as any part of the said Treasury Notes shall remain unredeemed, a Japanese subject to be Traffic Manager, and another Japanese subject to be Chief Accountant jointly with the Chinese Chief Accountant and with coordinate functions.

These officials shall all be under the direction, control and supervision of the Chinese Managing Director, and removable for cause.

ARTICLE XX

Financial details of a technical character relating to the said Treasury Notes, not provided for in this Section, shall be determined in common accord between the Chinese and Japanese authorities as soon as possible, and, in any case, not later than six months from the date of the coming into force of the present Treaty.

SECTION VI
Extensions of the Tsingtao-Tsinanfu Railway
ARTICLE XXI

The concession relating to the two extensions of the Tsingtao-Tsinanfu Railway, namely, the Tsinanfu-Shunteh and the Kaomi-Hsuchowfu lines, shall be made open to the common activity of an international financial group, on terms to be arranged between the Government of the Chinese Republic and the said group.

SECTION VII
Mines
ARTICLE XXII

The mines of Tsechwan, Fangtze and Chinlingchen, for which the mining rights were formerly granted by China to Germany, shall be handed over to a company to be formed under a special charter of the Government of the Chinese Republic, in which the amount of Japanese capital shall not exceed that of Chinese capital.

The mode and terms of such arrangements shall be determined by the Joint Commission provided for in Article II of the present Treaty.

SECTION VIII
Opening of the Former German Leased Territory of Kiaochow
ARTICLE XXIII

The Government of Japan declares that it will not seek the establishment of an exclusive Japanese settlement, or of an international settlement, in the former German Leased Territory of Kiaochow.

The Government of the Chinese Republic, on its part, declares that the entire area of the former German Leased Territory of Kiaochow will be opened to foreign trade, and that foreign nationals will be permitted freely to reside and to carry on commerce, industry and other lawful pursuits within such area.

ARTICLE XXIV

The Government of the Chinese Republic further declares that vested rights lawfully and equitably acquired by foreign nationals in the former German Leased Territory of Kiaochow, whether under the German régime or during the period of the Japanese administration, will be respected.

All questions relating to the status or validity of such vested rights acquired by Japanese subjects or Japanese companies shall be adjusted by the Joint Commission provided for in Article II of the present Treaty.

SECTION IX
Salt Industry
ARTICLE XXV

Whereas the salt industry is a Government monopoly in China, it is agreed that the interests of Japanese subjects or Japanese companies actually engaged in the said industry along the coast of Kiaochow Bay shall be purchased by the Government of the Chinese Republic for fair compensation, and that the exportation to Japan of a quantity of salt produced by such industry along the said coast is to be permitted on reasonable terms.

Arrangements for the above purposes, including the transfer of the said interests to the Government of the Chinese Republic, shall be made by the Joint Commission provided for in Article II of the present Treaty. They shall be completed as soon as possible, and, in any case, not later than six months from the date of the coming into force of the present Treaty.

SECTION X
Submarine Cables
ARTICLE XXVI

The Government of Japan declares that all the rights, title and privileges concerning the former German submarine cables between Tsingtao and Chefoo and between Tsingtao and Shanghai are vested in China, with the exception of those portions of the said two cables which have been utilized by the Government of Japan for the laying of a cable between Tsingtao and Sasebo; it being understood that the question relating to the landing and operation at Tsingtao of the said Tsingtao-Sasebo cable shall be adjusted by the Joint Commission provided for in Article II of the present Treaty, subject to the terms of the existing contracts to which China is a party.

SECTION XI
Wireless Stations
ARTICLE XXVII

The Government of Japan undertakes to transfer to the Government of the Chinese Republic the Japanese wireless stations at

Tsingtao and Tsinanfu for fair compensation for the value of these stations, upon the withdrawal of the Japanese troops at the said two places, respectively.

Details of such transfer and compensation shall be arranged by the Joint Commission provided for in Article II of the present Treaty.

ARTICLE XXVIII

The present Treaty (including the Annex thereto) shall be ratified, and the ratifications thereof shall be exchanged at Peking as soon as possible, not later than four months from the date of its signature.

It shall come into force from the date of the exchange of ratifications.

In witness whereof, the respective Plenipotentiaries have signed the present Treaty in duplicate, in the English language, and have affixed thereto their seals.

Done at the City of Washington this fourth day of February, One Thousand Nine Hundred and Twenty-two.

ANNEX

I

RENUNCIATION OF PREFERENTIAL RIGHTS

The Government of Japan declares that it renounces all preferential rights with respect to foreign assistance in persons, capital and material stipulated in the Treaty of March 6, 1898, between China and Germany.

II

TRANSFER OF PUBLIC PROPERTIES

It is understood that public properties to be transferred to the Government of the Chinese Republic under Article V of the present Treaty include (1) all public works, such as roads, water works, parks, drainage and sanitary equipment, and (2) all public enterprises such as those relating to telephone, electric light, stockyard and laundry.

The Government of the Chinese Republic declares that in the management and maintenance of public works to be so transferred to the Government of the Chinese Republic, the foreign community in the former German Leased Territory of Kiaochow shall have fair representation.

The Government of the Chinese Republic further declares that, upon taking over the telephone enterprise in the former German Leased Territory of Kiaochow, it will give due consideration to the requests from the foreign community in the said Territory for such extensions and improvements in the telephone enterprise as may be reasonably required by the general interests of the public.

With respect to public enterprises relating to electric light, stockyard and laundry, the Government of the Chinese Republic, upon taking them over, shall re-transfer them to the Chinese municipal authorities of Tsingtao, which shall, in turn, cause commercial companies to be formed under Chinese laws for the management and working of the said enterprises, subject to municipal regulation and supervision.

III

Maritime Customs at Tsingtao

The Government of the Chinese Republic declares that it will instruct the Inspector General of the Chinese Maritime Customs (1) to permit Japanese traders in the former German Leased Territory of Kiaochow to communicate in the Japanese language with the Custom House of Tsingtao; and (2) to give consideration, within the limits of the established service regulations of the Chinese Maritime Customs, to the diverse needs of the trade of Tsingtao, in the selection of a suitable staff for the said Custom House.

IV

Tsingtao-Tsinanfu Railway

Should the Joint Railway Commission provided for in Article XVI of the present Treaty fail to reach an agreement on any matter within its competence, the point or points at issue shall be taken up by the Government of the Chinese Republic and the Government of Japan for discussion and adjustment by means of diplomacy.

In the determination of such point or points, the Government of the Chinese Republic and the Government of Japan shall, if necessary, obtain recomendations of experts of a third Power or Powers who shall be designated in common accord between the two Governments.

V

CHEFOO-WEIHSIEN RAILWAY

The Government of Japan will not claim that the option for financing the Chefoo-Weihsien Railway should be made open to the common activity of the International Financial Consortium, provided that the said Railway is to be contructed with Chinese capital.

VI

OPENING OF THE FORMER GERMAN LEASED TERRITORY OF KIAOCHOW

The Government of the Chinese Republic declares that, pending the enactment and general application of laws regulating the system of local self-government in China, the Chinese local authorities will ascertain the views of the foreign residents in the former German Leased Territory of Kiaochow in such municpal matters as may directly affect their welfare and interests.

APPENDIX IV: STATEMENTS IN THE CONFERENCE REGARDING SIBERIA

JAPANESE STATEMENT

The statement by Baron Shidehara on behalf of Japan was as follows:

"The Military expedition of Japan to Siberia was originally undertaken in common accord and in cooperation with the United States in 1918. It was primarily intended to render assistance to the Czecho-Slovak troops who in their homeward journey across Siberia from European Russia, found themselves in grave and pressing danger at the hands of hostile forces under German command. The Japanese and American expeditionary forces together with other Allied troops fought their way from Vladivostok far into the region of the Amur and the Trans-Baikal Provinces to protect the railway lines which afforded the sole means of transportation of the Czecho-Slovak troops from the interior of Siberia to the port of Vladivostok. Difficulties which the Allied forces had to encounter in their operations in the severe cold winter of Siberia were immense.

"In January, 1920, the United States decided to terminate its military undertaking in Siberia, and ordered the withdrawal of its forces. For some time thereafter Japanese troops continued alone to carry out the duty of guarding several points along the Trans-Siberian Railways in fulfillment of Inter-Allied arrangements and of affording facilities to the returning Czecho-Slovaks.

"The last column of Czecho-Slovak troops safely embarked from Vladivostok in September, 1920. Ever since then Japan has been looking forward to an early moment for the withdrawal of her troops from Siberia. The maintenance of such troops in a foreign land is for her a costly and thankless undertaking, and she will be only too happy to be relieved of such responsibility. In fact, the evacuation of the Trans-Baikal and the Amur Provinces was already completed in 1920. The only region which now remains to be evacuated is a southern portion of the Maritime Province around Vladivostok and Nikolsk.

"It will be appreciated that for Japan the question of the withdrawal of troops from Siberia is not quite as simple as it was for other Allied Powers. In the first place, there is a considerable number of Japanese residents who had lawfully and under guarantees of treaty established themselves in Siberia long before the Bolshevik eruption, and were there entirely welcomed. In 1917, prior to the Joint American-Japanese military enterprise, the number of such residents was already no less than 9,717. In the actual situation prevailing there, those Japanese residents can hardly be expected to look for the protection of their lives and property to any other authorities than Japanese troops. Whatever district those troops have evacuated in the past have fallen into disorder, and practically all Japanese residents have had precipitately to withdraw, to seek for their personal safety. In so withdrawing, they have been obliged to leave behind large portions of their property, abandoned and unprotected, and their homes and places of business have been destroyed. While the hardships and losses thus caused the Japanese in the Trans-Baikal and the Amur provinces have been serious enough, more extensive damages are likely to follow from the evacuation of Vladivostok in which a larger number of Japanese have always been resident and a greater amount of Japanese capital invested.

"There is another difficulty by which Japan is faced in proceeding to the recall of her troops from the Maritime Province. Due to geographical propinquity, the general situation in the districts around Vladivostok and Nikolsk is bound to affect the security of Korean frontier. In particular, it is known that these districts have long been the base of Korean conspiracies against Japan. Those hostile Koreans, joining hands with lawless elements in Russia, attempted in 1920 to invade Korea through the Chinese territory of Chientao. They set fire to the Japanese Consulate at Hunchun, and committed indiscriminate acts of murder and pillage. At the present time they are under the effective control of Japanese troops stationed in the Maritime Province, but they will no doubt renew the attempt to penetrate into Korea at the first favorable opportunity that may present itself.

"Having regard to those considerations, the Japanese Government have felt bound to exercise precaution in carrying out the contemplated evacuation of the Maritime Province. Should they take hasty action without adequate provision for the future they would be delinquent in their duty of affording protection to a large number of their nationals resident in the districts in question and of maintaining order and security in Korea.

"It should be made clear that no part of the Maritime Province is under Japan's military occupation. Japanese troops are still stationed in the southern portion of that Province, but they have not set up any civil or military administration to displace local authorities. Their activity is confined to measures of self-protection against the menace to their own safety and to the safety of their country and nationals. They are not in occupation of those districts any more than American or other Allied troops could be said to have been in occupation of the places in which they were formerly stationed.

"The Japanese Government are anxious to see an orderly and stable authority speedily reestablished in the Far Eastern possessions of Russia. It was in this spirit that they manifested a keen interest in the patriotic but ill-fated struggle of Admiral Kolchak. They have shown readiness to lend their good offices for prompting the reconciliation of various political groups in Eastern Siberia. But they have carefully refrained from supporting one faction against another. It will be recalled, for instance, that they withheld all assistance from General Rozanow against the revolutionary movements which led to his overthrow in January, 1920. They maintained an attitude of strict neutrality, and refused to interfere in these movements, which it would have been quite easy for them to suppress if they had so desired.

"In relation to this policy of nonintervention, it may be useful to refer briefly to the past relations between the Japanese authorities and Ataman Semenoff, which seem to have been a source of popular misgiving and speculation. It will be remembered that the growing rapprochement between the Germans and the Bolshevik Government in Russia in the early part of 1918 naturally gave rise to apprehensions in the allied countries that a considerable quantity of munitions supplied by those countries and stored in Vladivostok might be removed by the Bolsheviks to European Russia for the use of the Germans. Ataman Semenoff was then in Siberia and was organizing a movement to check such Bolshevik activities and to preserve order and stability in that region. It was in this situation that Japan, as well as some of the Allies, began to give support to the Cossack chief. After a few months, such support by the other powers was discontinued. But the Japanese were reluctant to abandon their friend, whose efforts in the allied cause they had originally encouraged; and they maintained for some time their connection with Ataman Semenoff. They had, however, no intention whatever of interfering in the domestic affairs of Russia, and when it was found that the assistance rendered to the Ataman was likely to complicate the internal situation in Siberia, they terminated all relations with him, and no support of any kind has since been extended to him by the Japanese authorities.

"The Japanese Government are now seriously considering plans which would justify them in carrying out their decision of the complete withdrawal of Japanese troops from the Maritime Province, with reasonable precaution for the security of Japanese residents and of the Korean frontier regions. It is for this purpose that negotiations were opened some time ago at Dairen between the Japanese representatives and the agents of the Chita Government.

"Those negotiations at Dairen are in no way intended to secure for Japan any right or advantage of an exclusive nature. They have been solely actuated by a desire to adjust some of the more pressing questions with which Japan is confronted in relation to Siberia. They have essentially in view the conclusion of provisional commercial arrangements, the removal of the existing menace to the security of Japan and to the lives and property of Japanese residents in Eastern Siberia, the provision of guarantees for the freedom of lawful undertakings in that region, and the prohibition of Bolshevik propaganda over the Siberian border. Should adequate provisions be arranged on the line indicated the Japanese Government will at once proceed to the complete withdrawal of Japanese troops from the Maritime Province.

"The occupation of certain points in the Russian Province of Sakhalin is wholly different, both in nature and in origin, from the stationing of troops in the Maritime Province. History affords few instances similar to the incident of 1920 at Nikolaievsk, where more than seven hundred Japanese, including women and children, as well as the duly recognized Japanese Consul and his family and his official staff, were cruelly tortured and massacred. No nation worthy of respect will possibly remain forbearing under such a strain of provocation. Nor was it possible for the Japanese Government to disregard the just popular indignation aroused in Japan by the incident. Under the actual condition of things, Japan found no alternative but to occupy, as a measure of reprisal, certain points in the Russian Province of Sakhalin in which the outrage was committed, pending the establishment in Russia of a responsible authority with whom she can communicate in order to obtain due satisfaction.

"Nothing is further from the thought of the Japanese Government than to take advantage of the present helpless conditions of Russia for prosecuting selfish designs. Japan recalls with deep gratitude and appreciation the brilliant rôle which Russia played in the interest of civilization during the earlier stage of the Great War. The Japanese people have shown and will continue to show every sympathetic interest in the efforts of patriotic Russians aspiring to the unity and rehabilitation of their country. The military occupation of the Russian Province of Sakhalin is only a temporary measure, and will naturally come to an end as soon as a satisfactory settlement of the question shall have been arranged with an orderly Russian Government.

"In conclusion, the Japanese Delegation is authorized to declare that it is the fixed and settled policy of Japan to respect the territorial integrity of Russia, and to observe the principle of nonintervention in the internal affairs of that country, as well as the principle of equal opportunity for the commerce and industry of all nations in every part of the Russian possessions."

Statement of the United States

The reply on behalf of the American Government, by the Secretary of State, was as follows:

"The American Delegation has heard the statement by Baron Shidehara and has taken note of the assurances given on behalf of the Japanese Government with respect to the withdrawal of Japanese troops from the Maritime Province of Siberia and from the Province of Sakhalin. The American Delegation has also noted the assurance of Japan by her authorized spokesman that it is her fixed and settled policy to respect the territorial integrity of Russia, and to observe the principle of nonintervention in the internal affairs of that country, as well as the principle of equal opportunity for the commerce and industry of all nations in every part of the Russian possessions.

"These assurances are taken to mean that Japan does not seek, through her military operations in Siberia, to impair the rights of the Russian people in any respect, or to obtain any unfair commercial advantages, or to absorb for her own use the Siberian fisheries, or to set up an exclusive exploitation either of the resources of Sakhalin or of the Maritime Province.

"As Baron Shidehara pointed out, the military expedition of Japan to Siberia was originally undertaken in common accord and in cooperation with the United States. It will be recalled that public assurances were given at the outset by both Governments of a firm intention to respect the territorial integrity of Russia and to abstain from all interference in Russian internal politics. In view of the reference by Baron Shidehara to the participation of the American Government in the expedition of 1918, I should like to place upon our records for transmission to the Conference the purposes which were then clearly stated by both Governments.

" The American Government set forth its aims and policies publicly in July, 1918. The purposes of the expedition were said to be, first, to help the Czecho-Slovaks consolidate their forces; second, to steady any efforts at self-government or self-defense in which the Russians themselves might be willing to accept assistance; and, third, to guard the military stores at Vladivostok.

" The American Government opposed the idea of a military intervention, but regarded military action as admissible at the time solely for the purpose of helping the Czecho-Slovaks consolidate their forces and get into successful cooperation with their Slavic kinsmen, and to steady any efforts at self-government or self-defense in which the Russians themselves might be willing to accept assistance. It was stated that the American Government proposed to ask all associated in this course of action to unite in assuring the people of Russia in the most public and solemn manner that none of the Governments uniting in action either in Siberia or in northern Russia contemplated any interference of any kind with the political sovereignty of Russia, any intervention in her internal affairs, or any impairment of her territorial integrity either now or thereafter, but that each of the Associated Powers had the single object of affording such aid as should be acceptable, and only such aid as should be acceptable, to the Russian people in their endeavor to regain control of their own affairs, their own territory, and their own destiny.

" What I have just stated is found in the public statement of the American Government at that time.

" The Japanese Government, with the same purpose, set forth its position in a statement published by the Japanese Government on August 2, 1918, in which it was said:

" 'The Japanese Government, being anxious to fall in with the desires of the American Government and also to act in harmony with the Allies in this expedition, have decided to proceed at once to dispatch suitable forces for the proposed mission. A certain number of these troops will be sent forthwith to Vladivostok. In adopting this course, the Japanese Government remain unshaken in their constant desire to promote relations of enduring friendship with Russia and the Russian people, and reaffirm their avowed policy of respecting the territorial integrity of Russia and of abstaining from all interference in her internal politics. They further declare that, upon the realization of the project above indicated, they will immediately withdraw all Japanese troops from Russian territory and will leave wholly unimpaired the sovereignty of Russia in all its phases, whether political or military.'

"The United States of America withdrew its troops from Siberia in the spring of 1920, because it considered that the original purposes of the expedition had either been accomplished or would not longer be subserved by continued military activity in Siberia. The American Government then ceased to be a party to the expedition, but it remained a close observer of events in Eastern Siberia and has had an extended diplomatic correspondence upon this subject with the Government of Japan.

"It must be frankly avowed that this correspondence has not always disclosed an identity of views between the two Governments. The United States has not been unmindful of the direct exposure of Japan to Bolshevism in Siberia and the special problems which the conditions existing there have created for the Japanese Government, but it has been strongly disposed to the belief that the public assurances given by the two Governments at the inception of the joint expedition nevertheless required the complete withdrawal of Japanese troops from all Russian territory—if not immediately after the departure of the Czecho-Slovak troops, then within a reasonable time.

"As to the occupation of Sakhalin in reprisal for the massacre of the Japanese at Nikolaievsk, the United States, not unimpressed by the serious character of that catastrophe, but, having in mind the conditions accepted by both Governments at the outset of the joint expedition, of which the Nikolaievsk massacres must be considered an incident, it has regretted that Japan should deem necessary the occupation of Russian territory as a means of assuring a suitable adjustment with a future Russian Government.

APPENDICES 409

"The general position of the American Government was set forth in a communication to Japan of May 31, 1921. In that communication appears the following statement:

"'The Government of the United States would be untrue to the spirit of cooperation which led it, in the summer of 1918, upon an understanding with the Government of Japan, to dispatch troops to Siberia, if it neglected to point out that, in its view, continued occupation of the strategic centers in Eastern Siberia—involving the indefinite possession of the port of Vladivostok, the stationing of troops at Habarovsk, Nikolaievsk, De Castries, Mago, Sophiesk, and other important points, the seizure of the Russian portion of Sakhalin, and the establishment of a civil administration, which inevitably lends itself to misconception and antagonism—tends rather to increase than to allay the unrest and disorder in that region.

"'The military occupation'—I am still reading from the note of May 31, 1921—'The military occupation in reprisal for the Nikolaievsk affair is not fundamentally a question of the validity of procedure under the recognized rules of international law.'

"The note goes on to say that 'the issue presented is that of the scrupulous fulfillment of the assurances given to the Russian people, which were a matter of frank exchanges and of apparently complete understanding between the Government of the United States and of Japan. These assurances were intended by the Government of the United States to convey to the people of Russia a promise on the part of the two Governments not to use the joint expedition, or any incidents which might arise out of it, as an occasion to occupy territory, even temporarily, or to assume any military or administrative control over the people of Siberia.'

"Further, in the same note, the American Government stated its position as follows:

"'In view of its conviction that the course followed by the Government of Japan brings into question the very definite understanding concluded at the time troops were sent to Siberia, the Government of the United States must in candor explain its position and say to the Japanese Government that the Government of the United States can neither now nor hereafter recognize as valid any claims or titles arising out of the present occupation and control, and that it can not acquiesce in any action taken by the Government of Japan which might impair existing treaty rights or the political or territorial integrity of Russia.

" ' The Government of Japan will appreciate that, in expressing its views, the Government of the United States has no desire to impute to the Government of Japan motives or purposes other than those which have heretofore been so frankly avowed. The purpose of this Government is to inform the Japanese Government of its own conviction that, in the present time of disorder in Russia, it is more than ever the duty of those who look forward to the tranquilization of the Russian people, and a restoration of normal conditions among them, to avoid all action which might keep alive their antagonism and distrust toward outside political agencies. Now, especially, it is incumbent upon the friends of Russia to hold aloof from the domestic contentions of the Russian people, to be scrupulous to avoid inflicting what might appear to them a vicarious penalty for sporadic acts of lawlessness, and, above all, to abstain from even the temporary and conditional impairment by any foreign Power of the territorial status which, for them as for other peoples, is a matter of deep and sensitive national feeling transcending perhaps even the issues at stake among themselves.'

" To that American note the Japanese Government replied in July, 1921, setting forth in substance what Baron Shidehara has now stated to this Committee, pointing out the conditions under which Japan had taken the action to which reference was made, and giving the assurances, which have here been reiterated, with respect to its intention and policy.

" While the discussion of these matters has been attended with the friendliest feeling, it has naturally been the constant and earnest hope of the American Government—and of Japan as well, I am sure—that this occasion for divergence of views between the two Government might be removed with the least possible delay. It has been with a feeling of special gratification, therefore, that the American Delegation has listened to the assurances given by their Japanese colleague, and it is with the greatest friendliness that they reiterate the hope that Japan will find it possible to carry out within the near future her expressed intention of terminating finally the Siberian expedition and of restoring Sakhalin to the Russian people."

APPENDICES

French Statement

On behalf of the French Government M. Sarraut said—

" he gave his full and unreserved adherence to this resolution. In giving this unreserved adherence, he liked to remember that France was the oldest ally, perhaps, of Russia, and in this respect it was with a particular feeling of gratification that he would state that he had listened with great pleasure to the exchange of views that had just taken place before the Committee between the representatives of the United States and Japan. The French Government would hear with the same feelings the formal assurance given by Baron Shidehara of the intention of the Japanese Government concerning Siberia; of Japan's desire to withdraw her troops from Russia as soon as possible; of its firm intention not to interfere in the domestic affairs of Russia; and of its firm purpose to respect the integrity of Russia.

" France had full trust in Japan, who had always proved a loyal and trustworthy friend. It was quite certain that this assurance would be carried out. France accepted this with all the more pleasure because it was exactly the program which the French Government had adopted in 1918 and which led them to interfere in Siberia under the same conditions as those set forth so exactly by the Secretary of State of the United States. At this point he could not fail to restate quite clearly France's intention, like that of her Allies, to respect the integrity of Russia, and to have the integrity of Russia respected, and not to interfere in her internal policy.

" France remained faithful to the friendship of Russia, which she could not forget. She entertained feelings of gratitude to the Russian people, as she did to her other Allies. Russia had been her friend of the first hour, and she was loyal; she had stuck to her word until the Russian Government was betrayed in the way with which those present were familiar. France also remained faithful to the hope that the day would come when through the channel of a normal and regular government great Russia would be able to go ahead and fulfill her destiny. Then it would be good for her to find unimpaired the patrimony that had been kept for her by the honesty and loyalty of her allies. It was with this feeling that the French Delegation with great pleasure concurred in the adoption of the present resolution" [that the American and Japanese statements be spread upon the minutes of the Conference].

APPENDIX V: CHINA'S DELEGATION

DELEGATES.
- Mr. Sao-Ke Alfred Sze, Envoy Extraordinary and Minister Plenipotentiary to the United States of America.
- Mr. V. K. Wellington Koo, Envoy Extraordinary and Minister Plenipotentiary to the Court of St. James.
- Dr. Chung-Hui Wang, Chief Justice of the Supreme Court of the Republic of China.
- Mr. Chao-Chu Wu (appointed but did not go to Washington).

SUPERIOR ADVISERS.
- Mr. Yuho M. T. Liang, Ex-Minister for Foreign Affairs.
- Mr. Tzu-Chi Chow, Ex-Minister of Finance.

SECRETARY GENERAL.
- Mr. Philip K. C. Tyau, Envoy Extraordinary and Minister Plenipotentiary to Cuba.

ASSISTANT SECRETARY GENERAL.
- Mr. Yun-Siang Tsao, Counselor of the Ministry of Foreign Affairs.

ADVISERS.
- Vice Admiral Ting-Kan Tsai.
- Lieutenant General Fu Hwang.
- Mr. Chia-Jui Wang, Counselor of the Government Bureau of Printing.
- Mr. Wen-Kan Lo, Vice President of the Commission on Codification of Laws.
- Dr. Hawkling Yen, Adviser to the Ministry of Foreign Affairs.

COUNSELORS.
- Mr. Yen Liu.
- Mr. Chung-Yu Wang.
- Mr. Mun-Yew Chung.
- Mr. Tung-Fan Hsu.
- Mr. Nan-Ju Wu.
- Mr. Ta-Chen Wang.

COUNSELORS.
- Mr. Shih-Tsin Wen.
- Mr. Tien-Chi Yang.
- Mr. Kwai Yung.
- Mr. Pan-Chen King.
- Mr. En-Liang Tang.
- Mr. Shu-Jen Hsu.

APPENDICES 413

TECHNICAL DELEGATES.
  Mr. Yu-Chuan Chang.
  Mr. Hon-Nieng Wang.
  Mr. Yang-Pin Wang.
  Mr. Ching-Ming Li.
  Mr. Shih-Yi Chia.
  Lieutenant General Chung-Yo Lee.
  Rear Admiral King-Hsi Li.
  Mr. Fatting Tinsik Cheng.
  Mr. Tseu-Ying Teng.
  Mr. Chih-Chang Wang.
  Mr. Tien Chow.
  Dr. Te-Ching Yen.
  Mr. T. T. Tsang Ou.
  Dr. Koung-Ou Houx.
  Mr. Kwang-Yi Char.
  Mr. Tinph W. Tu.
  Mr. Lun Chan.

DIRECTORS OF DEPARTMENTS.
  Mr. Pau-Yien Wu.
  Mr. Chao-Hsinug Zee.
  Mr. Tzon-Fah Hwang.

ASSISTANT DIRECTOR OF DEPARTMENTS.
  Dr. Ung-Yu Yen.

SECRETARIES.
  Mr. Fu-Yun Chang.
  Mr. Shou-Mo Chang.
  Mr. Ziang-Ling Chang.
  Mr. Chuan Chao.
  Commander Tao Yuan Chen.
  Mr. Linson Dzau.
  Dr. Chi-Tai Hoo.
  Mr. Tsung-Ling Huang.
  Dr. Feng-Hua Huang.
  Dr. Thomas King.
  Mr. Wunsz King.

SECRETARIES.
  Mr. Telly Howard Koo.
  Mr. Gilford T. Kuan.
  Mr. Yun-Kuan Kuo.
  Mr. Yung-Chung Kwong.
  Mr. Kuang-Chao Lee.
  Mr. Wei-Shiu Lao.
  Dr. Tien-Lu Li.
  Mr. Pao-Heng Lin.
  Mr. Sy-Tchang Liou.
  Mr. Dakium K. Liou.
  Mr. Tsiun Lou.
  Mr. Pao Shen Shen.
  Mr. Tsu-Lieh Sun.
  Mr. Kwang Schu.
  Mr. Chiang-Ming Sung.
  Mr. I. Hsuan Si.
  Dr. T. Philip Sze.
  Mr. Hsia-Chang Szeping.
  Mr. Ching-Yi Tang.
  Dr. Ven-Four Tchou.
  Mr. Che-Tsien Tchou.
  Dr. M. T. Z. Tyau.
  Mr. Hong-Nien Tong.
  Mr. Yoeh-Liang Tong.
  Dr. Wen-Pin Wei.
  Mr. Tsen-Ngao Yang.
  Mr. Yung-Ching Yang.
  Mr. De-Djuen Yu.

ATTACHÉS.
  Brevet Brigadier General Ting-Chia Chen.
  Mr. Hsing-Hai Chang.
  Mr. Hung-Yeh Chao.
  Mr. Yen-Shu Che.
  Mr. Tien-Tsin Chen.
  Mr. Franklin Chiu.
  Mr. Tsu-hung Chu.

414 CHINA AT THE CONFERENCE

ATTACHÉS.
  Mr. Pao-Tien Hsieh.
  Mr. Mour Hsu.
  Mr. Teh-peh Kung.
  Mr. Shih-Sung Li.
  Mr. Yeh Li.
  Mr. Min-Chao Liu.
  Mr. Yuhu C. Liu.
  Mr. Kwang-Lai Lou.
  Mr. Mau-Dei Lu.
  Mr. Jones Lu.
  Mr. Keesing Sen.
  Mr. Dzu-Kun Shen.
  Mr. Chao-Wei Sze.
  Mr. Nai-Wen Tao.
  Mr. Teh Kwang Tsen.
  Mr. Yuan-Mow Wang.
  Mr. Yung-hsi Wei.
  Mr. Seu-Mei Woo.
  Mr. Ge-Zay Wood.
  Mr. Chao-Yung Wu.
  Mr. Shen-Kun Wu.
  Mr. Chao-Ying T. C. Yeh.
  Mr. Kih-Sung Yen.

ATTACHÉS.
  Mr. Kimpson Yu.
  Mr. Chun-Shieh Yu.
  Mr. Robert Yu, jr.

TRANSLATORS.
  Mr. Chi Chow.
  Mr. Ying Kao.
  Mr. Che-Yee Lee.
  Mr. Chia-Yu Liu.
  Mr. Gin-Ding Shen.
  Mr. Ching-Shang Tyau.

CLERKS.
  Mr. Tsong-Gee Chu.
  Mr. Tsung-Len Li.
  Mr. Chi-Seng Mong.
  Mr. Yu-Lean Shang.
  Mr. Shih-Yuan Yu.
  Mr. Hing-Ching Chu.
  Mr. Shao-Ying Fan.
  Mr. Vun-Kang Hang.
  Mr. Chun-Fang Lee.
  Mr. Tsen-Tung Lieu.
  Mr. Hsi-Chi Wang.
  Mr. Tso-Yung Tyau.

INDEX

Administrative Integrity, 41. See Territorial and Administrative Integrity.
Agenda, 25.
Agreements of May 25, 1915. See Twenty-One Demands, Manchuria, Spheres of Interests.
Anglo-Japanese Alliance, 344 ff.
Armed Forces in China, proposed resolution by the Powers regarding, 108; Chinese statement, 109; Sir Robert Borden's statement, 110; resolution adopted, 112.
Arms Embargo, 242 ff.; draft resolution, 244; amended resolution, 246; resolution withdrawn, 247.

Baker, John E., statement of, regarding Shantung settlement, 329; value of services of, 332, note.
Board of Reference, 210, 215.
Borden, Sir Robert, statement regarding armed forces in China, 110.

Cables, submarine, at Tsingtao, 308; railway, 309 ff.; valuation of, 310; joint railway commission, 313; payment for, 314.
Chefoo-Weihsien Railway, 325.
Chief Accountant, Shantung Railway, 315; Chinese Chief Accountant, 324.
China, invitation to, and acceptance by, 9; delegates of, 11, and appendix; handicapped by her weakness, 15; programme of, 27 ff.; fears of, 30 ff.; Ten Points, 32 ff.; defined, 39; sovereignty and administrative integrity, 45 ff.; neutral rights of, 53.
Chinese Eastern Railway, 226 ff.; report of Technical Committee, 227 ff.; views of Dr. Hawkling Yen, 229; resolutions adopted, 230.
Claims in Shantung, 325.
Commitments, China's, 261 ff.; Chinese proposals, 261; draft resolution, 264; resolution adopted, 271; without time limits, 273; construction of, 274.
Committees of the Whole, 19.
Communiques, to the press, 20, 23.
Conference, preliminary correspondence and invitations to, 3 ff.; one of sovereign Powers, 2; delegates to, 11; plenary sessions, 19; committees of the whole, 19; communiques, 20.
Consortium, International Banking and Special Interests, 194 ff.; and spheres of interest, 176; and the Open Door, 213; and Japanese rights in Manchuria, 258; character of, 268.
Convention, secretariat, 21; chairman, 22.
Conversations. See Shantung.
Customs Administration at Tsingtao, 302.
Customs, Maritime, maintenance of existing administrative system, 94, 104.

415

Delegates, names of, 11.

Electric Light, Tsingtao, 304.
Electrical Communications. See Wireless.
Embargo. See Arms Embargo.
Entity, Administrative, defined, 50 note.
Equality of Powers, 1 ff., 47.
Extraterritoriality, Chinese statement regarding, 114; resolution adopted, 118.

Finland, status of regarding Chinese tariff treaty, 83.
Forestry in Shantung, 325.
Four Power Pact, 21.

Garrett, Honorable John W., Secretary-General, 22.
Geddes, Sir Auckland, resolution of, regarding Consortium and the Open Door, 213; resolution of, regarding Chinese Railway, 223.
George, Lloyd, remarks in British House of Commons, July 11, 1921, 4 (footnote).
Good Offices. See Shantung.

Harding, President, interview with Mr. Sze, 322.
Hongkong. 187.
Hughes, Hon. Charles Evans, Chairman of convention and of committees, 22; opening address, 23.

Inter-Power Agreements, 235 ff.; statement of Dr. Koo, 236; resolution adopted, 240.
Invitations, to conference, 4 ff.

Japan, ambitions of, 15 ff.; hesitancy in accepting invitation to conference, 4 ff.
Joint Railway Commission, 313.

Koo, Dr. V. K. Wellington, defines China, 39; statement of, regarding Chinese tariff wishes, 55 ff.; remarks on tariff in sub-committee, 60 ff., 75; statement of, as to deposit of customs receipts, 97; as to maintenance of existing customs administration, 104; statement of, regarding Chinese Eastern Railway, 233; statement of, regarding Inter-Powers Agreements, 235; statement of, regarding China's commitments, 262; statement regarding Leased Areas, 181; statement regarding Kowloon, 188; statement regarding Manchuria, 198, 199; statement of, regarding stationing of troops, 153.
Kashgar, wireless station at, 160.
Kowloon, 186, statement of Dr. Koo concerning, 188.
Kiaochow. See Shantung.
Kwangchow-wan, statement of M. Viviani regarding surrender of, 183; statement of M. Sarraut, 192; wireless at, 160.
Kwantung. See Liaotung Peninsula.

Land Frontier Duties, 69 ff.
Lansing-Ishii Agreement, 193 ff.
Laundry, Tsingtao, 304.
Leased Areas, 181 ff.; Dr. Koo's statement, 181; Kwangchow-wan, 183, 192; Kiaochow, 185 (see also Shantung); Kwantung, 185, 190; Kowloon, 186; Weihaiwei, 188, 191; foreign post offices in, 134.
Liaotung Peninsula, 185, 190.
Light Railways, Shantung, 323.
Likin, 58.
Li-Lobanoff Treaty, 262.
Lodge, Senator, statement in United States Senate regarding Shantung, 281.

INDEX

Luxemburg, Grand Duchy of, status of, regarding Chinese tariff treaty, 83.

Manchuria, and the Consortium, 194, 197; Dr. Koo's statement, 198, 199.
Mines, Shantung, 307.
Mining Code, China's, 202.
Most Favored Nation Clause and Chinese tariff, 89, 92.

Neutrality, of China, 53.
Non-Treaty Powers, and Chinese tariff, 84, 103.

Open Door, 205 ff.; definition of, 206 ff.; consortium and, 213, Board of Reference, 215; Chinese statement, 218, resolutions adopted, 219; Chinese Railways and, 222 ff.

Pacific and Far Eastern Questions. need for discussion of, 14 ff.; committee of whole for discussion of, 19.
Plenary Sessions, of the conference, 19.
Poland, status of, regarding Chinese tariff treaty, 83.
Police, foreign, in China. See Troops.
Post Offices, foreign, in China statement by Mr. Sze, 121 ff.; discussion of, 129; resolutions reported, 129; Japanese statement, 132; Chinese statement, 133; in leased areas and railway zones, 134; Japanese, in Shantung. 325.

Radio. See Wireless.
Railway Guards, 155.
Railway Zones, foreign post offices in, 134; wireless in, 161.

Railways, Chinese, unification of, 222; resolution of Sir Auckland Geddes regarding, 223.
Roads, Tsingtao, 304.
Root, Senator, resolutions of, 40 ff.
Root Resolutions, 40 ff.
Russia, status of, regarding Chinese tariff treaty, 82.

Salt, Shantung, 306.
Sarraut, M., statement regarding Kwangchow-wan, 192.
Secretary-General, 21.
Shanghai, French wireless station at, 160.
Shantung, 277 ff.; reasons for Conversations, 280 ff.; statements of Senators Lodge and Underwood, 281; question as to scope of good offices, 283 note; scope of Conversations, 284; status of question reviewed, 285; Treaty of Versailles, 289; correspondence between China and Japan, 291 ff.; reasons why other Powers unwilling to have Shantung before the Conference, 297; Kiaochow to be restored, 301; customs administration, 302; public properties, 303; vested rights, 306; salt, 306; mines, 307; withdrawal of troops, 308; wireless, 308; cables, 308; Shantung Railway, 309 ff.; agreements reached, 323; understandings recorded, 323 ff.; joint commission, 326; merits of settlement, 327; statement of John E. Baker, 329.
Shantung Railway, 309 ff.
Shantung Treaty, 21.
Shidehara, Baron, statement of, regarding China's natural resources, 200; Mr. Sze's reply, 201.
Siberia, Japan's actions in, 17, 349 ff.

Sovereignty, defined and discussed in relation to territorial and administrative integrity, 45 ff.
Special Interests in China, 193 ff.; the Consortium and, 194 ff.; Manchuria, 198 f.; Shidehara's statement, 200; Mr. Sze's reply, 201.
Spheres of Influence, resolution adopted regarding, 273.
Spheres of Interest, Dr. Wang's statement, 174 ff.; status of, 175; Dr. Koo's statement, 177; resolution adopted, 179. See "Open Door."
Stockyard, Tsingtao, 304.
Subcommittee, 20.
Sze, Minister S. K. Alfred, statement of, regarding Chinese Railways, 222, 224; statement of, to Conference regarding Shantung Conversations, 278; interview with President Harding, 322; statement regarding wireless installations in China, 157, 166, 173; statement by, regarding foreign troops and police in China, 136 ff.; rejoinder to Japanese statement, 143; statement by, as to general right to station troops, 155; reply to Baron Shidehara's statement regarding China's natural resources, 201; reply to Hughes opening address, 24; introduction of China's Ten Points, 33; statement by, regarding foreign post offices in China. 121 ff.

Tariff, Chinese, deposit of receipts from, 95; report of Senator Underwood to plenary session, 98 ff.; Chinese statements, 103 ff.; draft, of treaty, 86; most favored nation clause, 89, 92; China's power to denounce tariff treaties, 92; maintenance of existing system of administration, 94; statement by Dr. Koo, 75; report from drafting committee, 80; Russia's status, 82; Luxemburg's status, 83; Finland and Poland, 83; non-treaty powers, 84, statement, 55; subcommittee discussions, 50 ff.; Japan objects to 7½ per cent, 63; Japanese statement, 64; draft agreement, 67, land frontier duties, 69 ff.; statement by Underwood, 72.
Telephone, Tsingtao, 304.
Ten Points of China, 32 ff., 43.
Territorial and Administrative Integrity, defined and discussed, 45 ff.
Traffic Manager, Shantung Railway, 315, staff of, 324.
Treaties and Agreements of May 25, 1915. See Twenty-One Demands.
Treasury Notes, in payment for Shantung Railway, 323, 324.
Troops, foreign, in China, Chinese statement, 136 ff.; Japanese statement, 139; police troops, 142; Chinese rejoinder, 143; Chinese argument, 144; Japanese reply, 150; commission of inquiry proposed, 151; Chinese objections to, 152; resolution adopted, 153; Chinese statement, 154.
Troops. Japanese, in Shantung, withdrawal of, 308.
Tsingtao. See Shantung.
Twenty-One Demands, 3, 16, 42; 249 ff.; statement of Dr. Wang, 249; Japanese statement, 250; reply by Dr. Wang, 253; statement of the United States, 256.

Unanimity, required, 2.
Underwood, Senator, remarks regarding Chinese tariff, 59, 72, 79; statement regarding China's power to denounce tariff treaties, 92; report of, upon Chinese tariff to

Augsburg College
George Sverdrup Library
Minneapolis, Minnesota 55404

INDEX 419

plenary session, 98 ff.; statement of, regarding wireless, 169; statements in U. S. Senate, 107 note; statement of, in United States Senate regarding Shantung, 281.

Unification of Chinese Railways, 222 ff.

Viviani, M., statement regarding Kwangchow-wan, 183.

Viviani Wireless Resolution, 164.

Walsh, Senator. resolution of, in United States Senate, 280.

Wang, Dr., presentation of Twenty-One Demands, 249, reply to Japanese statement, 253; statement regarding extraterritoriality, 114 ff.; statement regarding Spheres of Interest, 174.

Water-works, Tsingtao, 304.

Weihaiwei, 188, 191.

Wireless, withdrawal of in Shantung, 308.

Wireless Installations, in China. 157 ff.; Chinese statement, 157; draft resolution by Mr. Root, 159; at Kashgar, 160; Kwangchow-wan, 160; resolution of December 7, 162; Viviani resolution, 164; Chinese statement, 166; revised Root resolution, 168; statement by Underwood, 169; resolution of December 7, re-adopted, 172; statement by Mr. Sze, 173.

Yen, Dr. Hawkling, views of, regarding Chinese Eastern Railway, 229.